Moving from Turbo Pascal®
to Turbo C++®

MOVING FROM TURBO PASCAL® TO TURBO C++®

Namir Clement Shammas

SAMS PUBLISHING

A Division of Prentice Hall Computer Publishing
11711 North College, Carmel, Indiana 46032 USA

To my dear and special friends Jim and Anne DeArras.

International Standard Book Number: 0-672-30199-7

Library of Congress Catalog Card Number: 92-62688

96 95 94 93   4 3 2 1

Interpretation of the printing code: the rightmost double-digit number is the year of the book's printing; the rightmost single-digit, the number of the book's printing. For example, a printing code of 93-1 shows that the first printing of the book occurred in 1993.

Composed in AGaramond and MCPdigital by Prentice Hall Computer Publishing

Printed in the United States of America

Trademarks

Publisher
> Richard K. Swadley

Acquisitions Manager
> Jordan Gold

Acquisitions Editor
> Stacy Hiquet

Development Editor
> Greg Guntle

Senior Editor
> Grant Fairchild

Production Editor
> Grant Fairchild

Editors
> Mary Corder
> Sandra Doell

Editorial Coordinator
> Rebecca S. Freeman

Formatter
> Bill Whitmer

Editorial Assistant
> Rosemarie Graham

Technical Editor
> Greg Guntle

Cover Designer
> Dan Armstrong

Director of Production and Manufacturing
> Jeff Valler

Production Manager
> Corinne Walls

Imprint Manager
> Matthew Morrill

Book Designer
> Michele Laseau

Production Analyst
> Mary Beth Wakefield

Proofreading/Indexing Coordinator
> Joelynn Gifford

Production
> Christine Cook
> Lisa Daugherty
> Howard Jones
> John Kane
> Sean Medlock
> Roger Morgan
> Juli Pavey
> Susan M. Shepard
> Michelle Self
> Greg Simsic
> Angie Trzepacz

Indexers
> Jeannie Clark
> Loren Malloy
> John Sleeva

OVERVIEW

CONTENTS

ACKNOWLEDGMENTS

I would like to acknowledge the participation of the many people who made this book possible. I want to thank Publisher Richard Swadley and Acquisitions Manager Jordan Gold for their vision for this book. Many thanks to the editors of this book, Stacy Hiquet, Grant Fairchild, Mary Corder, and Sandy Doell. Also, I would like to thank the technical and developmental editor, Greg Guntle, for his valuable comments and corrections. Finally, I would like to thank all those who were involved in producing this book at Sams Publishing.

ABOUT THE AUTHOR

Namir Clement Shammas is a software engineer and an expert in object-oriented programming. He has written many articles for leading computer magazines and is responsible for many of the first books on object-oriented programming, including *Turbo Pascal 6 Object-Oriented Programming*. He is also the author of *Windows Programmer's Guide to ObjectWindows Library*, *Windows Programmer's Guide to Microsoft Foundation Class Library*, and *Advanced C++*.

INTRODUCTION

Learning different programming languages started out as a hobby for me. As a professional author, I enjoy writing a book like this one in which I build a bridge between two languages that I use regularly. This book will help you learn how to use Turbo C++ if you already program in Turbo Pascal. The approach that I use in most chapters is to first present a program example in Pascal and then present the same program written in C++. This strategy enables you to compare the code for Turbo Pascal (which you already know) with the similar code in Turbo C++. Because C++ evolved from C, I also point out the similarities and differences between C++ and C. My secondary goal is to make you comfortable with C (at least C code).

This book contains 14 chapters. Chapter 1, "A Quick Tour of C++," starts with a quick overview of C++. This chapter gives you a taste of the various features and constructors of C++.

Chapter 2, "Getting Started," is the formal kickoff of your journey to learn C++. The chapter looks at the basic components of a C++ program, simple data types, constants, and basic input/output.

Chapter 3, "C++ Operators," examines C++ operators and presents the various categories of operators: arithmetic, increment, assignment, relational, bit-manipulating, and other operators. This chapter shows you the richness and versatility of C++ operators.

Chapter 4, "The Preprocessor and Compiler Directives," discusses the preprocessor and compiler directives. The preprocessor is a tool, inherited from C, that allows you to create macros that emulate simple functions, data type aliases, or command shorthand. The compiler directives enable you to fine-tune compiler operations.

Chapter 5, "Decision-Making," presents the various decision-making constructors in C++. These constructs include various forms of the if statement and the switch statement.

Chapter 6, "Loops," discusses the various loops offered by C++. These loops include the versatile for loop and the conditional while and do-while loops. This chapter also shows you how to exit from a loop and how to skip the rest of a loop iteration.

Chapter 7, "Simple Functions," examines simple C++ functions. The aim of the chapter is to familiarize you with the basic syntax of C++ functions. The chapter also discusses recursive functions, exiting functions, the default argument feature, and the function overloading feature.

Chapter 8, "Pointers, Arrays, and Strings," introduces you to the more advanced aspects of C++ by discussing pointers, arrays, and strings. This chapter looks at the various types of storage for variables and their scope and discusses one-dimensional arrays, multidimensional arrays, strings, and how to access these structures using pointers.

Chapter 9, "Enumerated and Structured Data Types," presents user-defined data types. These types include enumerated types, structures, and unions.

Chapter 10, "Advanced Functions," discusses advanced aspects of using functions. These aspects include passing user-defined parameters and passing arguments by copy and by reference. This chapter also discusses access of command-line arguments, using pointers to functions, and writing functions with a varying number of arguments.

Chapter 11, "Object-Oriented Programming Basics," gives you a basic introduction to object-oriented programming (OOP). This chapter is written for readers who are not familiar with OOP. It discusses classes, objects, methods, inheritance, and polymorphism.

Chapter 12, "Turbo Pascal OOP Features," presents the basic object-oriented features of Turbo Pascal. This chapter was written with the assumption that you have used Turbo Pascal strictly to write non-OOP applications.

Chapter 13, "C++ Classes," covers C++ classes and OOP aspects that you need to quickly become familiar with. This chapter discusses topics that include declaring basic classes, declaring descendent classes, multiple inheritance, static members, nested classes, friend functions, operators, friend operators, and friend classes. When you finish reading this chapter, you should be comfortable enough with C++ to write your own classes.

Chapter 14, "Basic Stream File I/O," offers a practical and basic introduction to stream file I/O. This chapter covers sequential text file I/O, sequential binary file I/O, and random-access file I/O.

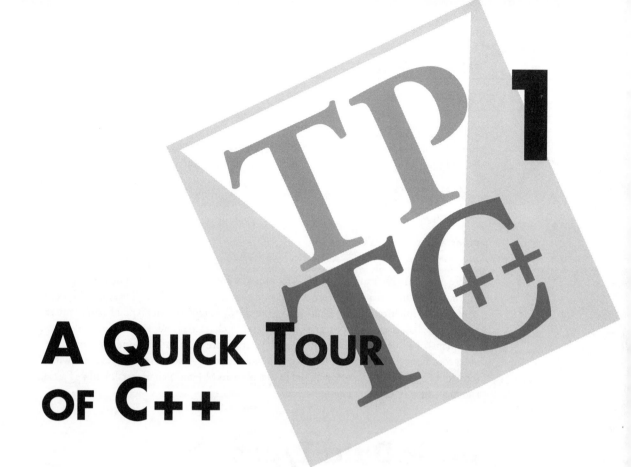

A Quick Tour
of C++

This chapter briefly looks at the various components of C++. It is designed to give you a taste of C++ before you delve into learning the language.

The General C++ Program Components

If you compare C++ to Pascal, C++ is more flexible in organizing programs and modules. C++ programs consist of global declarations and single-level functions. The general form of C++ is as follows:

```
// This is a comment that runs to the end of the line
/* This is the C-style comment
    that can run through multiple
    lines
*/
```

```
global declarations
function declarations
main()
{
  local declarations
  function statements
  return 0;
}
other function declarations
```

Every C++ program must contain the function main, a special function that indicates where program execution begins. C++ comments come in two forms. The first type uses // characters and creates a comment that runs to the end of a line. The second type of comment is inherited from C and uses /* and */ characters (this type of comment resembles the Pascal comment that employs (* and *) characters and works on just the Pascal comment). You can use the /* and */ comments to create multiline comments or to create a comment that is surrounded by compilable code. C++ statements always end with a semicolon and C++ blocks are enclosed in braces (pairs of { and } characters). Unlike Pascal, the identifiers in C++ are case-sensitive.

Basic Data Types and Variables

Note the following basic data types in C++:

Data Type Identifier	Meaning
char	character
int	integer
float	single-precision floating-point number
double	double-precision floating-point number

C++ also utilizes data type modifiers that manipulate the sign and precision of the preceding data types. Note the following data type modifiers:

Data Type Modifier	Meaning
signed	the high bit of an integer is used to indicate the sign
unsigned	the high bit of an integer contributes to the value of the integer

Data Type Modifier	Meaning
long	the number has an extended precision
short	the number has a reduced precision

Because C++ is flexible, you can abbreviate unsigned for unsigned int, long for long int, and short for short int. Declaring variables in C++ is similar to declaring variables in Pascal, although the data type comes first and no colon separates the data type and the variables in C++:

```
int index,
int i, j, k;
double rate = 1.23;
char drive_name = 'A';
long int offset = 0L;
long offset2 = offset;
```

C++, like Pascal, enables you to declare more than one variable at a time. Such variables are declared in a comma-delimited list. With C++, you can also initialize a variable when you declare it. The initializing values may be constants or the names of other variables.

Pointers are special variables in C++. Like pointers in Pascal, C++ pointers store data addresses. Typically, C++ pointers are associated with a specific data type. This association empowers the pointer to interpret the data it accesses. C++ also supports the "non-denominational" pointer of the type void. Such a pointer is similar to the Pointer type in Turbo Pascal. Declaring pointers in C++ is easy and straightforward. Simply place an asterisk (*) to the left of the identifier you want to declare as the pointer. Note the following declaring pointers examples:

```
int *p1, *p2; // p1 and p2 are pointers
int* p3, p4;  // p3 is a pointer, but p4 is an int!
```

In the preceding example, the identifiers p1 and p2 are clearly pointers to the int type because each identifier is preceded by the * character. What about the p3 and p4 identifiers? Are they both pointers? The answer is no! Only p3 is a pointer. The p4 identifier is an int-typed variable. C++ enables you to move the * character and place it directly after the type identifier. However, this makes only the first identifier a pointer. All other identifiers in the same list are not pointers unless each has a * character to its left. If you want to make the preceding statement declare both p3 and p4 as pointers, write this statement:

```
int* p3, *p4;  // both p3 and p4 are pointers
```

or this statement:

```
int *p3, *p4;  // both p3 and p4 are pointers
```

3

C++ enables you to assign the address of a variable to a pointer by placing the address-of operator, &, to the left of the variable's name. This operator is similar to the Turbo Pascal @ operator. To access data using the pointer, place a * character to the left of the pointer's name. You may use the latter notation on either side of the equal sign in an assignment operator. The following example illustrates these rules:

```
#include <iostream.h>

    main()
    {
        int a = 10;
        int b = 100;
        int *p;

        // assign address of a to p
        p = &a;
        cout << "p access the value " << *p << '\n';
        *p = *p * 2;
        cout << "p is now " << *p << '\n';
        cout << "a is now " << a << " ?=? " << *p << '\n';

        // assign address of b to p
        p = &b;
        cout << "p access the value " << *p << '\n';
        *p = *p * 2;
        cout << "p is now " << *p << '\n';
        cout << "b is now " << b << " ?=? " << *p << '\n';

        return 0;
    }
```

The program declares the int-typed variables a and b, and the pointer to the int type, p. The program assigns the address of variable a to p and performs the following tasks:

1. Displays the contents of variable a as accessed by the p pointer using the expression *p. The cout is the name of the standard output stream (the screen). The << symbols are stream extractor operators. The program displays the integer 10.

2. Doubles the value stored in variable a using the statement:

```
*p = *p * 2;
```

The *p on the right side of the equal sign recalls the value stored in the variable accessed by the p pointer. The *p located on the left side of the equal sign tells the compiler to assign the result to the variable accessed by the p pointer, not to the p pointer itself.

3. Displays the new value stored in the variable access by the p pointer. The program displays the integer 20.

4. Displays the new value stored in variable a. This value should also be 20.

The program then assigns the address of variable b to the pointer b and repeats the preceding steps with variable b.

Operators

C++ offers numerous powerful operators that can be categorized as follows:

1. Arithmetic operators: +, -, /, *, and % (the same as the Pascal MOD operator).

2. Relational operators (see Table 1.1).

Table 1.1. The C++ relational operators.

Operator	Function
==	equal to
!=	not equal to
<	less than
<=	less than or equal to
>	greater than
>=	greater than or equal to
&&	logical AND
||	logical OR
!	logical NOT

3. Bitwise operators (see Table 1.2, a list of operators that manipulate the individual bits of one or more bytes).

Table 1.2. The C++ bitwise operators.

Operator	Function
¦	bitwise OR
&	bitwise AND
^	bitwise XOR
~	bitwise NOT
>>	shift bits to the right
<<	shift bits to the left

4. The pointer operators—these include the address-of operator, &, and the access operator, *.

5. The reference operator, &, which allows you to create a variable that is an alias to another variable. The reference is used mostly in parameter lists of functions to create reference parameters that resemble VAR parameters in Pascal.

6. The increment and decrement operators: ++ and --. These operators increment and decrement by 1 the value stored in a variable, respectively. When applied to a pointer, these operators alter the address stored in that pointer by the size of its associated data type.

7. The assignment operators—these operators include the equal sign and other operators that are made up of a math or bitwise operator symbol followed by the equal sign. These operators are shorthand forms that enable you to specify the manipulated variable only once. Consider the following example:

```
index = 3 * index;
```

The following statement can replace the preceding multiplication of two items:

```
index *= 3;
```

Notice the *= operator multiplies the index variable by 3 and assigns the result back to index.

Constants

You can declare two types of constants in a C++ program. The first type is a carryover from C and uses the #define macro directive. For example:

```
#define MAX_SIZE 100
#define MIN_RATE 12.3
#define DEFAULT_DRIVE A
```

The #define macro directive tells the C++ compiler to first substitute 100, 12.3, and A for the MAX_SIZE, MIN_RATE, and DEFAULT_DRIVE identifiers, respectively. This substitution occurs before the compiler starts compiling the code.

The second constant type is based on the ANSI standard for C, which supports a formal type of constant. This new type uses the const keyword and may specify a data type for the constant. A few examples of this genre of constants follows.

```
const MAX_SIZE = 100;
const double MIN_RATE = 12.3;
const char DEFAULT_DRIVE = 'A';
```

Notice the MAX_SIZE constant has no associated type. In this case, the C++ compiler assumes the default type of int.

C-Style Console I/O

C++ and its parent language, C, lack built-in I/O functions. This unusual approach enables C and C++ to use I/O functions that suit special applications. Both C and C++ use standard libraries that contain popular I/O functions. In C, programmers use the stdio.h header file to employ basic console and file I/O. Header files in C and C++ contain the definitions of global data types, constants, variables, and functions. These are somewhat similar to the INTERFACE segment of a Turbo Pascal library UNIT. Turbo C programmers also use the conio.h header file, which Borland customized to include useful and commonly used console I/O functions.

The printf function provides flexible (it accepts a varying number of arguments), formatted output for various basic data types. The first argument must always be a string. The other optional arguments are of the basic data types and may include strings. If two or more arguments appear in a call to printf, then the first argument is a formatting string. The following code is a simple example of the printf function:

```
#include <stdio.h>
main()
{
    int x = 65;

    printf("The number is:");
    printf("\nx = %d\n", x);
    return 0;
}
```

The first `printf` merely produces text, and the second `printf` creates formatted output. The first argument of the second `printf` is the formatting string. Notice the following items in that string:

1. The first two characters in the formatting string are \n. These characters are part of a family of control characters. The \n requests a new line.

2. The x = characters appear as text.

3. The %d characters specify the format for displaying the contents of variable x. The %d request displays the number in variable x as a decimal integer. The % symbol is a format command used to specify the data type and the output width. In the case of integers, the format command % can also specify the output to appear as an octal, decimal, or hexadecimal number.

The counterpart of the `printf` function is the `scanf` function. This function accepts formatted input and takes at least two arguments. The first `scanf` argument is the format string. The other arguments are the addresses of the variables that receive the data. The following example shows an input using the `scanf` function and the output using the `printf` function:

```
#include <stdio.h>
main()
{
    int num1, num2;
    long product;
    printf("Enter two integers delimited by a single space : ");
    scanf("%d %d", &num1, &num2);
    product = num1 * num2;
    printf("%d * %d = %ld\n", num1, num2, product);
    return 0;
}
```

The first call to `printf` simply displays a promoting string. The `scanf` function accepts the two integers that must be separated by a single space. A single space must be used because the formatting string in `scanf` has a single space between the two %d format commands. Also notice that the second and third arguments of `scanf` are the addresses of the num1 and num2 variables, respectively.

The conio.h header file enables you to import functions that manage the cursor, the screen, and perform character I/O. The following code is an example of conio.h usage:

```
#include <conio.h>
#include <stdio.h>
main()
{
    char c;
    clrscr(); // clear the screen
    printf("Enter a character : ");
    // input a character and echo it back on the screen
    c = getche();
    printf("\n\nYou typed %c\n", c);
    return;
}
```

The clrscr() function clears the screen (just like ClrScr in Turbo Pascal). The getche() function reads a character from the keyboard and echoes it back on the screen. The conio.h also offers the getch() function, which reads a character without echo.

C++ Stream I/O

C++ also offers a new and more flexible mechanism for extendible I/O, called streams. Actually, the notion of streams has its roots in C. C++ extends streams and offers more flexible, extendible features. This chapter focuses on simple stream I/O.

C++ has a number of predefined streams: cout, cin, and cerr. cout is the standard output stream (usually the screen), cin is the standard input stream (usually the keyboard), and cerr is the standard error stream (usually the screen.) Stream I/O uses a number of functions, as well as the stream extractor operator, <<, and the stream inserter operator, >>. The advantage of using these operators is that they enable you to chain several items for input or output. The following sample statement illustrates chaining an output to the cout stream:

```
cout << 2 << ' ' << 2.3 << ' ' << 'A' << 3.4 << " abcs\n";
```

The << operators are predefined for the basic data types in C++, as well as for character arrays. Note the following example usage of simple stream I/O:

```
#include <iostream.h>
#include <conio.h>

main()
{
```

```
    int i, j;
    long k;

    cout << "Enter the first integer : ";
    cin >> i;
    cout << "Enter the second integer : ";
    cin >> j;
    k = i * j;
    cout << "\ni = " << i
         << "\nj = " << j
         << "\nk = " << k << '\n';

    return 0;
}
```

The << operator is used with the cout stream to display the prompting messages, echo the input values, and show the result. The >> operator and the cin stream are used to enter integers. String input using C++ stream requires a special function and does not work easily with the >> operator.

Decision-Making Constructs

C++ inherited the decision-making constructs of C. Boolean expressions in C and C++ are true only when they yield a nonzero value.

C++ supports the single-alternative if statement and the dual-alternative if-else statement. These statements use no then keyword and instead require that you enclose the tested condition in parentheses. The following program is an example of the single-alternative if statement:

```
#include <iostream.h>
#include <conio.h>
main()
{
    char c;
    cout << "Enter a disk drive name: ";
    c = getche();
    if (c < 'A' || c > 'E')
        count << "Invalid drive!\n\n";
    return 0;
}
```

The following example illustrates the dual-alternative if-else statement:

```
#include <stdio.h>

main()
{
    int x;
    double x0, y;

    printf("Enter a number: ")
    scanf("%d", &x);
    if (x > 0) {
        x0 = x * x;
        y = 1.5 + 3 * x0 / (1 + x0);
    }
    else {
        x0 =  2 * x * x - 12.4;
        y = 100 - x0 * x0;
    }
    printf("f(%d) = %g\n", x, y);
    return 0;
}
```

The preceding example shows the if-else statement using multistatement blocks for both alternatives. C++ requires that all statements in a block end with a semicolon, including the last statement.

In addition to if statements, C++ supports the multiple-alternative switch statement, which is similar to the CASE-OF statement in Pascal. The switch statement utilizes case labels with constants to choose the course of action. The break statement is used to jump out of the switch statement when a matching case label is found. The following example illustrates use of the switch statement:

```
#include <iostream.h>
#include <conio.h>
main()
{
    char c;
    cout << "Enter a character : ";
    cin >> c;
    cout << "\n\n";

    switch (c) {
        case '0':
        case '1':
        case '2':
        case '3':
```

```
           case '4':
           case '5':
           case '6':
           case '7':
           case '8':
           case '9':
                   cout << "You entered a digit!\n";
                   break;
           case 'i':
           case 'o':
           case 'u':
           case 'e':
           case 'a':
           case 'I':
           case 'O':
           case 'U':
           case 'E':
           case 'A':
                   cout << "You entered a vowel\n";
                   break;
           default:
                   cout << "You type a character";
                   break;
       }
     return 0;
}
```

The preceding example indicates that C++ does not support a mechanism to consolidate the case labels.

Loops

C++ supports three loop constructs: for, while, and do-while loops. The for loop in C++ is a superset of similar loops in other languages like Pascal, Modula-2, and BASIC. The for loop is able to work as a fixed-iteration loop, a conditional loop, and an open loop and is made up of three elements: the loop initialization, the loop continuation test, and the loop increment. All these elements of the for loop are optional. The following example shows a typical for loop using its three components. The loop writes the letters A to Z to the standard output stream:

```
#include <iostream.h>

main()
{
       char c;
```

```
    for (c = 'A';      // initialize loop control variable
         c <= 'Z';     // test condition to continue looping
         c++)          // increment loop control variable
         cout << c;
    cout << "\n\n";
    return 0;
}
```

The do-while loop iterates as long as the tested condition (located at the end of the loop) is true. The following example illustrates the do-while loop performing the same task as the for loop in the preceding example:

```
#include <iostream.h>

main()
{
    char c = 'A';
    do {
        cout << c;
        c++;
    } while (c <= 'Z');
    cout << "\n\n";
    return 0;
}
```

The while loop iterates while the tested condition is true. The following example shows the while loop performing the same task as the do-while loop in the preceding example:

```
#include <iostream.h>

main()
{
    char c = 'A';
    while (c <= 'Z') {
        cout << c;
        c++;
    }
    cout << "\n\n";
    return 0;
}
```

Arrays

C++ supports arrays. The declaration of an array in C++ specifies only the size of an array (enclosed in a pair of brackets). The lower bound of the array is always 0. The upper bound

13

is therefore equal to the array size minus 1. C++ also supports multidimensional arrays and requires that the size of every dimension be specified in a separate pair of brackets. Note the proceeding example of simple array usage:

```
#include <iostream.h>

main()
{
    double factorial[20];
    unsigned i;
    // initialize the first array member
    factorial[0] = 1;
    // loop to calculate the factorials
    for (i = 1; i < 20; i++)
        factorial[i] = i * factorial[i-1];
    // loop to display the factorials
    for (i = 0; i < 20; i++)
        cout << i << "! = " << factorial[i] << '\n';
    return 0;
}
```

In the preceding program, the for loops iterate until the loop control variables reach **20**, the size of the array. This is due to the fact that the array factorial has valid indices in the range of 0 to 19 (which is equal to 20 minus 1).

Accessing a multidimensional array in C++ involves using indices for each dimension. Each index must appear in a separate set of brackets. Here is an example for manipulating a matrix:

```
#include <iostream.h>

main()
{
    const max_rows = 5;
    const max_cols = 3;
    double mat[max_rows][max_cols];
    unsigned row, col;
    // assign value to first matrix members
    mat[0][0] = 5.3;
    // assign values to other matrix members
    for (row = 1; row < max_rows; row++)
        for (col = 1; col < max_cols; col++)
            mat[row][col] = mat[row-1][col-1] +
                            row + 10 * col - 4;
    // display matrix
    for (row = 0; row < max_rows; row++)
```

```
        for (col = 0; col < max_cols; col++)
            cout << "mat[" << row << "][" << col
                 << "] = " << mat[row][col] << '\n';
    return 0;
}
```

Strings

C++ does not support a formal data structure for strings. Instead, C++ considers a string as an array of characters that ends with the ASCII 0 character (the null character). This approach enables you to declare strings with custom-fit sizes and create strings that exceed the 255-character size limit of a Turbo Pascal string type. Keep in mind that you specify the size of a string variable in C++ to include space for the delimiting null character. The smallest usable string in C++, therefore, has the size of two elements.

Regarding string I/O in C++, you can use functions from either the stdio.h or the iostream.h header files, or from both. The stdio.h header file declares the string I/O functions gets and puts. The puts function is more efficient than the printf function if you want to output a single string. The following example illustrates string I/O using the gets and puts functions:

```c
#include <stdio.h>

main()
{
    unsigned i;
    int lowercaseShift = 'a' - 'A';
    char aString[81];

    printf("Enter a string : ");
    gets(aString);
    for (i = 0; aString[i] != '\0'; i++)
        // is the current character an uppercase?
        if (aString[i] >= 'A' && aString[i] <= 'Z')
        aString[i] += lowercaseShift;

    printf("\nThe lowercase string is : ");
    puts(aString);
    return 0;
}
```

The preceding program shows that the gets and puts functions accept the bare name of a character array. Why? These functions actually require the address of the first character in the array aString, which is &aString[0]. In C++, the bare name of an array is also interpreted as the address of the first element.

The string.h header file declares many string manipulating functions used by C programmers. You can also use these functions in C++. String manipulation, C-style, often involves the use of pointers to access the individual characters of a string. For example, you can replace the character reference of aString[i] in the preceding program with the expression *(ptr + i). The ptr identifier is a pointer to the first character in the aString array. You may rewrite the preceding program to use a separate pointer, as follows:

```c
#include <stdio.h>

main()
{
    unsigned i;
    int lowercaseShift = 'a' - 'A';
    char aString[81];
    char* ptr = aString;

    printf("Enter a string : ");
    gets(aString);
    for (i = 0; *(ptr + i) != '\0'; i++)
        // is the current character an uppercase?
        if (*(ptr + i) >= 'A' && *(ptr + i) <= 'Z')
        *(ptr + i) += lowercaseShift;

    printf("\nThe lowercase string is : ");
    puts(aString);
    return 0;
}
```

User-Defined Data Types

C++ enables you to declare enumerated data types that are similar to those of Pascal. Each enumerated type creates a set of unique identifiers. Each enumerated identifier is assigned an integer value, either explicitly or implicitly. If you have used enumerated values in Pascal, you know how much they enhance the readability of a program. Enumerated values replace cryptic numbers with more descriptive identifiers. For example, you can replace integer codes for the days of the week with enumerated values that spell out the names of the weekdays. The same approach enhances coding information related to colors, error status, and other characteristics defined by a finite set of values. A few examples of enumerated types follow:

```
enum boolean { false, true };
enum weekDays { Sunday = 1, Monday, Tuesday, Wednesday,
                Thursday, Friday, Saturday, No_Day = 100 };
enum stringError { no_error, bad_index, allocate_error };
```

C++ assigns 0 as the default value for the first member of the enumerated type. In addition, a subsequent enumerated member has a default value that is one greater than its predecessor. The second example shows that you can override this automatic assignment scheme. The first enumerated member, Sunday, is explicitly assigned the value of 1. This means the value for Monday is 2, the value for Tuesday is 3, and so on. The weekDays enumerated type also includes the special No_Day value with an explicit value of 100. Another feature of enumerated types is that C++ enables you to duplicate the integer values assigned to the enumerated members of the same set.

After you declare an enumerated type, you can use it to declare variables in the same way as any other predefined data type. The following example illustrates this.

```
#include <stdio.h>
#include <conio.h>
enum boolean { false, true };

main()
{
    unsigned i;
    int lowercaseShift = 'a' - 'A';
    char aString[81];
    char c;
    boolean goOn;

    do {
        printf("\nEnter a string : ");
        gets(aString);
        for (i = 0; aString[i] != '\0'; i++)
            // is the current character an uppercase?
            if (aString[i] >= 'A' && aString[i] <= 'Z')
                aString[i] += lowercaseShift;

        printf("\nThe lowercase string is : %s\n", aString);
        printf("Enter another string? (Y/N) ");
        c = getche();
        if (c == 'y' || c == 'Y')
            goOn = true;
        else
            goOn = false;
    } while (goOn == true);
    return 0;
}
```

C++ also supports structures and unions. Structures resemble the Pascal Record types. Unions resemble the variant records in Pascal. C++ enables you to declare structures that combine logically related fields of diversified data types. For example, the following C++ structure defines a phone number structure:

```
struct phone_rec {
     char last_name[15];
     char first_name[10];
     char phone[14];
     char fax[14];
     char company[30];
     unsigned yearsEmployed;
};
```

The preceding example demonstrates that the declaration of a structure incorporates the struct keyword. The next example declares the phone_rec structure that contains last_name, first_name, phone, fax, company, and yearsEmployed. After you declare a structure, you can use the name of the structure to declare variables and pointers:

```
phone_rec aPhone;                    // single variable
phone_rec phoneNumbers[100];         // array of structures
phone_rec *phonePtr = &aPhone;       // pointer to the structure
```

Using the aPhone variable, you can access the yearsEmployed field by the aPhone.yearsEmployed expression. The dot access operator works in C++ as it does in Pascal. To access the yearsEmployed field in the third element of the phoneNumbers array, you need the phoneNumbers[2].yearsEmployed expression. In this case, I used an index with the array, followed by the dot operator. To access the yearsEmployed field using the phonePtr pointer, you need the phonePtr->yearsEmployed expression (the -> symbol represents the structure-access operator for a pointer).

C++ unions enable you to include variant fields. These fields support automatic data conversion and mutually exclusive shared memory space. The following code is an example of a C++ union:

```
union intLong {
     int aInt[2];
     long aLong;
};
```

The preceding union uses four bytes to store either an array of two ints or a single long integer. You can use the union to easily obtain the upper or lower two bytes of a long integer.

Functions

C++, like its parent language C, is a function-oriented language. Every routine in C++ is a function. C++ has no formal procedures like Pascal has. The general syntax for a C++ function is:

```
<returnType> <functionName>(<parameterList>)
{
    <local declaration of data types, constants, and variables>
    <statements for the function body>
    return <functionValue>;
}
```

The function's `return` type appears first. C++ functions can return the predefined types as well as pointers and structures. This feature makes them more flexible than functions in Pascal. You can use the `void` return type to indicate that the function does not return any particular type. Thus, `void` functions are basically equivalent to procedures. The parameter list is optional. If a function has no parameters, you can either use the `void` keyword or not state any type at all. The parameters in a function appear in the following format:

```
<type1> param1, <type2> param2, ...
```

C++ forces you to declare each parameter with its own type. You cannot shorten the parameter list for two or more consecutive parameters that have the same data type.

C++ functions may declare their own data types, constants, variables, and pointers. However, nested functions are not supported. The `return` statement enables you to return the function value. In `void` functions, you can use the bare `return` statement to exit the function from any statement.

Influenced by the ANSI C standard, C++ requires you to prototype (that is, make a forward declaration) a function in a client function. This prototyping is necessary when the client function uses the `target` function before the `target` function is defined. In fact, that's what the header files do—they contain the prototypes of the various functions. Prototyping a function enables the compiler to perform type checking and reconcile the use of the function with its declaration.

The following is an example of a simple C++ function:

```
#include <iostream.h>
#include <conio.h>

main()
{
    // prototype the factorial function
    double fact(int);
```

19

```
        clrscr();
        cout << "3! = " << fact(3);
        getche();
        return 0;
}

double fact(int n)
{

        double p = 1;
        if (n < 2)
            return 1;
        for (int i = 2; i <= n; i++)
            p *= (double)i;
        return p;
}
```

The fact function calculates the factorial. Because the fact function is defined after the main function where it is used, the main function contains a prototype of the fact function. A better way to code the prototype of fact is to place it before any function, making it a global prototype. This solution enables you to make a single set of prototype declarations.

C++ functions have evolved in a couple of directions, making them more versatile than C functions. In C, arguments are strictly passed by value. If you pass a variable as an argument in a C function, you pass a copy of the value stored in that variable. Changing the value of the argument in the preceding example, therefore, does affect the copy and leaves the original variable intact. To alter the value of a variable outside a function, C requires that you pass a pointer to that variable. In fact, you are also passing a copy of the address of the targeted variable.

C++ allows reference parameters that are very similar to the Pascal VAR parameters. A reference parameter becomes an alias for its arguments. Change the reference variable in a C++ function and you change the variable supplied as the argument. Reference parameters are declared by using the & symbol. The following example illustrates a C++ function that uses a reference parameter:

```
#include <iostream.h>
#include <conio.h>

// prototype the factorial function
void fact(int, double&);

main()
{
```

```
    double x;
    clrscr();

    fact(3, x);
    cout << "3! = " << x;
    getche();
    return 0;
}

void fact(int n, double& p)
{

    p = 1;
    if (n < 2)
        return;
    for (int i = 2; i <= n; i++)
        p *= (double)i;
}
```

The preceding program passes the result of the factorial function via the p reference parameter. The change in the declaration of the fact function is also reflected in the global prototype of the function. The main function supplies the x variable as the argument for the p parameter in the fact function. The p parameter becomes a temporary alias for x. Any assignment made to p in the fact function is actually made to the x.

Other C++ extensions to functions include overloading functions and the support for operators. Overloaded functions are functions that have the same names but possess a different parameter list. Operators are special functions that enable you to extend the use of operators to include instances of classes.

Classes

Classes are the most significant feature that separates C++ from C. C++ classes are similar to the Object type in Turbo Pascal and encapsulate data members with the functions that manipulate these members. The following code is a sample class:

```
class complex {

    protected:
        double real;
        double imag;

    public:
        // constructors
```

21

```
        complex();
        complex(double Real, double Imag);
        ~complex();
        double absValue();
        double getReal()
            { return real; }
        double getImag()
            { return imag; }
        void getComplex(double& Real, double& Imag);
        complex add(complex& c1, complex& c2);
        complex sub(complex& c1, complex& c2);
        complex mul(complex& c1, complex& c2);
        complex div(complex& c1, complex& c2);
};
```

The class declaration starts with the class keyword. The preceding example shows that C++ uses the public and protected keywords (there is also a private keyword) to support data hiding and limited access. The class complex declares two protected data members, real and imag. As in Turbo Pascal, these protected members cannot be accessed by the instances of the complex class. The class also declares two class constructors and a set of member functions.

Constructors are special class members that are automatically invoked when you declare a class instance. C++ constructors must have the same class name. You can declare multiple constructors to enable the initialization of class instances in more than one way. The class complex declares two constructors. The first one is called the default or void constructor. This constructor has no parameters. To create instances of class complex using the default constructor, use declarations that resemble the following one:

```
complex c1; // create a default complex number
```

The second class constructor uses parameters that enable you to initialize the instances of class complex:

```
complex c2(1.2, 34.3);
complex c3(1, -9);
complex complexNum(0, 2);
```

The arguments used with declaring the class instances tell the compiler which constructor to use.

The complex class also declares a class destructor. The destructor also has the same name as the class and is preceded by a tilde (~) symbol. C++ enables you to declare only one destructor, which must have an empty parameter list.

The complex class declares a set of member functions. Notice that some of these member functions are also defined in the class declaration. Including the definition of a member function in a class should be limited to functions with one or two statements. Functions with a longer set of statements should be defined outside the class declaration. C++ requires that you follow a certain rule to indicate which class owns what function. The general syntax for defining a member function outside the class declaration is:

```
<returnType> <className>::<functionName>(<parameterList>)
```

Thus the class name, followed by two colons, must be inserted between the function's `return` type and the name of the function. This rule applies to constructors, destructors, and member functions. For example, the definition of the second constructor might appear as follows:

```
complex::complex(double Real, double Imag)
{
    real = Real;
    imag = Imag;
}
```

Similarly the definition of the function `getComplex` is:

```
void complex::getComplex(double& Real, double& Imag)
{
    Real = real;
    Imag = imag;
}
```

Notice that the preceding functions access the data members `real` and `imag` without any special qualifiers.

C++ enables you to create classes that are descendants of other classes. This scheme allows the descendant classes to inherit the data members and member functions of their parent and ancestor classes. C++ also allows descendant classes to override inherited member functions. Regarding inheritance lineage schemes, C++ supports both single and multiple inheritance. Single inheritance creates a line of descendant classes in such a way that each class has only one parent class. Multiple inheritance allows a descendant class to have two or more parent classes.

GETTING STARTED

Your journey through the world of C++ begins in this chapter, which covers the following basic topics:

- getting started with C++

- predefined C++ data types

- using constants in C++

- basic I/O in C++

A Simple C++ Program

The first C++ program that I present will probably take you down memory lane. It is a simple program that displays a one-line greeting message. This program enables you to see the basic components of a C++ program and how they differ from those of a Pascal program. Throughout this book, I will present Turbo Pascal programs followed by their equivalent Turbo C++ programs. Occasionally, I include refined versions of the Turbo C++ programs that contain code more typical of C++ programs written by practicing programmers.

Listing 2.1 contains the source code for program LST02_01.PAS. This is a trivial Turbo Pascal program that displays the "Hello Programmer!" string. Listing 2.2 shows the source code for program LST02_02.CPP, which contains the C++ code equivalent to LST02_01.PAS.

Listing 2.1. Source code for program LST02_01.PAS.

```
Program Howdee;

{ a trivial Turbo Pascal program that says hello }

BEGIN
  WRITE('Hello Programmer!');
END.
```

Listing 2.2. Source code for program LST02_02.CPP.

```cpp
// a trivial C++ program that says hello
#include <iostream.h>

main()
{
  cout << "Hello Programmer!";
  return 0;
}
```

The following characteristics of a C++ program are contained in the preceding C++ program code:

1. The comments in C++ use the // characters for comments that run to the end of the line. C++ also supports the C-style comments that begin with the /* characters and end with the */ characters. The second type of comment works very much like the (* and *) comments in Turbo Pascal.

2. The C++ program has no formal keywords (such as Pascal's PROGRAM and END keywords) that define the beginning and end of a C++ program. In fact, C++ uses a different scheme to organize a program. This scheme supports two levels of

code: global and single-level functions. In addition, the main function plays a special role because runtime execution begins with this function. Therefore, there can be only a single main function in C++. In Pascal, the main section in the program comes after the declarations of the labels, constants, data types, variables, procedures, and functions. In C++, you can place main anywhere in the code. Because main is a function, it can have local data types, constants, and variables like other C++ functions. The Pascal language does not have a similar scoping mechanism. In addition, all C++ functions have access to globally scoped constants, data types, and variables.

3. C++ strings and characters are enclosed in double and single quotes, respectively, and are handled differently—'A' is a character and "A" is a single-character string. Mixing C++ single-character strings and characters is not allowed (it is allowed in Turbo Pascal).

4. C++ defines blocks using the { and } characters instead of the BEGIN and END keywords.

5. Every statement in a C++ program must end with a semicolon. C++ has a more systematic approach to including statement delimiters than Pascal.

6. C++ contains the #include compiler directive that instructs the Turbo C++ compiler to include the iostream.h header file. The #include directive is similar to the Turbo Pascal {$I filename} directive. Header files contain the declarations of constants, data types, variables, and forward declarations of functions. They are similar to the interface parts of a library module. Although Turbo Pascal has no parallel to header files (because library units contain the code for both the definition and implementation), the Modula-2 language has separate definition and implementation modules. The iostream.h file provides the operations that support basic stream input and output. Unlike Pascal, C++ and C do not include I/O intrinsically as part of the core language. Instead, they rely on libraries specialized in various types of I/O.

7. The C++ program sends the "Hello Programmer!" string, using the extractor operator <<, to the standard output stream, cout, which is usually the screen.

8. The main function must return a value that reflects the error status of the C++ program. Returning the value 0 signals to the operating system that the program terminated normally.

C-Style Output

> Although the notion of streams is rooted in C, C++ has an extended and more flexible notion of stream I/O. Because I/O operations are not part of the core C++ language, C++ programmers may use stdio.h for C-style I/O or the various C++ libraries for stream I/O. Although it is a standard library, some C++ programmers feel that stdio.h should be abandoned altogether. These C++ programmers feel that stdio.h lacks the flexibility and the ability to offer abstract I/O for C++ classes. Of course, the C++ stream I/O libraries are not yet standardized among C++ compiler vendors. I feel that you should be exposed to both the C- and C++-style I/O, and you should decide what functions to use from each I/O library category. From a practical point of view, there is room for both C-style and C++-style I/O.

Now that you have heard the case for C-style I/O, take a look at a version of the last C++ program (Listing 2.2) that uses C-style output. Listing 2.3 shows the source code for program LST02_03.CPP, which uses the #include directive to include the stdio.h header file. This program displays the greeting message using the printf function.

Listing 2.3. Source code for program LST02_03.CPP.

```
// another trivial C++ program that says hello
// this version uses the C-style output

#include <stdio.h>

main()
{
  printf("Hello Programmer!");
  return 0;
}
```

Simple Data Types

Turbo Pascal's evolution includes the introduction of simple data types that parallel those used in C and C++. This similarity makes it easier to learn about the simple C++ data types. C++ contains the int, char, float, double, and void data types. The first four C++ data types are similar to Turbo Pascal's INTEGER, CHAR, REAL, and EXTENDED data types, respectively. The void data type is a special valueless type. C++ uses the void type with a function's returned values to indicate that the function acts as a procedure.

C++ adds more flexibility to data types by supporting what is known as data type modifiers. These modifiers alter the precision and range of values. The type modifiers are signed, unsigned, short, and long. Table 2.1 shows the predefined data types in C++ (and includes the type modifiers) and their sizes, ranges, and equivalent Turbo Pascal data types.

Table 2.1. Predefined data types in C++.

Data Type	Byte Size	Range	Turbo Pascal Type
char	1	-128 to 128	CHAR and SHORTINT
signed char	1	-128 to 128	SHORTINT
unsigned char	1	0 to 255	BYTE
int	2	-32,768 to 3,2767	INTEGER
signed int	2	-32,768 to 32,767	INTEGER
unsigned int (unsigned)	2	0 to 65,535	WORD
short int	2	-32,768 to 32,767	INTEGER
signed short int	2	-32,768 to 32,767	INTEGER
unsigned short int	2	0 to 65,535	WORD
long int (long)	4	-2,147,483,648 to 2,147,483,647	LONGINT
signed long int	4	-2,147,483,648 to 2,147,483,647	LONGINT
unsigned long int	4	0 to 4,294,967,295	none
float	4	3.4E-38 to 3.4E+38 and -3.4E-38 to -3.4E+38	SINGLE

continues

29

Table 2.1. continued

Data Type	Byte Size	Range	Turbo Pascal Type
long float	8	1.7E-308 to 1.7E+308 and -1.7E-308 to -1.7E+308	DOUBLE
double	8	1.7E-308 to 1.7E+308 and -1.7E-308 to -1.7E+308	DOUBLE
long double	10	3.4E-4,932 to 1.1E+4,932 and -3.4E-4,932 to -1.1E+4,932	

Listings 2.4 and 2.5 illustrate, respectively, a simple Turbo Pascal program that uses simple data types and an equivalent Turbo C++ program. Listing 2.4 contains the source code for the LST02_04.PAS program, which performs the following simple tasks:

- declares variables that have the simple data types

- assigns values to the variables

- displays the values of some of these variables and the results of expressions that involve some of these variables

Listing 2.5 contains the source code for an equivalent C++ program, LST02_05.CPP. Compare the code in both versions and note the following differences:

1. The C++ program declares its variables by stating the data type and declaring the variable. There is no semicolon between the data type and its associated variable. Instead, one space is placed between the data type and its associated variable. Like Pascal, however, a semicolon is placed after the declaration of each variable.

2. Unlike Pascal, the identifiers in C++ are case-sensitive. The identifiers anInt, AnInt, and ANINT refer to different items in C++.

3. The variables in the C++ program are initialized when they are declared. This feature enables you to reduce the number of statements and consolidate the declaration and initialization of variables.

4. C++ supports numeric constants that include type specifiers. The constant 65000U, for example, contains the letter U to indicate that the constant is an

unsigned integer. Similarly, the constant `2000000L` contains the letter `L` to signify that the constant is a long integer. If you omit these type specifiers, the C++ compiler makes the needed type conversions. Including type specifiers is a bit more efficient and gives you control over the interpretation of the numeric constant.

5. The assignment operator in C++ is the equal sign (no colon is placed before the equal sign).

6. I translated the Pascal `WRITELN` into the `printf` function to illustrate the formatting feature of `printf`. The first argument of the `printf` function is the formatting string that includes format code and the output text. The second and subsequent arguments are usually the values displayed by `printf`. I say "usually" because `printf` enables you to include arguments that fine-tune the formatted output. The `printf` function uses the `%` character to locate format code instructions. The `%` character may be followed by an optional number that specifies the output width for the corresponding argument. The `%` character is also followed by one or two letters that specify the data type. To further understand the `%` format, it may be useful to examine the way in which it is used in the C++ program. Consider the first call to `printf`:

```
printf("%3d + %2d = %3d\n", aByte, anInt, aByte + anInt);
```

The formatting string contains three instances of the `%` character. The first and last instances are `%3d`. The 3 that follows the `%` character indicates that a three-column width is reserved to display a value. The letter `d` indicates that the value appears as an `int` type. Similarly, the `%2d` format code specifies the display of an integer in a two-column width. Notice that the second and third arguments are the variables `aByte` and `anInt`. By contrast, the fourth argument of function `printf` is an expression.

How many arguments do you think `printf` accepts? Listing 2.3 shows one argument and Listing 2.5 shows four. This may not seem unusual because you might compare the `printf` function to the Pascal `WRITE` and `WRITELN` intrinsics. These Pascal intrinsics take a varying number of arguments. `printf` is a C function just like any other C function that you declare (okay, so `printf` is really a sophisticated function). C++ and C allow functions to have a variable number of arguments. Of course, these functions must be declared in a certain way. Although this topic is discussed later in more detail, for the moment you should be aware of this unusual language feature in C++.

The second call to the printf function is as follows:

```
printf("%4.1f / %4.1f = %f5.3\n", aSingle, aDouble,
    aSingle / aDouble);
```

The first two instances of the % characters are similar. Each has the number 4.1 followed by f. The number 4.1 specifies that the output occupies four columns and displays one decimal place. The letter f indicates that the output is a floating-point number. Likewise, the characters %5.3f specify a width of five columns and three decimal places.

The third call to the printf function displays a character. The %c format code specifies that the aChar variable appear as a character. The printf function also uses the %s format code to specify strings.

> The % format code in a printf function call can perform data conversion. The program, for example, declares the aByte variable as unsigned char, which is basically a character. Notice, however, that the first call to printf uses the %3d format code to display the aByte variable. When you run the program you see an integer instead of a character. The d character specifies that the aByte argument, a character, be converted into an integer.

Listing 2.4. Source code for program LST02_04.PAS.

```
Program Demo_Predefined_Data_Types;
{$N+}
{
  Program that demonstrates the simple
  predefined data types in Turbo Pascal.
}

VAR aShort  : SHORTINT;
    anInt   : INTEGER;
    aByte   : BYTE;
    aWord   : WORD;
    aLong   : LONGINT;
    aChar   : CHAR;
    aSingle : SINGLE;
    aDouble : DOUBLE;

BEGIN
  { assign values to the program's variables }
```

```
  aShort := 4;
  anInt := 67;
  aByte := 128;
  aWord := 65000;
  aLong := 2000000;
  aChar := '!';
  aSingle := 355.0;
  aDouble := 1.130E+002;
  { display sample expressions }
  WRITELN(aByte:3, ' + ', anInt:2, ' = ', (aByte + anInt):3);

  WRITELN(aSingle:4:1, ' / ', aDouble:4:1, ' = ',
          (aSingle / aDouble):5:3);

  WRITELN('The character saved in variable aChar is ', aChar);

END.
```

Listing 2.5. Source code for program LST02_05.CPP.

```
/*
  Program that demonstrates the simple
  predefined data types in Turbo C++.
*/

#include <stdio.h>

main()
{
  short    aShort    = 4;
  int      anInt     = 67;
  unsigned char aByte = 128;
  unsigned aWord     = 65000U;
  long     aLong     = 2000000L;
  char     aChar     = '!';
  float    aSingle   = 355.0;
  double   aDouble    = 1.130e+002;
  // display sample expressions
  printf("%3d + %2d = %3d\n", aByte, anInt, aByte + anInt);
  printf("%4.1f / %4.1f = %f5.3\n", aSingle, aDouble,
         aSingle / aDouble);
  printf("The character saved in variable aChar is %c\n", aChar);
  return 0;
}
```

Formatted Stream Output

Listing 2.5 shows you how to use printf to create formatted output. iostream.h contains functions that specify the width and number of digits for floating-point numbers. Listing 2.6 contains the source code for program LST02_06.CPP. This program is similar to LST02_05.CPP, except it uses C++ stream functions to generate formatted output. I have included this program for two reasons:

- to illustrate how to emit formatted output using C++ streams

- to demonstrate that a single call to printf succeeds in replacing multiple statements that provide C++ stream output

If you examine the statements that perform the stream output, you can see the first group of stream output statements are equivalent to the first call to printf in Listing 2.5. The program uses the width stream function to specify the output width for the next item displayed by a cout << statement. Notice how many statements it takes to display three integers. In addition, notice that the program uses the int(aByte) expression to typecast the unsigned char type into an int. Without this type conversion, the contents of variable aByte appear as a character. If I use the stream output to display integers that have default widths, then I can indeed replace the six stream output statements with a single one.

The second set of stream output statements generates the floating-point numbers. The program uses the precision stream function to specify the total number of digits to display. It takes six C++ statements to output three floating-point numbers. To reiterate, if I use the stream output to display numbers that have default widths, I can replace the six stream output statements with a single one.

This sample program shows that printf offers a viable tool for the formatted output of simple data types. Concerning code readability, printf is better than the equivalent stream output statements.

Listing 2.6. Source code for program LST02_06.CPP.

```
/*
  Program that demonstrates the simple
  predefined data types in Turbo C++.
  This version uses stream output.
*/

#include <iostream.h>
```

```
main()
{
  short    aShort    = 4;
  int      anInt     = 67;
  unsigned char aByte = 128;
  unsigned aWord     = 65000U;
  long     aLong     = 2000000L;
  char     aChar     = '!';
  float    aSingle    = 355.0;
  double   aDouble    = 1.130e+002;
  // display sample expressions
  cout.width(3);
  cout << int(aByte) << " + ";
  cout.width(2);
  cout << anInt << " = ";
  cout.width(3);
  cout << (aByte + anInt) << '\n';

  cout.precision(4);
  cout << aSingle << " / ";
  cout.precision(4);
  cout << aDouble << " = ";
  cout.precision(5);
  cout << (aSingle / aDouble) << '\n';

  cout << "The character saved in variable aChar is "
       << aChar << '\n';
  return 0;
}
```

Constants

Constants are identifiers associated with fixed values. Many languages, such as recent implementations of BASIC, Modula-2, Ada, C, Pascal, and C++ support constants. No one can deny that constants enhance the readability of a program by replacing numeric constants with identifiers that are more descriptive. Using constants enables you to alter the value of a program parameter by simply changing the value of that parameter in one location. This capability is definitely easier and less prone to generate errors that may occur when you order your text editor to replace certain numbers with other numbers.

C++ constants are available in two varieties: macro-based and formal constants. Macro-based constants are inherited from C and use the #define compiler directive. The general syntax for the #define directive is:

```
#define constantName constantValue
```

The #define directive causes the compiler to invoke the preprocessor and perform text substitution to replace the macro-based constants with their values. This replacement means that the compiler never sees the macro-based constants—only what they expand to.

The second type of constant in C++ is the formal constant. The general syntax for the formal constant is:

```
const dataType constantName = constantValue;
```

The dataType item is an optional item that specifies the data type of the constant values. If you omit the data type, the C++ compiler assumes the int type. The declaration of formal constants in C++ resembles that of type constants in Turbo Pascal. Keep in mind that a formal constant in C++ is a true constant. The Turbo Pascal type constant is really an initialized variable. You can alter the value of a Turbo Pascal type constant. This is not possible with the C++ constant.

Many C++ gurus don't recommend using the #define directive to define constants. They favor the formal constant because it enables the compiler to perform type checking.

Listing 2.8, the source code for the LST02_08.PAS program, shows a Turbo Pascal program that uses constants. Listing 2.8 is its equivalent Turbo C++ program. The Pascal program uses the formal Pascal constants and the Turbo Pascal-typed constants. The MSG, SLOPE, and TEMP_F_CHAR constants are formal Pascal constants, whose values cannot be altered. In contrast, the TEMP_C_CHAR and INTERCEPT identifiers are Turbo Pascal typed constants. The Turbo Pascal program uses a global declaration for all of these constants and calculates the Fahrenheit temperature based on the same temperature given in Celsius.

Looking at the Turbo C++ version, program LST02_08.CPP, which appears in Listing 2.8, you can see the C++ program declares the constants MSG, SLOPE, and TEMP_F_CHAR as macro-based constants. The program also declares the formal constants TEMP_C_CHAR and INTERCEPT. All the constants are declared as local to the function main. Looking at the various declarations of the constants in the C++ program, notice the following:

1. The macro-based constants do not use the equal sign and do not end with a semicolon.

2. The #define directive permits only one constant declared per line.

Listing 2.9 shows the source code for program LST02_09.CPP. This program is a variant of the C++ program in Listing 2.8 and makes the constant declarations global. This means that these constants are accessible to any other function in the C++ program that you may add.

Listing 2.7. Source code for program LST02_07.PAS.

```
Program Demo_Constants;

{ a trivial Turbo Pascal program that demonstrates constants }

CONST MSG = 'The temperature ';
      SLOPE = 1.8;
      TEMP_F_CHAR = 'F';
      { use Turbo Pascal typed constants }
      TEMP_C_CHAR : CHAR = 'C';
      INTERCEPT : REAL = 32;

VAR   tempC,
      tempF : REAL;

BEGIN
   tempC := 10;
   tempF := INTERCEPT + SLOPE * tempC;
   { show the values stored in the above variables }
   WRITE(MSG);
   WRITE(tempC:3:1, ' ', TEMP_C_CHAR, ' = ');
   WRITELN(tempF:3:1, ' ', TEMP_F_CHAR);
END.
```

Listing 2.8. Source code for program LST02_08.CPP.

```
// a trivial Turbo C++ program that demonstrates local constants

#include <stdio.h>

main()
{
```

continues

Listing 2.8. continued

```
#define MSG "The temperature "
#define SLOPE 1.8
#define TEMP_F_CHAR 'F'
const char TEMP_C_CHAR = 'C';
const double INTERCEPT = 32;

double tempC, tempF;

tempC = 10;
tempF = INTERCEPT + SLOPE * tempC;
// show the values stored in the above variables
printf(MSG);
printf("%3.1f %c = %3.1f %c", tempC, TEMP_C_CHAR,
                              tempF, TEMP_F_CHAR);
}
```

Listing 2.9. Source code for program LST02_09.CPP.

```
// a trivial Turbo C++ program that demonstrates global constants

#include <stdio.h>

#define MSG "The temperature "
#define SLOPE 1.8
#define TEMP_F_CHAR 'F'

const char TEMP_C_CHAR = 'C';
const double INTERCEPT = 32;

main()
{
    double tempC, tempF;

    tempC = 10;
    tempF = INTERCEPT + SLOPE * tempC;
    // show the values stored in the above variables
    printf(MSG);
    printf("%3.1f %c = %3.1f %c\n", tempC, TEMP_C_CHAR,
                                    tempF, TEMP_F_CHAR);
}
```

You probably noticed the \n characters in the format string of the printf function in the last two C++ programs. These characters are part of a special set of characters called the escape sequence. The \n characters result in a newline character (ASCII code 10). Table 2.2 shows the set of escape sequences. You can use these characters in strings sent to the output using either C-style output functions or the C++ stream output functions.

Table 2.2. The escape sequence.

Sequence	Decimal Value	Hex Value	Task
\a	7	0x07	Bell
\b	8	0x08	Backspace
\f	12	0x0C	Formfeed
\n	10	0x0A	Newline
\r	13	0x0D	Carriage return
\t	9	0x09	Horizontal Tab
\v	11	0x0B	Vertical Tab
\\	92	0x5C	Backslash
\'	44	0x2C	Single quote
\"	34	0x22	Double quote
\?	63	0x3F	Question mark
\000			1 to 3 digits for octal value
\Xhhh and \xhhh		0xhhh	Hexadecimal value

The *printf* Function

As a novice C++ programmer, you have a wealth of I/O functions to choose from. The printf function is powerful. It presents formatted controls that outdo the formatted output features of the Pascal WRITE and WRITELN intrinsics. In Listings 2.8 and 2.9, I gave you only a glimpse of what the printf function can do. To give you a good feel for the formatting features of printf, I will present the general form of the formatting options available to printf. The general syntax for the individual formatting instruction is as follows:

```
% [flags] [width] [.precision] [F ¦ N ¦ h ¦ l ¦ L] <type character>
```

The flags options indicate the output justification, numeric signs, decimal points, and trailing zeros. In addition, these flags specify the octal and hexadecimal prefixes. Table 2.3 shows the options for the flags in the format string of the printf function.

Table 2.3. The options for the *flags* in the format string of the *printf* function.

Format Option	Outcome
0	Add zeros until minimum field width is reached, if width is prefixed with zero.
-	Justifies to the left within the specified field.
+	Displays the plus or minus sign of a value.
blank	Displays a leading blank if the value is positive. Displays a minus sign if the value is negative.
#	No effect on decimal integers. Displays a leading 0X or 0x for hexadecimal integers. Displays a leading zero for octal integers. Displays the decimal point for reals.

The width option indicates the minimum number of displayed characters. The printf function uses zeros and blanks to pad the output if needed. When the width number begins with a 0, the printf function uses leading zeros, instead of spaces, for padding. When the * character appears instead of a width number, the printf function obtains the actual width number from the function's argument list. The argument that specifies the required width must be before the argument actually being formatted.

The precision option specifies the maximum number of displayed characters. If you include an integer, the precision option defines the minimum number of displayed digits. When the * character is used in place of a precision number, printf obtains the actual number from the argument list. The argument that specifies the required precision number must be before the argument actually being formatted.

The F, N, h, L, and l options are sized options utilized to overrule the argument's default size. The F and N options are used in conjunction with far and near pointers, respectively. The h, L and l options indicate short int or long, respectively.

The printf function requires that you specify a data type character with each % format code. Table 2.4 shows the data type characters utilized in the format string of printf.

Table 2.4. The data type characters utilized in the format string of *printf*.

Category	Type Character	Outcome
character	c	Single character
	d	Signed decimal int
	i	Signed decimal int
	o	Unsigned octal int
	u	Unsigned decimal int
	x	Unsigned hexadecimal int (the set of numeric characters used is 01234567890abcdef)
	X	Unsigned hexadecimal int (the set of numeric characters used is 01234567890ABCDEF)
pointer	p	Displays only the offset for near pointers as OOOO (displays far pointers as SSSS:OOOO)
pointer to int	n	
real	f	Displays signed value in the format [-]dddd.dddd
	e	Displays signed scientific value in the format [-]d.dddde[+|-]ddd
	E	Displays signed scientific value in the format [-]d.ddddE[+|-]ddd
	g	Displays signed value using either the f or e formats, depending on the value and the specified precision

continues

Table 2.4. continued

Category	Type Character	Outcome
	G	Displays signed value using either the f or E formats, depending on the value and the specified precision
string pointer	s	Displays characters until the null terminator of the string is reached

Translation Hints

The translation of the Pascal WRITE statements into printf statements employ the following general forms:

```
Pascal:
WRITE(stringVar:<width>);

C++:
    printf("%<width>s", stringVar);

Pascal:
    WRITE(integerVar:<width>);

C++:
    printf("%<width>d", integerVar);

Pascal:
    WRITE(longVar:<width>);

C++:
    printf("%<width>ld", longVar);

Pascal:
    WRITE(realVar:<width>:<decimals>);

C++:
    printf("%<width>.<decimals>f", realVar);
```

The *scanf* Function

The scanf function is a console input function that can be regarded as the counterpart to the printf function. Like the printf function, the first argument of scanf is an input format string. This string tells scanf the number of input items, their types, and formats. The other arguments of scanf are pointers to the variables that receive the input values. In the case of a single variable, you need to place the address-of operator & before the name of the variable. Using the & operator provides the address of a variable to function scanf. Using scanf to input a single value is easy. In the case of multiple input, the role of the input format string becomes more critical because it specifies how many spaces (typically one space) delimit the various input data. This means that you must use the same number of spaces when you type your data. For example, if you want to enter two floating-point numbers in two variables, s and y, use the function call scanf("%f %f", &x, &y) to point out that the two numbers are input with a single space between them. On the other hand, if you specify the input format string of "%f %f" you must enter two spaces between the numbers you enter.

Listing 2.10 contains the source code for program LST02_10.CPP, an example that uses the scanf function for input. The program carries out the following tasks:

1. Prompts you to enter an integer. The program stores the integer in the anInt variable. Notice that the call to scanf uses the input format string of "%d". The function call also uses the &anInt expression as the argument that specifies the address of the anInt variable.

2. Displays the contents of anInt as decimal, octal, and hexadecimal numbers. These various numeric representations are generated using the %d, %o, and %X format codes, respectively, in the printf function.

3. Prompts you to enter an unsigned integer. The program stores the integer in the aWord variable. Notice that the call to scanf uses the input format string of "%u". The function call also uses the &aWord expression as the argument that specifies the address of the aWord variable.

4. Displays the contents of aWord as decimal, octal, and hexadecimal numbers. These various numeric representations are generated using the %u, %o, and %X format codes, respectively, in the printf function.

5. Prompts you to enter a long integer. The program stores the integer in the aLong variable. Notice that the call to scanf uses the input format string of "%ld". The function call also uses the &aLong expression as the argument that specifies the address of the aLong variable.

43

6. Displays the contents of aLong as decimal, octal, and hexadecimal numbers. These various numeric representations are generated using the %ld, %lo, and %lX format codes, respectively, in the printf function.

7. Prompts you to enter a floating-point number. The program stores your input in the aFloat variable. Notice that the call to scanf uses the "%f" input format string to specify a floating-point number. The second argument of scanf is the &aFloat expression, which provides the function with the address of the aFloat variable.

8. Displays the value stored in the aFloat variable using the %f, %E, and % format codes.

9. Calculates the square of your input and stores the result in the aLongFloat variable.

10. Displays the value stored in the aLongFloat variable using the %f, %E, and % format codes.

11. Prompts you to enter a sequence of three characters (with no delimiting spaces between them). The call to scanf uses the "%c%c%c" input format. The scanf function uses the &char1, &char2, and &char3 arguments to specify the addresses of the char1, char2, and char3 variables, respectively.

12. Displays the input characters and the ASCII code for the character stored in char1. Notice that for the latter output, printf displays the char1 variable twice, first using the %c format code and the second time using the %d format code. The %d format code displays the contents of char1 as an integer—the ASCII code of the character.

A sample session using the LST02_10.CPP program yields the following results.

```
Enter an integer : 67

decimal 67 = octal 103 = hexadecimal 43

Enter a positive integer : 255

decimal 255 = octal 377 = hexadecimal FF

Enter a long integer : 123456

decimal 123456 = octal 361100 = hexadecimal 1E240

Enter a floating point number : 3.456
```

```
number =
        3.456000 (in %f format)
        3.456000E+00 (in %E format)
        3.456 (in %g format)

number =
        11.943937 (in %lf format)
        1.194394E+01 (in %lE format)
        11.9439 (in %lg format)


Type three characters followed by [Enter] : and

You typed and

The ASCII code of a is 97
```

Listing 2.10. Source code for program LST02_10.CPP.

```c
/*
  program to demonstrate output formatting with printf()
  and keyboard input using scanf()
*/

#include <stdio.h>

main()
{
  int anInt;
  long aLong;
  unsigned aWord;
  char char1, char2, char3;
  float aFloat;
  long float aLongFloat;

  // test keyboard I/O for an integer
  printf("Enter an integer : ");
  scanf("%d", &anInt);
  printf("\ndecimal %d = octal %o = hexadecimal %X",
          anInt, anInt, anInt);

  // illustrate keyboard I/O for an unsigned integer
  printf("\n\nEnter a positive integer : ");
  scanf("%u", &aWord);
  printf("\ndecimal %u = octal %o = hexadecimal %X",
          aWord, aWord, aWord);
```

continues

45

Listing 2.10. continued

```c
// illustrate keyboard I/O for a long integer
printf("\n\nEnter a long integer : ");
scanf("%ld", &aLong);
printf("\ndecimal %ld = octal %lo = hexadecimal %lX",
       aLong, aLong, aLong);

// illustrate keyboard I/O for a single precision
// floating point number
printf("\n\nEnter a floating point number : ");
scanf("%f", &aFloat);
printf("\nnumber = \n");
printf("          %f (in %%f format)\n", aFloat);
printf("          %E (in %%E format)\n", aFloat);
printf("          %g (in %%g format)\n", aFloat);

// illustrate keyboard I/O for a double precision
// floating point number
aLongFloat = aFloat * aFloat;
printf("\nnumber = \n");
printf("          %lf (in %%lf format)\n", aLongFloat);
printf("          %lE (in %%lE format)\n", aLongFloat);
printf("          %lg (in %%lg format)\n", aLongFloat);

// illustrate keyboard I/O for characters
printf("\n\n\n\n");
printf("Type three characters followed by [Enter] : ");
/*-----------------------------------------------------
   if you experience a bug with the program properly
   reading 3 characters, uncomment the following line
   and enclose the next one in a comment.
   scanf("%c%c%c%c", &char1, &char1, &char2, &char3);
-----------------------------------------------------*/
scanf("%c%c%c", &char1, &char2, &char3);
printf("\nYou typed %c%c%c\n\n", char1, char2, char3);
printf("The ASCII code of %c is %d\n\n\n", char1, char1);
return 0;
}
```

Character I/O Functions

The preceding C++ program should give you a good feel for the power and flexibility of the printf function, as well as for the input capabilities of scanf. These I/O features have

no parallel in Turbo Pascal. The ability of a single printf call to issue multiple newline characters exemplifies printf's flexibility.

> Listing 2.10 also illustrates the advantage of using scanf in the input of integers and floating-point numbers. The scanf function is not a good choice for entering characters and strings. (I'll discuss string input in Chapter 8.) Turbo C++ offers other functions to support character I/O. Some of these functions are prototyped in the conio.h header file and may not be portable to other C++ implementations.

The character input functions are:

1. The getche function, which returns a character from the console and echoes that character on the screen. This function is prototyped in the conio.h header file.

2. The getch function, which returns a character from the console but does not echo that input character. This function is also prototyped in the conio.h header file.

3. The getchar function, which returns a character from the console. This function is prototyped in the stdio.h header file.

The character output functions are:

1. The putch function, which outputs a single character to the console. This function is prototyped in the conio.h header file.

2. The putchar function, which outputs a single character to the console. This function is also prototyped in the stdio.h header file.

The getchar and putchar functions work with input and output devices in general and not just the console.

> The character input functions need no argument and return an int type to represent the ASCII code of the input character. Why not return a char type? The answer points back to the traditional C approach, inherited by C++, that draws a close association between integers and characters (which are always stored using their numeric ASCII code). Each character input function, therefore, is merely returning a character in its raw form—an ASCII code integer. The same logic is applied to the character output functions that accept the int type rather than a char type.

Listing 2.11 shows the source code for program LST02_11.PAS, which puts some of the character I/O functions to work. This simple program prompts you to enter three characters. The program reads each character using the ReadKey function imported from the CRT unit. To echo each character, the Pascal program uses the WRITELN intrinsic.

Listing 2.11. Source code for program LST02_11.PAS.

```
{ simple Turbo Pascal program to demonstrate character I/O }

PROGRAM Demo_Char_IO;

Uses CRT;

VAR Char1, Char2, Char3, aKey : CHAR;

BEGIN

    WRITELN; WRITELN;
    WRITE('Enter the first  character : ');
    Char1 := ReadKey;
    WRITELN(Char1);
    WRITE('Enter a second character   : ');
    Char2 := ReadKey;
    WRITELN(Char2);
    WRITE('Enter a third  character   : ');
    Char3 := ReadKey;
    WRITELN(Char3);
    WRITELN; WRITELN;
    WRITE('You entered ', Char1, Char2, Char3);
    WRITELN; WRITELN;
    aKey := ReadKey;
END.
```

Listing 2.12 shows the source code for program LST02_12.CPP, the C++ program equivalent to the preceding Pascal program. The C++ program uses the getche, getch, and getchar functions to enter each character. Notice that the call to getch is followed by a call to putchar to echo the input character on the console. The call to getchar requires you to press Enter after you type in the character. In contrast, the getche and getch functions do not require you to press Enter. Consequently, these functions support faster character input, but you have no chance to correct erroneous input! The program uses the putch function to emit the three characters you type. Listing 2.13 contains the source code for the LST02_13.CPP program, which uses getch to support character input without echo.

Listing 2.12. Source code for program LST02_12.CPP.

```
/*
    program to demonstrate character I/O using getche and
    putchar.  The program demonstrates how getche is used
    in character console-input with echoing.
*/

#include <stdio.h>
#include <conio.h>

main()
{
    char char1, char2, char3;

    printf("\n\n");
    printf("\nType the first  character : ");
    char1 = getche();
    printf("\nEnter a second character  : ");
    char2 = getch();
    putchar(char2); // echo the character
    printf("\nEnter a third character   : ");
    char3 = getchar();

    printf("\n\nYou entered ");
    putch(char1);
    putch(char2);
    putch(char3);
    printf("\n\n");
    getche();
    return 0;
}
```

Listing 2.13. Source code for program LST02_13.CPP.

```
/*
    program to demonstrate character I/O using getch and
    putchar.  The program demonstrates how getch is used
    in character console-input without echoing.
*/

#include <stdio.h>
#include <conio.h>
```

continues

Listing 2.13. continued

```
main()
{
    char char1, char2, char3;

    printf("\n\n");
    printf("\nType the first  character : ");
    char1 = getch();
    printf("\nEnter a second character  : ");
    char2 = getch();
    printf("\nEnter a third character   : ");
    char3 = getch();

    printf("\n\nYou entered ");
    putchar(char1);
    putchar(char2);
    putchar(char3);
    printf("\n\n");
    getch();
    return 0;
}
```

C++ Stream Character I/O

To offer the C++ streams "equal airtime," so to speak, I would like to turn your attention to character I/O using C++ streams. Listing 2.14 shows the source code for program LST02_14.CPP, which performs the same tasks as the last two C++ programs, except it uses the C++ streams. Notice that the program includes the iostream.h header file instead of the stdio.h header file. The program also uses the cin standard input stream and the >> operator to obtain a character from the standard input stream, the console. The cin stream requires you to confirm your input by pressing Enter. In that regard, the cin stream and the >> operator together work like the getchar function. The program sends the characters you type using a single stream output statement. The output statement uses the cout stream and a chained sequence of << operators and output operands.

Listing 2.14. Source code for program LST02_14.CPP.

```
/*
    program to demonstrate character I/O using C++ stream
    >> and << operators.
*/

#include <iostream.h>
#include <conio.h>

main()
{
    char char1, char2, char3;

    cout << "\n\n\nType the first  character : ";
    cin >> char1;
    cout << "Enter a second character  : ";
    cin >> char2;
    cout << "Enter a third character   : ";
    cin >> char3;

    cout << "\n\nYou entered "
         << char1
         << char2
         << char3
         << "\n\n";
    getch();
    return 0;
}
```

Summary

In this chapter, you started your C++ journey and learned about the following topics:

- The basic components of C++ programs. This includes comments, the main function, and the declaration of simple variables.

- The simple predefined C++ data types.

- The formatted output using the versatile printf function.

- C++ constants that are declared using either the #define compiler directive or the const declaration.

51

- The format code involved in the format string of the printf function.
- Data input from the console using the scanf function.
- Character I/O using functions prototyped in the stdio.h and conio.h header files.
- Character I/O using C++ streams.

C++ OPERATORS

3

Operators are vital components of a language that is employed to write terms, factors, and expressions. This chapter presents the C++ operators and covers the following topics:

- arithmetic operators

- increment operators

- arithmetic assignment operators

- character operators

- typecasting and data conversion

- relational operators and conditional expressions

- bit-manipulating operators

- comma operator

Many operators in C++ (and in its parent language, C) parallel those used in Turbo Pascal. Keep in mind, however, that C++ has operators that enable you to write more terse statements.

Arithmetic Operators

Table 3.1 lists the C++ operators and their equivalent Turbo Pascal operators. The / operator in C++ works like the / and DIV operators in Turbo Pascal. The compiler performs floating-point or integer division depending on the operands. If both operands are integer expressions, the compiler produces the code for an integer division. If either or both operands are floating-point expressions, then the compiler yields code for floating-point division.

Table 3.1. The C++ arithmetic operators and their equivalent Turbo Pascal operators.

C++ Operator	Purpose	Data Type	Turbo Pascal Operator
+	unary plus	numeric	+
-	unary minus	numeric	-
+	add	numeric	+
-	subtract	numeric	-
*	multiply	numeric	*
/	divide	numeric	/ (reals)
			DIV
%	modulus	integers	MOD

Listings 3.1 and 3.2 contain the source code for LST03_01.PAS and LST03_02.CPP, programs that perform simple math operations. Listing 3.1 is Turbo Pascal and Listing 3.2 is the equivalent Turbo C++ program. Listing 3.1 carries out the following tasks:

1. Prompts you to enter two integers. The program stores your input in the int1 and int2 variables.

2. Adds, subtracts, multiplies, divides, and takes the modulus of the two integers you typed. The program assigns the result of each operation to a LONGINT-typed variable. This type of assignment ensures that the variable storing the result will not overflow (except when dividing by zero).

3. Displays the contents of the long1, long2, long3, long4, and long5 variables that store the results of the preceding math operations.

4. Prompts you to enter two floating-point numbers. The programs store your input in the x and y variables.

5. Adds, subtracts, multiplies, and divides the two numbers that you typed. The program assigns the result of each operation to a REAL-typed variable.

6. Displays the contents of the real1, real2, real3, and real4 variables that store the results of the preceding math operations.

The following code is a sample session of the Turbo Pascal program:

```
[BEGIN SESSION]
Type first  integer : 67
Type second integer : 11

67 + 11 = 78
67 - 11 = 56
67 * 11 = 737
67 / 11 = 6
67 mod 11 = 1


Type first  real number : 355.0
Type second real number : 113.0

 3.5500000000E+02 +  1.1300000000E+02 =  4.6800000000E+02
 3.5500000000E+02 -  1.1300000000E+02 =  2.4200000000E+02
 3.5500000000E+02 *  1.1300000000E+02 =  4.0115000000E+04
 3.5500000000E+02 /  1.1300000000E+02 =  3.1415929204E+00
[END SESSION]
```

Listing 3.1. Source code for program LST03_01.PAS.

```
PROGRAM Demo_Numeric_Math;

{
  simple Turbo Pascal program to illustrate simple math operations
}

VAR int1, int2 : INTEGER;
    long1, long2, long3, long4, long5 : LONGINT;
    x, y, real1, real2, real3, real4 : REAL;

BEGIN
    WRITE('Type first  integer : '); READLN(int1);
    WRITE('Type second integer : '); READLN(int2);
```

continues

55

Listing 3.1. continued

```
    WRITELN;
    long1 := int1 + int2;
    long2 := int1 - int2;
    long3 := int1 * int2;
    long4 := int1 div int2;
    long5 := int1 mod int2;
    WRITELN(int1,' + ',int2,' = ', long1);
    WRITELN(int1,' - ',int2,' = ', long2);
    WRITELN(int1,' * ',int2,' = ', long3);
    WRITELN(int1,' / ',int2,' = ', long4);
    WRITELN(int1,' mod ',int2,' = ', long5);
    WRITELN; WRITELN;
    WRITE('Type first  real number : '); READLN(x);
    WRITE('Type second real number : '); READLN(y);
    WRITELN;
    real1 := x + y;
    real2 := x - y;
    real3 := x * y;
    real4 := x / y;
    WRITELN(x,' + ',y,' = ', real1);
    WRITELN(x,' - ',y,' = ', real2);
    WRITELN(x,' * ',y,' = ', real3);
    WRITELN(x,' / ',y,' = ', real4);
    WRITELN; WRITELN;
END.
```

Listing 3.2, the source code for the LST03_02.CPP program, is the C++ equivalent to LST03_01.PAS. The program uses the int, long, and float data types in place of the Turbo Pascal INTEGER, LONGINT, and REAL types. The C++ program performs the same tasks as the Pascal program and uses C++ stream input and output.

The following code is a sample session of the Turbo C++ program:

```
[BEGIN SESSION]
Type first  integer : 67
Type second integer : 11

67 + 11 = 78
67 - 11 = 56
67 * 11 = 737
67 / 11 = 6

67 mod 11 = 1
```

```
Type first  real number : 355.0
Type second real number : 113.0

355 + 113 = 468
355 - 113 = 242
355 * 113 = 40115
355 / 113 = 3.141593
[END SESSION]
```

Listing 3.2. Source code for program LST03_02.CPP.

```cpp
// simple C++ program to illustrate simple math operations

#include <iostream.h>

main()
{
    int int1, int2;
    long long1, long2, long3, long4, long5;
    float x, y, real1, real2, real3, real4;

    cout << "\nType first  integer : ";
    cin >> int1;
    cout << "Type second integer : ";
    cin >> int2;
    cout << "\n";
    long1 = int1 + int2;
    long2 = int1 - int2;
    long3 = int1 * int2;
    long4 = int1 / int2;
    long5 = int1 % int2;
    cout << int1 << " + " << int2 << " = " << long1 << '\n';
    cout << int1 << " - " << int2 << " = " << long2 << '\n';
    cout << int1 << " * " << int2 << " = " << long3 << '\n';
    cout << int1 << " / " << int2 << " = " << long4 << '\n';
    cout << int1 << " mod " << int2 << " = " << long5 << '\n';
    cout << "\n\n";
    cout << "Type first  real number : ";
    cin >> x;
    cout << "Type second real number : ";
    cin >> y;
    cout << "\n";
    real1 = x + y;
    real2 = x - y;
    real3 = x * y;
```

continues

57

Listing 3.2. continued

```
    real4 = x / y;
    cout << x << " + " << y << " = " << real1 << '\n';
    cout << x << " - " << y << " = " << real2 << '\n';
    cout << x << " * " << y << " = " << real3 << '\n';
    cout << x << " / " << y << " = " << real4 << '\n';
    cout << "\n\n";
    return 0;
}
```

The Increment Operators

C++ supports special increment operators that enable you to increment and decrement by one the value stored in a variable. These operators are somewhat similar to, but more versatile than, the Turbo Pascal INC and DEC intrinsics. The ++ and -- are the increment and decrement operators and have the following general syntax:

```
variable++  // post-increment

++variable  // pre-increment

variable--  // post-decrement

--variable  // pre-decrement
```

The general syntax in the preceding code indicates that there are two ways to apply the ++ and -- operators. Placing these operators to the left of their operand alters the value of the operand before the operand contributes its value in an expression. Similarly, placing these operators to the right of their operands changes the value of the operand after the operand contributes its value in an expression. If the ++ or -- operators are the only operators in a statement, there is no difference between using the pre- or post forms.

You should note the following simple examples:

```
int i, j, k = 5;

k++; // k is now 6, same effect as ++k
--k; // k is now 5, same effect as k--
k = 5;
i = 4 * k++; // k is now 6 and i is 20
k = 5;
j = 4 * ++k; // k is now 6 and i is 24
```

The first statement uses the post-increment ++ operator to increment the value of the k variable. If you wrote ++k instead, you get the same result once the statement finishes executing. The second statement uses the pre-decrement -- operator. Again, if you write k-- instead, you get the same result. The next two statements assign 5 to k and then use the post-increment ++ operator in a simple math expression. This statement multiplies 4 by the current value of k (that is, 5), assigns the result of 20 to the i variable, and then increments the values in k to 6. The last two statements show a different result. The statement first increments the value in k (the value in k becomes 6), performs the multiplication, and then assigns the result of 24 to the i variable.

The Assignment Operators

As a Pascal programmer, you often see statements like this:

```
IndexOfFirstElement := IndexOfFirstElement + 4;
GraphicsScaleRatio := GraphicsScaleRatio * 3;
CurrentRateOfReturn := CurrentRateOfReturn DIV 4;
DOSfileListSize := DOSfileListSize - 10;
IndexOfLastElement = IndexOfLastElement MOD 23;
```

The variable that receives the result of an expression is also the first operand. (Of course, the addition and multiplication are communicative operations. The assigned variable, therefore, can be either operand with these operations.) I chose relatively long names to remind you, perhaps, that you need to shorten the expression without making the names of the variables shorter.

While C++ supports similar forms of statements, it also offers assignment operators that combine simple math operators and the assignment operator. C++, for example, enables you to write the following statements:

```
IndexOfFirstElement += 4;
GraphicsScaleRatio *= 3;
CurrentRateOfReturn /= 4;
DOSfileListSize -= 10;
IndexOfLastElement %= 23;
```

Notice that the name of the variable appears only once and that the statements use the +=, *=, /=, -=, and %= operators. Table 3.2 shows the arithmetic assignment operators. C++ also supports other types of assignment operators, and I will explain these other operators later in this chapter.

In addition to having an arithmetic assignment operator for each arithmetic operator (which is more than Turbo Pascal offers), these assignment operators work on characters, integers, and even floating-point numbers!

Table 3.2. The arithmetic assignment operators.

Assignment Operator	Long Form	Equivalent Pascal Intrinsic
x += y	x = x + y	INC(x, y)
x -= y	x = x - y	DEC(x, y)
x *= y	x = x * y	
x /= y	x = x / y	
x %= y	x = x % y	

First, I'll present a simple Turbo Pascal program that uses the various arithmetic operators and increment intrinsics. Listing 3.3 contains the source code for the Pascal program, LST03_03.PAS, which performs the following tasks:

- prompts you to enter two integers (the program stores your input in the i and j variables)

- uses the INC and DEC intrinsics and performs two math operations using the i and j variables

- displays the current values stored in the i and j variables

- prompts you to enter two floating-point numbers (the program stores these numbers in the x and y variables)

- performs various math operations using the x and y variables

- displays the current values stored in the x and y variables

Listing 3.3. Source code for program LST03_03.PAS.

```pascal
PROGRAM Demo_Numeric_Math2;

{
  simple Turbo Pascal program to illustrate additional
  simple math operations
}

VAR i, j : INTEGER;
    x, y : REAL;

BEGIN
    WRITE('Type first  integer : '); READLN(i);
    WRITE('Type second integer : '); READLN(j);
    WRITELN;
    INC(i, j);
    DEC(j, 6);
    i := i * 4;
    j := j div 3;
    INC(i);
    DEC(j);
    WRITELN('i = ',i); WRITELN;
    WRITELN('j = ',j); WRITELN;
    WRITELN; WRITELN;
    WRITE('Type first  real number : '); READLN(x);
    WRITE('Type second real number : '); READLN(y);
    WRITELN;
    x := x + y;
    y := y - 4.0;
    x := x * 4.0;
    y := y / 3.0;
    x := x + 1.0;
    y := y - 1.0;
    WRITELN('x = ',x); WRITELN;
    WRITELN('y = ',y); WRITELN;
END.
```

Listing 3.4 shows the source code for program LST03_04.CPP, the C++ program that is equivalent to Listing 3.3. This program example shows the increment and assignment operators in use. Compare the Pascal and C++ code and notice the following program aspects:

1. C++ offers a set of arithmetic assignment operators that function more consistently with the various numeric data types. These operators also cover the floating-point data types.

61

2. The increment and decrement operators also work with floating-point data types. This feature makes them more flexible than the Turbo Pascal INC and DEC intrinsics.

 ## Listing 3.4. Source code for program LST03_04.CPP.

```cpp
// simple C++ program to illustrate simple math operations

#include <iostream.h>

main()
{
    int i, j;
    float x, y;

    cout << "Type first  integer : ";
    cin >> i;
    cout << "Type second integer : ";
    cin >> j;
    cout << "\n";
    i += j;  // same as Pascal's INC(i, j)
    j -= 6;  // same as Pascal's DEC(j, 6)
    i *= 4;  // same as Pascal's i := i * 4
    j /= 3;  // same as Pascal's j := j div 3
    i++;     // same as Pascal's INC(i)
    j--;     // same as Pascal's DEC(j)
    cout << "\ni = " << i << "\n";
    cout << "\nj = " << j << "\n\n";

    cout << "\nType first  real number : ";
    cin >> x;
    cout << "Type second real number : ";
    cin >> y;
    cout << "\n";
    // abbreviated assignments also work with floats in C++
    x += y;    // no similar operations are allowed for
    y -= 4.0;  // reals in Turbo Pascal
    x *= 4.0;
    y /=  3.0;
    x++; // cannot be matched by Turbo Pascal's INC() and
    y--; // DEC() since they only work on ordinal-valued
         // data types
    cout << "x = " << x << '\n';
    cout << "y = " << y << "\n\n\n";
    return 0;
}
```

The next example, LST03_05.CPP, is a simple Turbo C++ program that illustrates the features of the pre-increment and post-increment operators. To get a better feel for how these operators work, use the built-in debugger and watch the k and i variables. Step through the program in Listing 3.5 and observe the current values in the watched variables. When the program executes the following statement:

```
i = 10 * (k++);
```

the k variable contributes the value of 5 to the multiplication expression. Consequently, the statement assigns 50 to the i variable. When the program executes the statement:

```
i = 10 * (++k)
```

the k variable is first incremented from 5 to 6. It then contributes its new value to the multiplication expression. Consequently, the statement assigns 60 to i.

Listing 3.5. Source code for program LST03_05.CPP.

```
/*
    C++ program illustrates the feature of the increment operator.
    The ++ or -- may be included in an expression.  The value
    of the associated variable is altered after the expression
    is evaluated if the var++ (or var--) is used, or before
    when ++var (or --var) is used.
*/

#include <iostream.h>

main()
{
    int i, k = 5;

    // use post-incrementing
    i = 10 * (k++); // k contributes 5 to the expression
    cout << "i = " << i << "\n\n"; // displays 50 (= 10 * 5)
    k--; // restores the value of k to 5

    // use pre-incrementing
    i = 10 * (++k); // k contributes 6 to the expression
    cout << "i = " << i << "\n\n"; // displays 60 (= 10 * 6)
    return 0;

}
```

The Character Operators

C++ and its parent language, C, support a close association between characters and integers. In Chapter 2, "Getting Started," I indicated that the character-typed variables store their information as ASCII numeric values. This feature paves the way for the arithmetic operators to manipulate characters as though they were integers.

The next two program examples illustrate the two-way automatic conversion between characters and integers. Listing 3.6 contains the source code for the Pascal program, LST03_06.PAS, and Listing 3.7 contains the source code for the equivalent C++ program, LST03_07.CPP. Look at the Pascal program first, which performs the following tasks:

- prompts you to type in a lowercase character
- converts the character to uppercase
- displays the uppercase character
- prompts you to type in an uppercase character
- converts the character to lowercase
- displays the lowercase character

The Turbo Pascal program relies on the ORD and CHR intrinsics to convert between characters and integers. Compare the Turbo Pascal program with its Turbo C++ counterpart. Notice that the character case conversion uses the += and -= arithmetic assignment operators. No special functions are needed to convert between characters and integers in C++. The integer math operators are able to shift the ASCII code of a character.

Listing 3.6. Source code for program LST03_06.PAS.

```
PROGRAM ASCII_Code;

Uses CRT;

{
   Turbo Pascal program to convert characters between
   uppercase and lowercase.
}

VAR ch : CHAR;
    ASCIIshift : BYTE;
```

```
BEGIN

    ASCIIshift := ORD('a') - ORD('A');

    { convert lowercase character to uppercase }
    WRITE('Type a lowercase character : ');
    ch := ReadKey; WRITELN(ch); WRITELN;

    ch := CHR(ORD(ch) - ASCIIshift);

    WRITE('The character in uppercase is : ', ch);
    WRITELN; WRITELN;

    { convert uppercase character to lowercase }
    WRITE('Type an uppercase character : ');
    ch := ReadKey; WRITELN(ch); WRITELN;

    ch := CHR(ORD(ch) + ASCIIshift);

    WRITE('The character in lowercase is : ', ch);
    WRITELN; WRITELN;

END.
```

Listing 3.7. Source code for program LST03_07.CPP.

```
// program to convert characters between uppercase and lowercase

#include <stdio.h>
#include "conio.h"

main()
{
    char ch;
    int ASCIIshift = 'a' - 'A';

    // convert lowercase to uppercase
    printf("Type a lowercase character : ");
    ch = getche();
    ch -= ASCIIshift;
    printf("\n\nThe character in uppercase is : %c\n\n", ch);
```

continues

[]

Listing 3.7. continued

```
// convert uppercase to lowercase
printf("Type an uppercase character : ");
ch = getche();
ch += ASCIIshift;
printf("\n\nThe character in lowercase is : %c\n\n", ch);
return 0;

}
```

The *sizeof* Operator

Your programs may often need to know the byte size of a data type or a variable. Turbo Pascal offers the SizeOf intrinsic, which takes either a data type or the name of a variable (scalar, array, record, and so on) for an argument. The SizeOf intrinsic in Turbo Pascal is not part of the standard Pascal. In fact, Borland added this useful intrinsic to emulate the C sizeof operator. C++ inherited the same operator from C. The general syntax for the sizeof operator is:

```
sizeof(variable_name ¦ data_type)
```

Listing 3.8 contains the source code for program LST03_08.PAS, which uses the SizeOf intrinsic with both data types and variables. The program prints a simple table that shows the byte sizes for some of the basic predefined data types. The following code is the output of the program:

```
[BEGIN SESSION]
Table 1. Data sizes using SizeOf(variable)

       Data type        Memory used
                          (bytes)
     ------------------  -----------
            byte              1
          integer             2
       long integer           4
         character            1
            real              6
```

Table 2. Data sizes using SizeOf(dataType)

Data type	Memory used (bytes)
byte	1
integer	2
long integer	4
character	1
real	6

[END SESSION]

Listing 3.8. Source code for program LST03_08.PAS.

```
PROGRAM Demo_Sizing_Data;

{
  simple Turbo Pascal program that displays the data sizes
  using the SizeOf() function with variables and data types.
}

VAR aByte : BYTE;
    anInt : INTEGER;
    aLong : LONGINT;
    aChar : CHAR;
    aReal : REAL;

BEGIN
    WRITELN('Table 1. Data sizes using SizeOf(variable) ');
    WRITELN;
    WRITELN('    Data type        Memory used ');
    WRITELN('                        (bytes)');
    WRITELN('------------------    ------------');
    WRITELN('        byte        ', sizeof(aByte));
    WRITELN('        integer     ', sizeof(anInt));
    WRITELN('    long integer    ', sizeof(aLong));
    WRITELN('      character     ', sizeof(aChar));
    WRITELN('        real        ', sizeof(aReal));
    WRITELN; WRITELN; WRITELN;

    WRITELN('Table 2. Data sizes using SizeOf(dataType) ');
    WRITELN;
    WRITELN('    Data type        Memory used ');
    WRITELN('                        (bytes)');
    WRITELN('------------------    ------------');
```

continues

67

Listing 3.8. continued

```
        WRITELN('      byte          ', sizeof(BYTE));
        WRITELN('      integer       ', sizeof(INTEGER));
        WRITELN('      long integer  ', sizeof(LONGINT));
        WRITELN('      character     ', sizeof(CHAR));
        WRITELN('      real          ', sizeof(REAL));
        WRITELN; WRITELN; WRITELN;
END.
```

Listing 3.9 shows the source code for program LST03_09.CPP. This program uses the sizeof operator in a manner similar to the SizeOf intrinsic in Turbo Pascal. The following code is the output of the Turbo C++ program:

```
[BEGIN SESSION]
Table 1. Data sizes using sizeof(variable)

        Data type        Memory used
                           (bytes)
    . . . . . . . . . . . . .      . . . . . . . . . . .
        short int             2
        integer               2
    long integer              4
        character             1
        float                 4


Table 2. Data sizes using sizeof(dataType)

        Data type        Memory used
                           (bytes)
    . . . . . . . . . . . . .      . . . . . . . . . . .
        short int             2
        integer               2
    long integer              4
        character             1
        float                 4
[END SESSION]
```

Notice that the float type in Turbo C++ requires four bytes, compared to six bytes needed by the Turbo Pascal type (on a machine that has a math coprocessor).

Listing 3.9. Source code for program LST03_09.CPP.

```c
/*
  simple program that returns the data sizes using the sizeof()
  operator with variables and data types.
*/

#include <stdio.h>

main()

{
    short int aShort;
    int anInt;
    long aLong;
    char aChar;
    float aReal;

    printf("Table 1. Data sizes using sizeof(variable)\n\n");
    printf("      Data type         Memory used\n");
    printf("                           (bytes)\n");
    printf("-----------------     ----------\n");
    printf("       short int          %d\n", sizeof(aShort));
    printf("         integer          %d\n", sizeof(anInt));
    printf("    long integer          %d\n", sizeof(aLong));
    printf("       character          %d\n", sizeof(aChar));
    printf("           float          %d\n", sizeof(aReal));
    printf("\n\n\n");

    printf("Table 2. Data sizes using sizeof(dataType)\n\n");
    printf("      Data type         Memory used\n");
    printf("                           (bytes)\n");
    printf("-----------------     ----------\n");
    printf("       short int          %d\n", sizeof(short int));
    printf("         integer          %d\n", sizeof(int));
    printf("    long integer          %d\n", sizeof(long));
    printf("       character          %d\n", sizeof(char));
    printf("           float          %d\n", sizeof(float));
    printf("\n\n\n");

    return 0;
}
```

Typecasting

Automatic data conversion is one of the duties of a compiler. This data conversion simplifies expression and relieves some frustration of both novice and veteran programmers. With behind-the-scenes data conversion, you don't need to study each expression that mixes somewhat similar data types in your program. For example, the compiler handles most expressions that mix various types of integers or integers and floating-point types. A compile-time error occurs if you try to do something illegal!

In some cases, you need to force the compiler into a particular (and compatible) data type. The early versions of Turbo Pascal did not support typecasting. Borland added this C-like data conversion feature a few years ago. If you've been using typecasting in Turbo Pascal, you can easily use it in C++. C++ supports the following forms of typecasting:

```
type_cast(expression)
```

and

```
(type_cast) expression
```

> Typecasting in C++ is more flexible than in Turbo Pascal. You can apply formal typecasting on integer types to obtain a floating-point type result.

Listing 3.10 contains the source code for the Pascal program, LST03_10.PAS. This program performs a series of math operations twice—once without typecasting, once with typecasting. The data conversion in the first set of operations relies on the compiler's decision to convert data. You specify the type of the result in the second set of operations.

The following code is the output of the Turbo Pascal program:

```
[BEGIN SESSION]
shortInt1 = 10
shortInt2 = 6
aByte = 16
anInt = 4
aLong = 60
aChar is C
aReal =  6.0250000000E+01

shortInt1 = 10
shortInt2 = 6
```

```
aByte = 16
anInt = 4
aLong = 60
aChar is C
[END SESSION]
```

Listing 3.10. Source code for program LST03_10.PAS.

```pascal
PROGRAM Demo_Type_Cast;

{
  simple Turbo Pascal program that demonstrates data
  conversion using typecasting
}

VAR shortInt1, shortInt2 : SHORTINT;
    aByte : BYTE;
    anInt : INTEGER;
    aLong : LONGINT;
    aChar : CHAR;
    aReal : REAL;

BEGIN
    { assign values }
    shortInt1 := 10;
    shortInt2 := 6;
    { perform operations without user-specified typecasting }
    aByte := shortInt1 + shortInt2;
    anInt := shortInt1 - shortInt2;
    aLong := shortInt1 * shortInt2;
    aChar := CHR(aLong + 7);
    aReal := shortInt1 * shortInt2 + 0.25;

    WRITELN('shortInt1 = ',shortInt1);
    WRITELN('shortInt2 = ',shortInt2);
    WRITELN('aByte = ',aByte);
    WRITELN('anInt = ',anInt);
    WRITELN('aLong = ',aLong);
    WRITELN('aChar is ',aChar);
    WRITELN('aReal = ',aReal);
    WRITELN; WRITELN;

    { perform operations with typecasting }
    aByte := BYTE(shortInt1 + shortInt2);
    anInt := INTEGER(shortInt1 - shortInt2);
```

continues

Listing 3.10. continued

```
aLong := LONGINT(shortInt1 * shortInt2);
aChar := CHR(BYTE(aLong + 7));
{ aReal := REAL(shortInt1 * shortInt2 + 0.15); IS NOT A
                                                VALID TYPECAST }

WRITELN('shortInt1 = ',shortInt1);
WRITELN('shortInt2 = ',shortInt2);
WRITELN('aByte = ',aByte);
WRITELN('anInt = ',anInt);
WRITELN('aLong = ',aLong);
WRITELN('aChar is ',aChar);
WRITELN; WRITELN;

END.
```

Now look at the equivalent Turbo C++ program, Listing 3.11. This program performs two sets of operations similar to the operation in the preceding Turbo Pascal program. Compare the two programs and note the following differences:

1. Regarding the automatic data conversion, both languages have expressions that are nearly equivalent. The one exception, though, is that the Turbo Pascal program needs the CHR intrinsic, but C++ has no need for a similar function. Both programs handle the rest of the expression properly. This includes the ability of Turbo Pascal to convert integer types into floating-point types.

2. Notice that the C++ program contains the following statement, which typecasts short int types to a float:

   ```
   aReal = (float) (shortInt1 * shortInt2 + 0.5);
   ```

   The Turbo Pascal program has no parallel executable statement because the Turbo Pascal compiler regards typecasting an integer type into a floating-point type as invalid.

3. The C++ program uses the expression (unsigned char) aLong + 5 to store the ASCII code for A.

4. Typecasting in C++ has a higher precedence than the +, -, *, /, and % operators— this is why the code encloses the arithmetic expressions in parentheses to typecast the result of the expression instead of a single operand. If you remove the parentheses in the Turbo C++ program, you get the same answers, but by a different route. In this alternate routine, typecasting is applied only to the

operand that immediately follows the typecast. The C++ compiler then promotes the data type of the other operands to get an expression that has a consistent data type.

The following code is the output of the Turbo C++ program:

```
[BEGIN SESSION]
shortInt1 = 10
shortInt2 = 6
aByte = 16
anInt = 4
aLong = 60
aChar is A
aReal = 60.5


shortInt1 = 10
shortInt2 = 6
aByte = 16
anInt = 4
aLong = 60
aChar is A
aReal = 60.5
[END SESSION]
```

Listing 3.11. Source code for program LST03_11.CPP.

```
// simple C++ program that demonstrates typecasting

#include <iostream.h>

main()
{
    short shortInt1, shortInt2;
    unsigned short aByte;
    int anInt;
    long aLong;
    char aChar;
    float aReal;

    // assign values
    shortInt1 = 10;
    shortInt2 = 6;
    // perform operations without typecasting
    aByte = shortInt1 + shortInt2;
    anInt = shortInt1 - shortInt2;
```

continues

73

Listing 3.11. continued

```
aLong = shortInt1 * shortInt2;
aChar = aLong + 5; // conversion is automatic to character
aReal = shortInt1 * shortInt2 + 0.5;

cout << "shortInt1 = " << shortInt1 << '\n'
     << "shortInt2 = " << shortInt2 << '\n'
     << "aByte = " << aByte << '\n'
     << "anInt = " << anInt << '\n'
     << "aLong = " << aLong << '\n'
     << "aChar is " << aChar << '\n'
     << "aReal = " << aReal << "\n\n\n";

// perform operations with typecasting
// note that C++ encloses the data type in parentheses
// and not the expression, as does Turbo Pascal
aByte = (unsigned short) (shortInt1 + shortInt2);
anInt = (int) (shortInt1 - shortInt2);
aLong = (long) (shortInt1 * shortInt2);
aChar = (unsigned char) (aLong + 5);
// the assignment below is valid in C++, but not in Pascal
aReal = (float) (shortInt1 * shortInt2 + 0.5);

cout << "shortInt1 = " << shortInt1 << '\n'
     << "shortInt2 = " << shortInt2 << '\n'
     << "aByte = " << aByte << '\n'
     << "anInt = " << anInt << '\n'
     << "aLong = " << aLong << '\n'
     << "aChar is " << aChar << '\n'
     << "aReal = " << aReal << "\n\n\n";

return 0;
}
```

Relational and Logical Operators

The relational and logical operators are the basic building blocks of decision-making constructs in any programming language. Table 3.3 shows the C++ relational and logical operators and their equivalent Turbo Pascal operators. Notice that C++ does not spell out

the AND, OR, and NOT operators. Instead, it uses single and dual character symbols. Also notice that C++ does not support the relational XOR operator. You can use the following #define macro directives to define AND, OR, and NOT identifiers as macros:

```
#define AND &&
#define OR ¦¦
#define NOT !
```

Although these macros are permissible in C++, you may get a negative reaction from veteran C++ programmers who read your code. Who said programming is always objective?

> I want to warn you against erroneously using the = operator as the equality rela-tional operator. This common mistake is a source of logical bugs in C++ programs. Although you may be accustomed to using the = operator in Pascal for testing the equality of two data items, in C++ you must use the == operator. What happens if you employ the = operator in C++? Do you get a compiler error? You may get a compiler warning. Other than that, your C++ program should run. Of course, a session with such a program will probably lead to bizarre program behavior or even a system hang! When the program reaches the expression that is supposed to test for equality it will actually attempt to assign the operand on the right of the = sign to the operand on the left of the = sign.

C++ uses a precedence level for the relational and logical operators that is different from that of Turbo Pascal. In C++, relational operators have a higher precedence than logical operators. This means that Turbo Pascal expressions, such as:

```
(N < 0) OR (N > 100)
(J <> 0) AND (500 DIV J)
```

can be translated into the following C++ expressions:

```
N < 0 ¦¦ N > 100
J != 0 && 500 / J
```

> The C++ expressions are equivalent to the Pascal ones. Adding parentheses to the C++ expressions gives no extra advantage to the code. However, it tells veteran C++ programmers looking at your code that you just moved from programming in Turbo Pascal to programming in C++.

If you look at Table 3.3, you might notice the last operator, ?:. This special operator supports the conditional expression, which is shorthand for a dual-alternative, simple if-else statement:

```
if (condition)
    variable = expression1;
else
    variable = expression2;
```

The equivalent conditional expression is:

```
variable = (condition) ? expression1 : expression2;
```

The conditional expression tests the condition. If that condition is true, it assigns expression1 to the target variable. Otherwise, it assigns expression2 to the target variable.

Table 3.3. The C++ relational and logical operators.

C++ Operator	Equivalent Turbo Pascal Operator
&&	AND
||	OR
!	NOT
N/A	XOR
<	<
<=	<=
>	>
>=	>=
==	=
!=	<>
?:	N/A

The next Turbo Pascal program tests relational operators, logical operators, and the conditional expression. Listing 3.12 contains the source code for program LST03_12.PAS. The program carries out the following tasks:

1. Prompts you to type in three integers.

2. Determines if the first integer is in the range of 30 to 199.

3. Determines if any two of the three numbers you typed are equal.

4. Performs a series of logical tests to drill the various relational operators.

The following is a sample session:

```
[BEGIN SESSION]
Type first  integer : 67
Type second integer : 55
Type third  integer : 41
67 is in the range of 30 to 199 : TRUE
at least two integers you typed are equal : FALSE
67 <> 55 : TRUE
NOT (67 < 55) : TRUE
67 <= 55 : FALSE
41 > 55 : FALSE
(41 = 67) AND (55 <> 41) : FALSE
(41 <= 67) XOR (55 >= 41) : TRUE
(41 > 67) AND (55 <= 41) : FALSE
[END SESSION]
```

Listing 3.12. Source code for program LST03_12.PAS.

```
PROGRAM Demo_Logical_Expressions_1;

{ simple Turbo Pascal program that uses logical expressions }

CONST MIN_NUM = 30;
      MAX_NUM = 199;

VAR i, j, k : INTEGER;
    flag1, flag2,
    in_range, same_int  : BOOLEAN;

BEGIN
    WRITE('Type first  integer : '); READLN(i);
    WRITE('Type second integer : '); READLN(j);
    WRITE('Type third  integer : '); READLN(k);

    { test for range [MIN_NUM..MAX_NUM] }
    flag1 := i >= MIN_NUM;
    flag2 := i <= MAX_NUM;
```

continues

77

Listing 3.12. continued

```
      in_range := flag1 AND flag2;
      WRITELN(i,' is in the range ', MIN_NUM, ' to ',
                                     MAX_NUM, ' : ',in_range);

      { test if two or more entered numbers are equal }
      same_int := (i = j) OR (i = k) OR (j = k);
      WRITELN('at least two integers you typed are equal : ',
              same_int);

      { miscellaneous tests }
      WRITELN(i,' <> ',j,' : ', (i <> j));
      WRITELN('NOT (',i,' < ',j,') : ', NOT(i < j));
      WRITELN(i,' <= ',j,' : ', (i <= j));
      WRITELN(k,' > ',j,' : ', (k > j));
      WRITELN('(',k,' = ',i,') AND (',j,' <> ',k,') : ',
              ((k = i) AND (j <> k)));
      WRITELN('(',k,' <= ',i,') XOR (',j,' >= ',k,') : ',
              ((k <= i) XOR (j <= k)));
      WRITELN('(',k,' > ',i,') AND (',j,' <= ',k,') : ',
              ((k > i) AND (j <= k)));

      WRITELN; WRITELN;
END.
```

Listing 3.13 contains the source code for program LST03_13.CPP, the equivalent Turbo C++ program. The following is a sample session with the Turbo C++ program:

```
[BEGIN SESSION]
Type first  integer : 67
Type second integer : 55
Type third  integer : 41

67 is in the range of 30 to 199 : TRUE
at least two integers you typed are equal : FALSE
67 != 55 : TRUE
NOT (67 < 55) : TRUE
67 <= 55 : FALSE
41 > 55 : FALSE
(41 = 67) AND (55 <> 41) : FALSE
(41 <= 67) XOR (55 >= 41) : FALSE
(41 > 67) AND (55 <= 41) : FALSE
[END SESSION]
```

Comparing the Turbo Pascal and Turbo C++ versions reveals the following aspects of C++:

1. C++ does not support a predefined Boolean type as Pascal does. Consequently, if you convert Turbo Pascal programs into C++, you should convert BOOLEAN variables into int-typed variables. C++ regards an expression as true if it is not zero, and false if it is zero. The Turbo C++ program uses TRUE and FALSE constants to represent Boolean identifiers.

2. The lack of a formal BOOLEAN type in C++ also requires you to devise a way to display the TRUE and FALSE strings to emulate Turbo Pascal's support for emitting BOOLEAN values. The Turbo C++ program shows how the conditional expression provides the method for displaying TRUE or FALSE.

3. Translating the Turbo Pascal logical operator XOR requires a simple program trick that involves the following two steps:

   - adds the result of the conditions (k <= i) and (j >= k) to the variable xor_flag (the value stored in xor_flag is either 0 or 2)

   - updates the xor_flag variable with FALSE if the xor_flag variable was assigned 2 in the preceding step (otherwise, it assigns TRUE to xor_flag)

Listing 3.13. Source code for program LST03_13.CPP.

```
/*
    simple C++ program that uses logical expressions.
    This program uses the conditional expression to display
    TRUE or FALSE messages, since C++ does not support the
    BOOLEAN data type.
*/

#include <stdio.h>

const MIN_NUM = 30;
const MAX_NUM = 199;
const int TRUE = 1;
const FALSE = 0;

main()
{
    int i, j, k;
    int flag1, flag2, in_range,
        same_int, xor_flag;

    printf("Type first  integer : "); scanf("%d", &i);
    printf("Type second integer : "); scanf("%d", &j);
    printf("Type third  integer : "); scanf("%d", &k);
```

continues

Listing 3.13. continued

```
// test for range [MIN_NUM..MAX_NUM]
flag1 = i >= MIN_NUM;
flag2 = i <= MAX_NUM;
in_range = flag1 && flag2;
printf("\n%d is in the range %d to %d : %s", i,
                MIN_NUM, MAX_NUM,
                (in_range) ? "TRUE" : "FALSE" );

// test if two or more entered numbers are equal
same_int = i == j || i == k || j == k;
printf("\nat least two integers you typed are equal : %s",
                (same_int) ? "TRUE" : "FALSE");

// miscellaneous tests
printf("\n%d != %d : %s", i, j, (i != j) ? "TRUE" : "FALSE");
printf("\nNOT (%d < %d) : %s", i, j,
        ( !(i < j) ) ? "TRUE" : "FALSE");
printf("\n%d <= %d : %s",i,j, (i <= j) ? "TRUE" : "FALSE");
printf("\n%d > %d : %s",k,j,(k > j) ? "TRUE" : "FALSE");
printf("\n(%d = %d) AND (%d <> %d) : %s", k, i, j, k,
        (k == i && j != k) ? "TRUE" : "FALSE");

// NOTE: C++ does NOT support the logical XOR operator for
// boolean expressions.
// add numeric results of logical tests.  Value is in 0..2
xor_flag = (k <= i) + (j >= k);
// if xor_flag is either 0 or 2 (i.e. not = 1), it is
// FALSE therefore interpret 2 as false.
xor_flag = (xor_flag == 2) ? FALSE : TRUE;
printf("\n(%d <= %d) XOR (%d >= %d) : %s", k, i, j, k,
                (xor_flag) ? "TRUE" : "FALSE");

printf("\n(%d > %d) AND (%d <= %d) : %s", k, i, j, k,
        (k > i && j <= k) ? "TRUE" : "FALSE");
printf("\n\n");

    return 0;
}
```

Bit-Manipulation Operators

C++, like C, is suitable for system development. System development requires bit-manipulating operators to toggle, set, query, and shift the bits of a byte or a word. Table 3.4 shows the bit-manipulating operators in C++ and their equivalent Turbo Pascal operators. Notice that C++ uses & and ¦ to represent the bit-wise AND and OR. (The && and ¦¦ characters represent the logical AND and OR operators.) In addition to the bit-manipulating operators, C++ supports the C++ bit-manipulating assignment operators, shown in Table 3.5.

Table 3.4. The bit-manipulating operators in C++ and the Turbo Pascal equivalents.

C++ Operator	Turbo Pascal Operator
&	AND
¦	OR
^	XOR
~	NOT
<<	SHL
>>	SHR

Table 3.5. The C++ bit-manipulating assignment operators.

C++ Operator	Long Form
x &= y	x = x & y
x ¦= y	x = x ¦ y
x ^= y	x = x ^ y
x <<= y	x = x << y
x >>= y	x = x >> y

The following programming examples compare bit-manipulation in Turbo Pascal and Turbo C++. Listing 3.14 shows the source code for program LST03_14.PAS. Compile and run the Turbo Pascal program. The program output follows.

```
[BEGIN SESSION]
 26 AND 240 =  16
 26 OR  240 = 250
 26 XOR  28 =   6
240 shifted left by 2 bits = 960
240 shifted right by 2 bits =  60
[END SESSION]
```

Listing 3.14. Source code for program LST03_14.PAS.

```pascal
PROGRAM Demo_Bit_Manipulation;

{ Turbo Pascal program that illustrates bit manipulations }

VAR i, j, k : INTEGER;

BEGIN
    { assign values to i and j }
    i := $F0;
    j := $1A;

    k := j AND i;
    WRITELN(j:3,' AND ',i:3,' = ',k:3);

    k := j OR i;
    WRITELN(j:3,' OR  ',i:3,' = ', k:3);

    k := j XOR $1C;
    WRITELN(j:3,' XOR ',$1C:3,' = ', k:3);

    k := i Shl 2;
    WRITELN(i:3,' shifted left by 2 bits = ', k:3);

    k := i Shr 2;
    WRITELN(i:3,' shifted right by 2 bits = ', k:3);

    WRITELN; WRITELN;

END.
```

Listing 3.15 contains the source code for the LST03_15.CPP program, a Turbo C++ program. Compile and run this program. You should get an output similar to that of the Turbo Pascal version. The two programs show how similar the bit-manipulating operators work in both implementations.

Listing 3.15. Source code for program LST03_15.CPP.

```c
// C++ program to perform bit manipulations

#include <stdio.h>

main()
{

    int i, j, k;

    // assign values to i and j
    i = 0xF0;
    j = 0x1A;

    k = j & i;
    printf("%3d AND %3d = %3d", j, i, k);

    k = j | i;
    printf("\n%3d OR  %3d = %3d", j, i, k);

    k = j ^ 0x1C;
    printf("\n%3d XOR %3d = %3d", j, 0x1C, k);

    k = i << 2;
    printf("\n%3d shifted left  by 2 bits = %3d", i, k);

    k = i >> 2;
    printf("\n%3d shifted right by 2 bits = %3d", i, k);

    printf("\n\n");

    return 0;
}
```

The next program illustrates the use of C++ bit-manipulation assignment operators. Listing 3.16 shows the source code for program LST03_16.CPP. Compile and run the program. The following code is the program output:

```
[BEGIN SESSION]
 26 AND 240 =  16
 16 OR  240 = 240
240 XOR 225 =  17
240 shifted left  by 2 bits = 960
960 shifted right by 2 bits = 240
[END SESSION]
```

Listing 3.16. Source code for program LST03_16.CPP.

```cpp
// C++ program to perform bit manipulation assignments

#include <stdio.h>

main()
{

    int i, j;

    // assign values to i and j
    i = 0xF0;
    j = 0x1A;

    printf("\n%3d AND %3d = ", j ,i);
    j &= i; // same as j = j & i
    printf("%3d", j);

    printf("\n%3d OR  %3d = ", j, i);
    j |= i; // same as j = j ¦ i
    printf("%3d", j);

    printf("\n%3d XOR %3d = ", j, (i - 0xF));
    j ^= i - 0xF; // same as j = j ^ (i - 0xF)
    printf("%3d", j);

    printf("\n%3d shifted left  by 2 bits = ", i);
    i <<= 2; // same as i = i << 2
    printf("%3d", i);


    printf("\n%3d shifted right by 2 bits = ", i);
    i >>= 2; // same as i = i >> 2
    printf("%3d\n\n", i);

}
```

The Comma Operator

The C++ comma operator has no equivalent in Turbo Pascal. The general syntax for the comma operator is:

```
expression1, expression2
```

The comma operator requires that the program completely evaluate the first expression before evaluating the second expression. Both expressions are located in the same C++ statement!

What does located in the same C++ statement mean? Why utilize this rather unusual operator in the first place? These questions have a lot of merit. The peculiar role of the comma operator does serve a specific and very important purpose in the for loop. Briefly, using the comma operator enables you to create multiple expressions that initialize multiple loop-related variables. Typically, Pascal code employs a single loop control variable that appears in the FOR-DO loop. You also initialize additional variables that are affected by each loop iteration before the loop body. In comparison, C++ offers more flexibility in initializing a for loop. I'll discuss this topic further in Chapter 6, "Loops."

Now that I've presented most of the C++ operators (a few more operators deal with pointers and addresses), there are two related aspects you need to know: the precedence of the C++ operators and the direction (or sequence) of evaluation. Table 3.6 shows the C++ precedence of the C++ operators covered so far and indicates the evaluation direction.

Table 3.6. C++ operators and their precedence.

Category	Name	Symbol	Eval. Direction	Precedence
Monadic				
	post-increment	++	left to right	2
	post-decrement	--	left to right	2
	address	&	right to left	2
	bitwise NOT	~	right to left	2
	typecast	(type)	right to left	2

continues

Table 3.6. continued

Category	Name	Symbol	Eval. Direction	Precedence
	logical NOT	!	right to left	2
	negation	-	right to left	2
	plus sign	+	right to left	2
	pre-increment	++	right to left	2
	pre-decrement	--	right to left	2
	size of data	sizeof	right to left	2
Multiplicative				
	modulus	%	left to right	3
	multiply	*	left to right	3
	divide	/	left to right	3
Additive				
	add	+	left to right	4
	subtract	-	left to right	4
Bitwise shift				
	shift left	<<	left to right	5
	shift right	>>	left to right	5
Relational				
	less than	<	left to right	6
	less or equal	<=	left to right	6
	greater than	>	left to right	6
	greater or equal	>=	left to right	6

Category	Name	Symbol	Eval. Direction	Precedence
	equal to	==	left to right	7
	not equal to	!=	left to right	7
Bitwise				
	AND	&	left to right	8
	XOR	^	left to right	9
	OR	¦	left to right	10
Logical				
	AND	&&	left to right	11
	OR	¦¦	left to right	12
Ternary				
	cond. express.	?:	right to left	13
Assignment				
	arithmetic	=	right to left	14
		+=	right to left	14
		-=	right to left	14
		*=	right to left	14
		/=	right to left	14
		%=	right to left	14
	shift	>>=	right to left	14
		<<=	right to left	14

continues

Table 3.6. continued

Category	Name	Symbol	Eval. Direction	Precedence
	bitwise	&=	right to left	14
		¦=	right to left	14
		^=	right to left	14
Comma		,	left to right	15

Summary

This chapter covered the following C++ topics:

- the arithmetic operators, including +, -, *, /, and % (modulus)

- the increment and decrement operators, which are in pre- and post forms. C++ enables you to apply these operators to variables that store characters, integers, and floating-point numbers

- the arithmetic assignment operators enable you to write shorter arithmetic expressions where the primary operand is also the variable receiving the result of the expression

- the sizeof operator returns the byte size of either a data type or a variable

- typecasting that enables you to force the type conversion of an expression

- relational and logical operators used to build logical expressions (C++ does not support a predefined Boolean type and instead considers 0 as false and any non-zero value as true)

- the conditional expression offers you a short form for the simple dual-alternative if-else statement

- the bit-manipulation operators that perform bitwise AND, OR, XOR, and NOT operations (in addition, C++ supports the << and >> bitwise shift operators)

- the bit-manipulation assignment operators that offer short forms for simple bit-manipulation statements

THE PREPROCESSOR AND COMPILER DIRECTIVES

Compiler directives enable you to instruct a language compiler to process the source code of an application. Turbo Pascal offers a number of directives that perform a wide variety of tasks such as including files, manipulation file I/O error, and toggling the shortcut mode for emulating Boolean expressions. C++, like C, also supports compiler directives. C++ also supports the special #define macro-building directive that defines macros. When you start the compilation process, the first step that occurs is the transparent invocation of the preprocessor. The preprocessor substitutes the macros created by the #define directive for their values. This chapter covers the following topics:

- the preprocessor
- compiler directives
- predefined macros

These topics are important programming language aspects of C++ that are inherited from C.

The Preprocessor

The preprocessor examines your C++ source code to locate the #define macro directive. In Chapter 2, "Getting Started," I presented the #define directive as a tool for defining constants. Chapter 2, however, featured a limited use (the first form) of the #define directive. The general syntax for this directive is:

```
#define macro macro_text_or_value
#define macro(argument_list) macro_expression
```

The second form of the #define directive reveals that you can include parameters with the macro. This feature makes macros very flexible. C++ requires that a line cannot contain more than one #define directive. If you cannot contain the macro expression on one line, you can use the \ (with a leading space) character as a line continuation character. Macros that possess parameters enable you to create pseudofunctions. Compared with formal functions, these macro-based functions are faster but require more code space because the preprocessor substitutes every occurrence of these macros with their respective expressions.

C++ gurus and many C++ programmers find a great fault with the #define macro. Their opinion is that for practically every macro, instances occur in which macro substitution produces an error in the code. In addition, these C++ programmers note the lack of type checking with macros created by the #define directive. They suggest that you use inline functions (refer to Chapter 7, "Simple Functions," for more information). The C++ compiler substitutes inline functions with their expressions (like the defined macros) and provides type checking.

The #define directive serves the following purposes:

- defines constants
- replaces reserved words or symbols with others
- creates pseudodata-type identifiers using standard data types
- creates shorthand commands
- defines macro-based pseudofunctions

You can undefine a macro using the #undef directive. The general syntax for the #undef directive is:

#undef macro

C++ enables you to reuse a macro name by simply placing it in another #define directive. You need not use the #undef directive to explicitly clear a macro definition between two #define directives.

Listing 4.1, source code for LST04_01.CPP, is a program that uses #define directives to creates various types of macros.

Listing 4.1. Source code for program LST04_01.CPP.

```
/*
   C++ program that demonstrates the many uses of the #define
   preprocessor directives to create pseudo types, functions
   and keywords.
*/

#include <stdio.h>
#include <conio.h>

// define a keyword macro
#define MAIN_PROGRAM main()
#define BEGIN {
#define begin {
#define END_PROGRAM }
#define END }
#define end }

// define data type macros
#define BOOLEAN char
#define BYTE unsigned char
#define REAL double
#define INTEGER int

#define PRINT printf
#define WRITE printf
#define INPUT scanf
#define READ scanf
#define ReadKey getch()
#define ReadChar getche()
#define WRITELN printf("\n")
#define WRITELN2 printf("\n\n")
#define WRITELN3 printf("\n\n\n")
```

continues

91

Listing 4.1. continued

```
// macros for popular shorthand command sequences
#define readvar(msg,frmt,var) printf(msg); scanf(frmt, &var)
#define read2var(msg,frmt,x,y) printf(msg); scanf(frmt, &x, &y)
#define readchar(msg,var) printf(msg); var = getche()
#define wait_for_key akey = getch()

// define screen macros.  The ANSI.SYS driver MUST be installed
#define clrscr printf("\x1b[2J")
#define gotoxy(col,row) printf("\x1b[%d;%dH",col,row)
#define clreol printf("\x1b[K")

// define boolean constants
#define FALSE 0
#define TRUE 1

// boolean pseudofunctions
#define boolean(x) ((x) ? "TRUE" : "FALSE")
#define yesno(x) ((x) ? "Yes" : "No")

// macros that define pseudo one-line functions
#define abs(x) (((x) >= 0) ? (x) : -(x))
#define max(x,y) (((x) > (y)) ? (x) : (y))
#define min(x,y) (((x) > (y)) ? (y) : (x))
#define sqr(x) ((x) * (x))
#define cube(x) ((x) * (x) * (x))
#define reciprocal(x) (1 / (x))
#define XOR(t1,t2) (((t1 + t2) == TRUE) ? TRUE : FALSE)

// macros useful in translating Turbo Pascal programs
#define inc(x) x++
#define dec(x) x--
#define dinc(x,y) x += (y)
#define ddec(x,y) x -= (y)

// macros used for character testing
#define islower(c) (c >= 'a' && c <= 'z')
#define isupper(c) (c >= 'A' && c <= 'Z')
#define isdigit(c) (c >= '0' && c <= '9')
#define isletter(c) ((c >= 'A' && c <= 'Z') ¦¦ (c >= 'a' && c <= 'z'))

// macros used in character case conversions
#define tolowercase(c) (c - 'A' + 'a')
#define touppercase(c) (c - 'a' + 'A')
```

```
MAIN_PROGRAM

BEGIN

    BOOLEAN bool;
    BYTE i, j;
    INTEGER k, m;
    char ch, akey;
    REAL x = 0.10;

    readvar("Enter an integer : ","%d",k);
    WRITELN;
    WRITE("You entered %d", k);
    WRITELN2;

    WRITE("Enter another integer : "); READ("%d", &k);
    WRITELN;
    WRITE("%d squared = %d ", k, sqr(k));
    WRITELN2;

    WRITE("1 / %f = %f", x, reciprocal(x));
    WRITELN2;

    ch = 'B';
    WRITE("The lowercase of %c is %c", ch, tolowercase(ch));
    WRITELN2;

    ch = 'f';
    WRITE("The uppercase of %c is %c", ch, touppercase(ch));

    printf("\n\npress any key to continue");
    wait_for_key;
    clrscr;

    WRITE("\n\nType a letter or a digit : "); ch = ReadChar;
    WRITELN2;
    bool = isupper(ch);
    gotoxy(5,10);
    WRITE("character is uppercase : %s\n",boolean(bool));
    bool = islower(ch);
    gotoxy(6,10);
    WRITE("character is lowercase : %s\n",boolean(bool));
    bool = isletter(ch);
    gotoxy(7,10);
    WRITE("character is a letter  : %s\n",boolean(bool));
    bool = isdigit(ch);
    gotoxy(8,10);
```

continues

93

Listing 4.1. continued

```
WRITE("character is a digit   : %s\n",boolean(bool));
WRITELN;
read2var("Enter two integers (separated by a space) : ",
        "%d %d",k,m);
WRITELN2;
WRITE("The largest of the two numbers is %d\n\n",max(k,m));
WRITE("The smallest of the two numbers is %d\n\n",min(k,m));
WRITE("ABS(%d) = %d\n\n", k, abs(k));

WRITE("%d + 1 = ", k);
inc(k);
WRITE("%d\n\n", k);

WRITE("%d - 1 = ", m);
dec(m);
WRITE("%d\n\n", m);

END_PROGRAM
```

Now examine the various groups of macros that appear in the preceding program. The first group of macros merely redefines C++ keywords, as follows:

```
#define MAIN_PROGRAM main()
#define BEGIN {
#define begin {
#define END_PROGRAM }
#define END }
#define end }
```

To make macro substitution easier for you, I named the macros to match Pascal keywords. Interestingly, by using enough of these macros you can disguise your C++ programs to look like Pascal programs! Although the processor and C++ compiler enable you to disguise your code in this manner, other C++ programmers will most likely find such code unamusing. Therefore, for practical coding practices, avoid using the #define macros in such a way. I included this type of macro merely to show you the extent of their use (or should I say misuse).

The second group of macros is similar to the first group. However, they serve a sounder purpose. These macros emulate commonly used predefined Turbo Pascal data types. You may recall that C++ does not implement a predefined Boolean data type. Consequently, programmers associate the integer 0 with the logical false and the integers 1 or -1 with the logical true value. In most cases, programmers use the two-byte int type to store Boolean

values. The one-byte char type can serve the same purpose and uses half as much memory space. The following macro defines the BOOLEAN identifier as an alias for the char data type:

```
#define BOOLEAN char
```

The C++ data type that is similar to the Turbo Pascal BYTE type is the unsigned char. The subsequent macros define the BYTE type accordingly:

```
#define BYTE unsigned char
```

The rest of the macros in this group are simply optional, convenient redefinitions of the C++ double and int data types:

```
#define REAL double
#define INTEGER int
```

The third set of macros builds shorthand commands. I purposely used Pascal keywords for the following macros:

```
#define PRINT printf
#define WRITE printf
#define INPUT scanf
#define READ scanf
#define ReadKey getch()
#define ReadChar getche()
#define WRITELN printf("\n")
#define WRITELN2 printf("\n\n")
#define WRITELN3 printf("\n\n\n")
```

The fourth set of macros also builds shorthand commands. These macros differ from the preceding group in their use of parameters, which add a lot of flexibility to the macros and make them work like procedures. Most of the macros in this set expand to multiple C++ statements:

```
#define readvar(msg,frmt,var) printf(msg); scanf(frmt, &var)
#define read2var(msg,frmt,x,y) printf(msg); scanf(frmt, &x, &y)
#define readchar(msg,var) printf(msg); var = getche()
#define wait_for_key akey = getch()
```

The fifth collection of macros, though similar to the last set of macros, specializes in screen and cursor management. These macros require that you install the ANSI.SYS driver (or any equivalent driver). Although the conio.h header file declares the screen and cursor management functions, these macros show you how to perform the same tasks if you work with a C++ compiler that lacks this capability.

```
#define clrscr printf("\x1b[2J")
#define gotoxy(col,row) printf("\x1b[%d;%dH",col,row)
#define clreol printf("\x1b[K")
```

The sixth set of macros is not new to you (refer to Chapter 2). In spite of their simplicity, these macros are relevant and are frequently used in C++ programs:

```
#define FALSE 0
#define TRUE 1
```

The seventh set of macros implements special pseudofunctions that return "TRUE" or "FALSE" and "Yes" or "No" strings based on the value of the x macro parameter:

```
#define boolean(x) ((x) ? "TRUE" : "FALSE")
#define yesno(x) ((x) ? "Yes" : "No")
```

The eighth group of macros implements one-line math functions. Notice that every macro parameter is enclosed in parentheses in the macro expression. Enclosing each parameter in parentheses ensures that the macro is correctly expanded when expressions are used as arguments for the macro parameters:

```
#define abs(x) (((x) >= 0) ? (x) : -(x))
#define max(x,y) (((x) > (y)) ? (x) : (y))
#define min(x,y) (((x) > (y)) ? (y) : (x))
#define sqr(x) ((x) * (x))
#define cube(x) ((x) * (x) * (x))
#define reciprocal(x) (1 / (x))
#define XOR(t1,t2) (((t1 + t2) == TRUE) ? TRUE : FALSE)
```

The ninth set of macros emulates the Turbo Pascal intrinsics INC and DEC. The inc and dec macros emulate the INC and DEC intrinsics with one argument. The dinc and ddec macros emulate the INC and DEC intrinsics with two arguments:

```
#define inc(x) x++
#define dec(x) x--
#define dinc(x,y) x += (y)
#define ddec(x,y) x -= (y)
```

Because macros perform no type checking, the preceding macros also work with floating-point data types. Consequently, these macros present an expanded emulation of the INC and DEC intrinsics.

The tenth set of macros carries out character classification tests. These tests include determining if a character is lowercase, uppercase, digit, and letter:

```
#define islower(c) (c >= 'a' && c <= 'z')
#define isupper(c) (c >= 'A' && c <= 'Z')
#define isdigit(c) (c >= '0' && c <= '9')
#define isletter(c) ((c >= 'A' && c <= 'Z') ¦¦ (c >= 'a' && c <= 'z'))
```

The last collection of macros implements pseudofunctions that perform character case conversion:

```
#define tolowercase(c) (c - 'A' + 'a')
#define touppercase(c) (c - 'a' + 'A')
```

Compile and run Listing 4.1. The program performs the following steps:

1. Prompts you to enter an integer. Type 67. The program then displays your input. The program uses the readvar macro to obtain your input and utilizes the WRITE macro to display what you typed.

2. Prompts you to enter another integer. Type 41. The program displays the number you typed and its square value. The program uses the sqr and WRITE macros to obtain the square and display the input and the square value.

3. Displays the following output without requiring any input:

   - the reciprocal of 0.1 (the program uses the reciprocal macro to obtain the reciprocal value)

   - the letter B and its lowercase (the program uses the tolowercase macro to obtain the lowercase of B)

   - the letter f and its uppercase (the program uses the touppercase macro to obtain the uppercase of f)

4. Prompts you to press any key to proceed. This prompt appears by using the wait_for_key macro. When you press any key, the program clears the screen by using the clrscr macro.

5. Prompts you to type in a letter or a digit. Enter the letter H. The program uses the macros islower, isupper, isdigit, and isletter to classify your input. The Boolean macro generates the TRUE or FALSE output.

6. Prompts you to type in two integers on the same line, separated by a space. Enter 34 and 89. The program uses the min and max macros to determine and display the smaller and larger of these two numbers.

7. Displays the absolute value of the first number you typed by using the abs macro.

8. Uses the inc and dec macros with the first and second numbers you entered, respectively. The program displays the incremented and decremented values.

The following code is the output of a session using the preceding Turbo C++ program:

```
[BEGIN SESSION]
Enter an integer : 67

You entered 67
```

```
Enter another integer : 41

41 squared = 1681

1 / 0.100000 = 10.000000

The lowercase of B is b

The uppercase of f is F

press any key to continue

Type a letter or a digit : H

        character is uppercase : TRUE
        character is lowercase : FALSE
        character is a letter  : TRUE
        character is a digit   : FALSE

Enter two integers (separated by a space) : 34 89


The largest of the two numbers is 89

The smallest of the two numbers is 34

ABS(34) = 34
34 + 1 = 35

89 - 1 = 88
[END SESSION]
```

Although the preceding program works fine, some of its macros represent undesired extremes. Because I don't want to leave you with a strange looking Turbo C++ program, I've included a toned-down version. Listing 4.2 contains the source code for this version, program LST04_02.CPP. Notice that this new version includes the screen.h header file, which contains the following three lines:

```
// screen.h
#define clrscr printf("\x1b[2J")
#define gotoxy(col,row) printf("\x1b[%d;%dH", row, col)
#define clreol printf("\x1b[K")
```

Listing 4.2. Source code for program LST04_02.CPP.

```
/*
   C++ program that demonstrates the many uses of the #define
   preprocessor directives to create pseudotypes and
```

```
   functions. This version avoids macros that 'redefine'
   important C++ keywords and symbols.
*/


#include <stdio.h>
#include <conio.h>
#include "screen.h"

// define data type macros
#define BOOLEAN char
#define BYTE unsigned char

// define boolean constants
#define FALSE 0
#define TRUE 1

// define macro used in waiting for a key to be pressed
#define wait_for_key  akey = getch()

// boolean pseudofunctions
#define boolean(x) (x) ? "TRUE" : "FALSE"
#define yesno(x) (x) ? "Yes" : "No"

// macros that define pseudo one-line functions
#define abs(x) (((x) >= 0) ? (x) : -(x))
#define max(x,y) (((x) > (y)) ? (x) : (y))
#define min(x,y) (((x) > (y)) ? (y) : (x))
#define sqr(x) ((x) * (x))
#define cube(x) ((x) * (x) * (x))
#define reciprocal(x) (1 / (x))
#define XOR(t1,t2) (((t1+t2) != 1) ? 0 : 1)

// macros useful in translating Turbo Pascal programs
#define inc(x) x++
#define dec(x) x--
#define dinc(x,y) x += (y)
#define ddec(x,y) x -= (y)

// macros used for character testing
#define islower(c) (c >= 'a' && c <= 'z')
#define isupper(c) (c >= 'A' && c <= 'Z')
#define isdigit(c) (c >= '0' && c <= '9')
#define isletter(c) ((c >= 'A' && c <= 'Z') ¦¦ (c >= 'a' && c <= 'z'))

// macros used in character case conversions
#define tolowercase(c) (c - 'A' + 'a')
#define touppercase(c) (c - 'a' + 'A')
```

continues

99

Listing 4.2. continued

```
main()
{
    BOOLEAN bool;
    BYTE i, j;
    int k, m;
    char ch, akey;
    double x = 0.10;

    printf("Enter an integer : "); scanf("%d", &k);
    printf("\n");
    printf("You entered %d", k);
    printf("\n\n");

    printf("Enter another integer : "); scanf("%d", &k);
    printf("\n");
    printf("%d squared = %d ", k, sqr(k));
    printf("\n\n");

    printf("1 / %f = %f", x, reciprocal(x));
    printf("\n\n");

    ch = 'B';
    printf("The lowercase of %c is %c", ch, tolowercase(ch));
    printf("\n\n");

    ch = 'f';
    printf("The uppercase of %c is %c", ch, touppercase(ch));

    printf("\n\npress any key to continue");
    wait_for_key;
    clrscr;

    printf("\n\nType a letter or a digit : "); ch = getche();
    bool = isupper(ch);
    gotoxy(10,5);
    printf("character is uppercase : %s\n",boolean(bool));
    bool = islower(ch);
    gotoxy(10,6);
    printf("character is lowercase : %s\n",boolean(bool));
    bool = isletter(ch);
    gotoxy(10,7);
    printf("character is a letter  : %s\n",boolean(bool));
    bool = isdigit(ch);
    gotoxy(10,8);
    printf("character is a digit   : %s\n",boolean(bool));
```

```
printf("\n");
printf("Enter two integers (delimited by a space) : ");
scanf("%d %d", &k, &m);
printf("\n\n");
printf("The largest of the two numbers is %d\n\n",max(k,m));
printf("The smallest of the two numbers is %d\n\n",min(k,m));
printf("ABS(%d) = %d\n\n", k, abs(k));

printf("%d + 1 = ", k);
inc(k);
printf("%d\n\n", k);

printf("%d - 1 = ", m);
dec(m);
printf("%d\n\n", m);

}
```

Predefined Macros

Turbo C++ predefines the following macros:

- the _ _CDECL_ _ macro is specific to the Borland C and C++ compilers

- the _ _cplusplus_ _ macro tells the compiler to work as in C++ mode

- the _ _DATE_ _ macro provides the date when the preprocessor started processing the source code files

- the _ _FILE_ _ macro specifies the name of the file being processed

- the _ _LINE_ _ macro offers the line number of the current line being processed

- the _ _MSDOS_ _ macro is specific to the Borland C and C++ compilers

- the _ _OVERLAY_ _ macro specifies whether you are compiling a module

- the _ _PASCAL_ _ macro indicates whether you are compiling your functions using the Pascal calling convention

- the _ _STDC_ _ macro indicates whether you are compiling your source code following the ANSI C standards

- the __TCPLUSPLUS__ macro stores the Turbo C++ version number (the value of the macro in version 3.0 is 0x300)

- the __TEMPLATES__ macro indicates whether or not Turbo C++ supports templates

- the __TIME__ macro provides the time when the preprocessor started processing the source code files

- the __TURBOC__ macro specifies the C compiler version (the value for this macro in Turbo C++ version 3.0 is 0x400)

Compiler Directives

C++ supports other compiler directives: #include, #error, #if (and other related directives), #line, and #pragma.

The *#include* Directive

The #include directive is similar to the Turbo Pascal {$Ifilename} directive. The general syntax for the #include directive is:

```
#include <filename>
#include "filename"
```

The filename represents the name of the included file. The two forms differ in how the #include directive searches for the included file. The first form searches for the file in the special directory for included files. The second form expands the search to include the current directory. All the programs that I have presented so far use the #include directive. C++ also allows you to use a macro name with the #include directive:

```
#include macro_name
```

The *#error* Directive

The #error directive generates an error message. The general syntax for the #error directive is:

```
#error errmsg
```

The preceding directive yields an error message that has the following general form:

```
Error: filename line # : Error directive : errmsg
```

Conditional Compilation Directives

The #if directive enables you to perform conditional compilation of your C++ program. This directive is similar to the Turbo Pascal {$IFDEF} directive. Turbo C++ provides the #if, #elif, #else, and #endif directives to support conditional compilation. The general syntax for conditional compilation directives is:

```
#if condition1
      sequence of statements to compile if condition1 is true
[#elif condition2
      sequence of statements to compile if condition2 is true
[#elif condition3
      sequence of statements to compile if condition3 is true
...
[#elif conditionN
      sequence of statements to compile if conditionN is true]
...]
[#else
      sequence of statements to compile if no condition is true]
#endif
```

C++ also offers the #ifdef and #ifndef directives that allow you to test whether or not a macro is already defined. Listing 4.3 contains the source code for the LST04_03.CPP program. This program uses a macro-based pseudofunction with a single variable and offers the following alternatives to evaluate its first derivative (its slope at a particular argument):

- using another function (also macro-based)
- using a numerical method with good accuracy
- using a numerical method with acceptable accuracy

The program can select one of these three methods by using the USE_MACRO and MORE_ACCURATE macros. The current program listing compiles the statement after the #elif directive and ignores the statements after the #if and #else directives.

Listing 4.3. Source code for program LST04_03.CPP.

```
// C program to demonstrate conditional directives
#include <stdio.h>

#define f_of_x(x) ((x) * (x) * (x) - 5.0L)
#define first_derivative(x) (3.0L * (x) * (x))
#define INCREMENT 0.01L

/*
   the following macro switches cause the numerical evaluation of
   the first derivative to be used.
*/
#define USE_MACRO 0
/*
  the following macro causes more accurate numerical
  evaluation to be used.
*/
#define MORE_ACCURATE 1

main()
{
     double x, derivative;

     printf("Enter nonzero value : "); scanf("%lf", &x);
     printf("\n\n");

     #if USE_MACRO == 1
        derivative = first_derivative(x);
     #elif MORE_ACCURATE == 1
        derivative = (f_of_x(x+INCREMENT)-f_of_x(x-INCREMENT))
                             /(2.0L * INCREMENT);
     #else
        derivative = (f_of_x(x+INCREMENT)-f_of_x(x))/INCREMENT;
     #endif

     printf("df/dx = %lf at %lf\n\n", derivative, x);

}
```

The *#line* Directive

The #line directives enable you to specify the line number to a program for cross-referencing or reporting an error. The general syntax for the #line directive is:

```
#line number ["filename"]
```

The #line directive enables you to specify the line number of the original file instead of the actual line number. The latter may vary if you include other files—a likely event. The filename clause is needed only the first time you use the #line directive.

The *#pragma* Directive

The #pragma directive supports implementation-specific directives that have the following general form:

```
#pragma directive_name
```

The Turbo C++ version 3.0 compiler has the following #pragma directives:

- #pragma startup specifies the function that is called before the main function when you start a program. The general syntax for this directive is:

  ```
  #pragma startup function [priority]
  ```

- #pragma exit specifies the function that is called after the main function when you end a program. The general syntax for this directive is:

  ```
  #pragma exit function [priority]
  ```

- #pragma hrdfile specifies the name of the file that stores the precompiled headers. The default name for that file is TCDEF.SYM. The general syntax for this directive is:

  ```
  #pragma hrdfile "filename.SYM"
  ```

- #pragma hrdstop ends the list of files that are eligible for precompilation.

- #pragma inline tells the compiler that inline assembly language is in the source code.

- #pragma option enables you to specify command-line options in your source code. The general syntax for this directive is:

  ```
  #pragma option [options...]
  ```

- #pragma saveregs ensures that a huge function will not alter the values of any registers when the huge function is called.

- #pragma warn enables you to check the display warning or override the -wxxx command-line option. The general syntax for the #pragma warn is:

  ```
  #pragma warn [+ ¦ - ¦ .]xxx
  ```

- The + symbol turns on #pragma warn. The - symbol turns off #pragma warn. The dot symbol, ., restores the #pragma warn.

105

> The compiler ignores a #pragma directive if Turbo C++ does not support the directive.

Summary

Turbo C++ supports the following directives:

- the #define directive used to define macros—the general syntax for this directive is:

```
#define macro macro_text_or_value
#define macro(argument_list) macro_expression
```

- the #undef directive enables you to undefine a macro—the general syntax for this directive is:

```
#undef macro
```

- the #include directive enables you to include files to be compiled with the currently compiled source file—the general syntax for this directive is:

```
#include <filename>
#include "filename"
```

- The #error directive generates an error message—the general syntax for this directive is:

```
#error errmsg
```

- the conditional compilation directives enable you to perform conditional compilation of your C++ program—the general syntax for the conditional compilation directives is:

```
#if condition1
    sequence of statements to compile if condition1 is true
[#elif condition2
    sequence of statements to compile if condition2 is true
[#elif condition3
    sequence of statements to compile if condition3 is true
...
[#elif conditionN
    sequence of statements to compile if conditionN is true]
...]
```

```
[#else
    sequence of statements to compile if no condition is true]
#endif
```

- the #line directive enables you to specify the line number to a program for cross-referencing or reporting an error—the general syntax for this directive is:

#line number ["filename"]

- the #pragma directive supports implementation-specific directives that have the following general form:

#pragma directive_name

DECISION-MAKING

5

In any programming language, decision-making constructs enable your application to examine conditions and specify a course of action. The exact workings of decision-making constructs vary in different programming languages. This chapter examines the decision-making constructs in C++ and covers the following topics:

- the single-alternative `if` statement
- the dual-alternative `if-else` statement
- the multiple-alternative `if-else` statement
- the multiple-alternative `switch` statement

The various forms of the `if` statement in C++ resemble similar forms of the `IF` statement in Pascal. The C++ `switch` statement is similar to the Pascal `CASE` statement.

The Single-Alternative *if* Statement

C++ does not use the `then` keyword in any form of the `if` statement. How does the `if` statement delimit the tested condition from the executable statements? In C++, you must enclose the tested condition in parentheses. The general syntax of the single-alternative `if` statement for a sequence of executable statements follows:

```
if (condition)
statement;
```

for a single executable statement, and:

```
if (tested_condition) {
<sequence of statement>
}
```

C++ uses curly braces ({}) to enclose a block of statements. The location of the braces as shown in the preceding general syntax is customary but not mandatory. You may also use the following form:

```
if (tested_condition)
{
<sequence of statements>
}
```

 Unlike Pascal, every C++ statement in a block must end with a semicolon, and the close brace must not be followed by a semicolon!

The translation of a single-alternative IF statement in Pascal into a similar `if` statement in C++ uses the following general syntax:

```
Pascal:
        IF condition THEN statement;

C++:
        if (condition) statement;

Pascal:
        IF condition THEN BEGIN
            <sequence of statements>
        END;

C++:
        if (condition) {
            <sequence of statements>
        }
```

The following examples in both Turbo Pascal and Turbo C++ illustrate the single-alternative `if` statement. The next program solves for only the real roots of the following quadratic equation:

$$A X^2 + B X + C = 0$$

The program prompts you to sequentially enter the values for the coefficients A, B, and C. The program calculates the value of the discriminant, which is equal to the square root of $B^2 - 4AC$. If the program determines that the value of the discriminant is positive, it calculates and displays the two roots. If the discriminant is negative, the roots are imaginary and the program displays a warning message.

This program illustrates the two forms of the single-alternative `if` statement. The first `if` statement executes a single statement when the tested condition is true. The second statement executes a block of statements when the tested condition is true. Listing 5.1 contains the source code for the LST05_01.PAS program.

Listing 5.1. Source code for the LST05_01.PAS program.

```
PROGRAM Decision_Making_1;

{
   Turbo Pascal program that solves for the real roots of
   a quadratic equation
}

VAR a, b, c,
    discriminant,
    root1, root2  : REAL;

BEGIN

    WRITE('SOLVE FOR THE REAL ROOTS OF A QUADRATIC EQUATION':60);
    WRITELN; WRITELN; WRITELN;
    WRITELN('The equation is Y = A X^2 + B X + C');
    WRITELN; WRITELN;
    WRITE('Enter A : '); READLN(a); WRITELN;
    WRITE('Enter B : '); READLN(b); WRITELN;
    WRITE('Enter C : '); READLN(c); WRITELN;

    discriminant := b * b - 4.0 * a * c;

    IF discriminant < 0 THEN
       WRITELN('Imaginary roots');
```

continues

Listing 5.1. continued

```
IF (discriminant >= 0) AND (a <> 0.0) THEN BEGIN
    root1 := (-b + SQRT(discriminant)) / (2 * a);
    root2 := (-b - SQRT(discriminant)) / (2 * a);

    WRITELN('Root1 = ',root1); WRITELN;
    WRITELN('Root2 = ',root2); WRITELN;

END; { IF }

END.
```

Listing 5.2 contains the source code for the LST05_02.CPP program. The empty macros THEN and then are declared for the benefit of Pascal programmers. (They are empty because they have no expressions. The use of such macros, however, is not recommended.)

Examine the Pascal and C++ listings and look at the second if statement in both programs. The Pascal IF statement is

```
IF (discriminant >= 0) AND (a <> 0.0) THEN BEGIN
```

The C++ if statement is

```
if (discriminant >= 0 && a != 0.0) {
```

Notice the following differences:

1. The Pascal logical operator AND is replaced with the C++ && operator.

2. The Pascal <> relational operator is replaced by the C++ != operator.

3. The tested condition in the C++ if statement is enclosed in parentheses.

4. C++ has no equivalent to the Pascal THEN keyword.

5. The Pascal statement block delimiters BEGIN and END are replaced by the { and } characters.

Listing 5.2. Source code for the LST05_02.CPP program.

```
/*
   C++ program that solves for the real roots
   of a quadratic equation
*/
```

```
// These macros make THEN and then harmless.
// They are provided for the die-hard Pascal programmer.
// NOT recommended by veteran C++ programmers!!
#define THEN
#define then

#include <iostream.h>
#include <math.h>

main()
{
    float a, b, c;
    float discriminant;
    float root1, root2;

    cout << "\t\t" // tab twice
        << "SOLVE FOR THE REAL ROOTS OF A QUADRATIC EQUATION"
        << "\n\n"
        << "The equation is Y = A X^2 + B X + C\n";
    cout << "\nEnter A : ";
    cin >> a;
    cout << "\nEnter B : ";
    cin >> b;
    cout << "\nEnter C : ";
    cin >> c;

    cout << "\n\n";

    discriminant = b * b - 4.0 * a * c;

    // note logical expression MUST be enclosed in
    // parentheses in C++
    if (discriminant < 0) THEN
        cout << "Imaginary roots\n";

    if (discriminant >= 0 && a != 0.0) {
        root1 = (-b + sqrt(discriminant)) / (2 * a);
        root2 = (-b - sqrt(discriminant)) / (2 * a);

        cout << "Root1 = " << root1 << "\n\n"
            << "Root2 = " << root2 << "\n\n";

    }

    return 0;

}
```

113

The Dual-Alternative
if-else Statement

This form of the if statement offers you two alternate routes of action based on the tested condition. The if-else statement resembles the Pascal IF-THEN-ELSE statement. The else keyword separates the statements used to execute each alternative. The general syntax for the if-else statement is

```
if (condition)
    statement1;
else
    statement2;
```

for a single executable statement, and

```
if (tested_condition) {
    <sequence #1 of statements>
}
else {
    <sequence #2 of statements>
}
```

for a sequence of executable statements.

The translation of a dual-alternative IF statement in Pascal to a similar if statement in C++ uses the following general syntax:

```
Pascal:
        IF condition THEN statement1;
                    ELSE statement2;


C++:
        if (condition)
            statement1;
        else
            statement2;

Pascal:
        IF condition THEN BEGIN
            <sequence #1 of statements>
        END
        ELSE BEGIN
            <sequence #2 of statements>
```

```
        END;

C++:
        if (condition) {
            <sequence of statements>
        }
```

The following modified version of the preceding program illustrates the dual-alternative if statement. This new version uses the if-else statement to obtain the real roots if the discriminant is non-negative and the imaginary roots if the discriminant is negative. Listing 5.3 shows the source code for the LST05_03.PAS program, and Listing 5.4 shows the source code for the LST05_04.CPP program. Notice how C++ uses curly braces to define a block of statements (the close brace is not followed by a semicolon).

Listing 5.3. Source code for the LST05_03.PAS program.

```
PROGRAM Decision_Making_2;

{
  Turbo Pascal program that solves the roots of a quadratic
  equation. This version uses IF-THEN-ELSE clauses.
}

VAR a, b, c,
    discriminant,
    real_part, imag_part,
    root1, root2          : REAL;

BEGIN

    WRITELN('SOLVE FOR THE ROOTS OF A QUADRATIC EQUATION':60);
    WRITELN; WRITELN;
    WRITELN('The equation is Y = A X^2 + B X + C');
    WRITELN; WRITELN;
    WRITE('Enter A : '); READLN(a); WRITELN;
    WRITE('Enter B : '); READLN(b); WRITELN;
    WRITE('Enter C : '); READLN(c); WRITELN;

    discriminant := b * b - 4.0 * a * c;

    IF discriminant >= 0.0  THEN BEGIN
      root1 := (-b + SQRT(discriminant)) / (2 * a);
```

continues

115

Listing 5.3. continued

```
      root2 := (-b - SQRT(discriminant)) / (2 * a);

      WRITELN('Root1 = ',root1); WRITELN;
      WRITELN('Root2 = ',root2); WRITELN;
   END
   ELSE BEGIN
      real_part := SQRT(-discriminant) / (2 * a);
      imag_part := -b / (2 * a);

      WRITELN('Root1 = (',real_part,') + i (',imag_part,')');
      WRITELN;
      WRITELN('Root2 = (',real_part,') - i (',imag_part,')');
      WRITELN;
   END; { IF }

END.
```

Listing 5.4. Source code for the LST05_04.CPP program.

```
/*
   C++ program that solves for the roots of a quadratic equation
   This version uses if-else clauses.
*/
#include <iostream.h>
#include <math.h>

main()
{

   float a, b, c, discriminant;
   float real_part, imag_part, root1, root2;

   cout << "\t\tSOLVE FOR THE ROOTS OF A QUADRATIC EQUATION"
        << "\n\n"
        << "The equation is Y = A X^2 + B X + C\n";
   cout << "\nEnter A : ";
   cin >> a;
   cout << "\nEnter B : ";
   cin >> b;
   cout << "\nEnter C : ";
   cin >> c;
```

```
    cout << "\n\n";

    discriminant = b * b - 4.0 * a * c;

    if (discriminant >= 0.0)    {
        root1 = (-b + sqrt(discriminant)) / (2 * a);
        root2 = (-b - sqrt(discriminant)) / (2 * a);

        cout << "Root1 = " << root1 << "\n\n"
             << "Root2 = " << root2 << "\n\n";
    }
    else {
        real_part = sqrt(-discriminant) / (2 * a);
        imag_part = -b / (2 * a);

        cout << "Root1 = (" << real_part << ") + i ("
             << imag_part << ")\n\n"
             << "Root2 = (" << real_part << ") - i ("
             << imag_part << ")\n\n";
    }

    return 0;
}
```

The Multiple-Alternative *if-else* Statement

Like Pascal, C++ enables you to nest if-else statements to create a multiple-alternative form. The general syntax for this form is

```
if (tested_condition1)
     statement1; ¦ { <sequence #1 of statement> }
else if (tested_condition2)
     statement2; ¦ { <sequence #2 of statement> }
else if (tested_condition3)
     statement3; ¦ { <sequence #3 of statement> }
...
else if (tested_conditionN)
     statementN; ¦ { <sequence #N of statement> }
[else
     statementN+1; ¦ { <sequence #N+1 of statement> }]
```

The multiple-alternative if-else statement performs a series of cascaded tests until one of the following events occurs:

1. One of the conditions in the if or the else-if clause is true. If true, the accompanying statements are executed.

2. None of the tested conditions is true. In this case, the program executes the statements in the else clause (if an else clause exists).

The following version of the quadratic equation solver illustrates the multiple-alternative if-else statement. Listing 5.5 contains the source code for the LST05_05.PAS program.

The multiple-alternative if-else statement works well because there are three types of discriminant values:

- a positive discriminant—the roots are real and distinct

- a positive discriminant—the roots are real and identical

- a negative discriminant—the roots are imaginary and distinct

Listing 5.5. Source code for the LST05_05.PAS program.

```
PROGRAM Decision_Making_3;

{
  Turbo Pascal program that solves the roots of a quadratic
  equation. This version uses IF-THEN-ELSE IF clauses.
}
VAR a, b, c,
    discriminant,
    real_part, imag_part,
    root1, root2          : REAL;

BEGIN

    WRITELN('SOLVE FOR THE ROOTS OF A QUADRATIC EQUATION':60);
    WRITELN; WRITELN;
    WRITELN('The equation is Y = A X^2 + B X + C');
    WRITELN; WRITELN;
    WRITE('Enter A : '); READLN(a); WRITELN;
    WRITE('Enter B : '); READLN(b); WRITELN;
    WRITE('Enter C : '); READLN(c); WRITELN;

    discriminant := b * b - 4.0 * a * c;
```

```
    IF (discriminant > 0.0) THEN BEGIN
        root1 := (-b + SQRT(discriminant)) / (2 * a);
        root2 := (-b - SQRT(discriminant)) / (2 * a);

        WRITELN('Root1 = ',root1); WRITELN;
        WRITELN('Root2 = ',root2); WRITELN;
    END
    ELSE IF discriminant = 0.0 THEN BEGIN { two identical roots }
        root1 := -b / (2 * a);

        WRITELN('Root1 = ',root1); WRITELN;
        WRITELN('Root2 = ',root1); WRITELN;
    END
    ELSE BEGIN { discriminant < 0.0 }
        real_part := SQRT(-discriminant) / (2 * a);
        imag_part := -b / (2 * a);

        WRITELN('Root1 = (',real_part,') + i (',imag_part,')');
        WRITELN;
        WRITELN('Root2 = (',real_part,') - i (',imag_part,')');
        WRITELN;
    END; { IF }

END.
```

Compile and run the Pascal program. A sample session with the Turbo Pascal program follows:

```
[BEGIN SESSION]
                SOLVE FOR THE ROOTS OF A QUADRATIC EQUATION


The equation is Y = A X^2 + B X + C


Enter A : 1

Enter B : 1

Enter C : 1

Root1 = ( 8.6602540379E-01) + i (-5.0000000000E-01)

Root2 = ( 8.6602540379E-01) - i (-5.0000000000E-01)
[END SESSION]
```

Listing 5.6 shows the source code for the LST05_06.CPP program.

Listing 5.6. Source code for the LST05_06.CPP program.

```
/*
   C++ program that solves for the roots of a quadratic equation
   This version uses nested if-else clauses.
*/

#include <iostream.h>
#include <math.h>

main()
{
    float a, b, c, discriminant;
    float real_part, imag_part;
    float root1, root2;

    cout << "\t\tSOLVE FOR THE ROOTS OF A QUADRATIC EQUATION"
         << "\n\n"
         << "The equation is Y = A X^2 + B X + C\n";
    cout << "\nEnter A : ";
    cin >> a;
    cout << "\nEnter B : ";
    cin >> b;
    cout << "\nEnter C : ";
    cin >> c;

    cout << "\n\n";

    discriminant = b * b - 4.0 * a * c;

    if (discriminant > 0.0)
    {
        root1 = (-b + sqrt(discriminant)) / (2 * a);
        root2 = (-b - sqrt(discriminant)) / (2 * a);

        cout << "Root1 = " << root1 << "\n\n"
             << "Root2 = " << root2 << "\n\n";
    }
    else if (discriminant == 0.0)
    { // two identical roots
        root1 = -b / (2 * a);

        cout << "Root1 = " << root1 << "\n\n"
             << "Root2 = " << root1 << "\n\n";
```

```
    }
    else
    { // discriminant < 0.0
        real_part = sqrt(-discriminant) / (2 * a);
        imag_part = -b / (2 * a);

      cout << "Root1 = (" << real_part << ") + i ("
            << imag_part << ")\n\n"
            << "Root2 = (" << real_part << ") - i ("
            << imag_part << ")\n\n";
    }

    return 0;
}
```

Compile and run the Turbo C++ program. Note the following sample session:

```
[BEGIN SESSION]
                SOLVE FOR THE ROOTS OF A QUADRATIC EQUATION

The equation is Y = A X^2 + B X + C

Enter A : 1

Enter B : 1

Enter C : 1


Root1 = (0.866025) + i (-0.5)

Root2 = (0.866025) - i (-0.5)
[END SESSION]
```

Another example of the multiple-alternative if-else statement follows. This program implements a simple four-function calculator that is invoked to perform a single operation. The program prompts you to enter the first operand, the operator, and the second operand. It then performs the requested operation (if it is valid and possible) and displays your input and the result. An error message appears if you attempt to divide by zero or enter an invalid operator. An equivalent version of this program (using the switch statement) is presented later in this chapter.

Listing 5.7 contains the source code for the LST05_07.PAS program. Listing 5.8 contains the source code for the LST05_08.CPP program.

121

Listing 5.7. Source code for the LST05_07.PAS program.

```pascal
PROGRAM Decision_Making_4;

Uses CRT;

{
  simple Turbo Pascal program that implements
  a one-time, four-function calculator
}

VAR ok : BOOLEAN;
    op : CHAR;
    operand1, operand2, result : REAL;

BEGIN

    WRITE('Enter first operand : ');
    READLN(operand1); WRITELN;
    WRITE('Enter operation [in +-/*] : ');
    op := ReadKey;
    WRITELN(op); WRITELN;
    WRITE('Enter second operand : ');
    READLN(operand2); WRITELN;

    ok := TRUE; { assign optimistic default }

    IF op = '+' THEN
        result := operand1 + operand2

    ELSE IF op = '-' THEN
        result := operand1 - operand2

    ELSE IF op = '*' THEN
        result := operand1 * operand2

    ELSE IF op = '/' THEN
        IF operand2 <> 0.0 THEN
            result := operand1 / operand2
        ELSE BEGIN { division by zero }
            WRITELN('Error: Cannot divide by zero!');
            ok := FALSE
        END

    ELSE BEGIN { bad operator }
        WRITELN('You typed an invalid operator!');
        ok := FALSE
    END; { IF }
```

```
WRITELN; WRITELN;
IF ok THEN BEGIN { display results if available }
   WRITELN(operand1,' ',op,' ',operand2,' = ',result);
   WRITELN; WRITELN
END;

END.
```

Listing 5.8. Source code for the LST05_08.CPP program.

```
/*
   simple C++ program that implements a one-time,
   four-function calculator
*/

#include <iostream.h>
#include <conio.h>

#define BOOLEAN char
#define TRUE 1
#define FALSE 0

main()
{

   BOOLEAN ok = TRUE;
   char op;
   float operand1, operand2, result;

   cout << "Enter first operand : ";
   cin >> operand1;
   cout << "\nEnter operation [in +-/*] : ";
   cin >> op;
   cout << "\nEnter second operand : ";
   cin >> operand2;
   cout << "\n";

   if (op == '+')
      result = operand1 + operand2;

   else if (op == '-')
      result = operand1 - operand2;
```

continues

Listing 5.8. continued

```
else if (op == '*')
   result = operand1 * operand2;

else if (op == '/')
 { if (operand2 != 0.0)
      result = operand1 / operand2;
   else
   { // division by zero
      cout << "Error: Cannot divide by zero!\n";
      ok = FALSE;
   }
 }
 else
 { // bad op
   cout << "You typed an invalid operator";
   ok = FALSE;
 }

cout << "\n";
if (ok)  // display results if available
   cout << operand1 << ' '
        << op << ' '
        << operand2 << " = "
        <<  result << "\n\n";

return 0;
}
```

Note the following characteristics of the Turbo C++ program:

- The program uses character constants (enclosed in single quotes) to compare the valid operators with the operator you enter.

- The program uses the == relational operator to test for equality.

- The final `else` clause in the `if-else` statement detects invalid operators.

As you examine the Pascal version of this program, it may occur to you that a CASE statement would serve the program better. You are right! In the next section, the switch statement (which is similar to the Pascal CASE statement) is applied to create a new version of the preceding program.

The *switch* Statement

The switch statement works similarly (but not identically) to the Pascal CASE statement. The general syntax for the switch statement is

```
switch (expression) {
     case constant1_1:
[    case constant1_2: ...]
          <one or more statements>
          break;
     case constant2_1:
[    case constant2_2: ...]
          <one or more statements>
          break;
...
     case constantN_1:
[    case constantN_2: ...]
          <one or more statements>
          break;
     default:
          <one or more statements>
          break;
}
```

Note the following differences between the C++ switch statement and the Pascal CASE statement:

1. The switch requires an integer-compatible value. This value may be a constant, variable, function call, or an expression. The C++ switch statement does not work with floating-point data types.

2. The value after each case label must be a constant.

3. C++ does not support case labels with ranges of values. Each value must appear in a separate case label.

4. You should use a break statement after each set of executable statements. The break statement causes program execution to resume when the current switch statement ends. If you do not use a break statement, the program execution resumes at the subsequent case labels.

5. The default clause is similar to the catch-all ELSE clause in Pascal. Although using the break statement in the default clause is optional, it is a safe programming practice.

125

6. The set of statements in each case label or grouped case labels need not be enclosed by curly braces.

The lack of single case labels with ranges of values makes it more appealing to use a multiple-alternative if-else statement if you have a large contiguous range of values.

The translation of a CASE statement in Pascal to a similar switch statement in C++ uses the following general syntax:

Pascal:

```
CASE caseVar OF
     case_list_1 :   statement1 ¦
                     BEGIN <sequence of statements 1> END;
     case_list_1 :   statement1 ¦
                     BEGIN <sequence of statements 2> END;
     <other case lists>
     case_list_N :   statement1 ¦
                     BEGIN <sequence of statements N> END;
     ELSE            statementN+1 ¦
                     BEGIN <sequence of statements N+1> END;
```

C++:

```
switch (caseVar) {
     case constant1_1:
     case constant1_2:
     <other case labels>
         <one or more statements>
         break;
     case constant2_1:
     case constant2_2:
     <other case labels>
         <one or more statements>
         break;
     ...
     case constantN_1:
     case constantN_2:
     <other case labels>
         <one or more statements>
         break;
```

```
    default:
         <one or more statements>
         break;
}
```

The C++ switch statement is applied in the following program. The Turbo Pascal and Turbo C++ versions of the preceding example use CASE and switch statements, respectively. Listing 5.9 contains the source code for the LST05_09.PAS program, and Listing 5.10 contains the source code for the LST05_10.CPP program. The Turbo C++ listing is a straightforward translation of the Pascal code and does not contain any unusual coding.

Listing 5.9. Source code for the LST05_09.PAS program.

```
PROGRAM Decision_Making_5;

Uses CRT;

{
  simple Turbo Pascal program that implements a one-time,
  four-function calculator using the CASE statement.
}

VAR ok : BOOLEAN;
    op : CHAR;
    operand1, operand2, result : REAL;

BEGIN

    WRITE('Enter first operand : ');
    READLN(operand1); WRITELN;
    WRITE('Enter operation [in +-/*] : ');
    op := ReadKey;
    WRITELN(op); WRITELN;
    WRITE('Enter second operand : ');
    READLN(operand2); WRITELN;

    ok := TRUE; { assign optimistic default }

    CASE op OF

      '+' : result := operand1 + operand2;
      '-' : result := operand1 - operand2;
```

continues

127

Listing 5.9. continued

```
       '*' : result := operand1 * operand2;
       '/' : BEGIN
                IF operand2 <> 0.0 THEN
                    result := operand1 / operand2
                ELSE BEGIN { division by zero }
                    WRITELN('Error: Cannot divide by zero!');
                    ok := FALSE
                END
             END

    ELSE BEGIN { bad operator }
      WRITELN('You typed an invalid operator!');
      ok := FALSE
    END;
  END; { CASE }

  WRITELN; WRITELN;
  IF ok THEN BEGIN { display results if available }
    WRITELN(operand1,' ',op,' ',operand2,' = ',result);
    WRITELN; WRITELN
  END;

END.
```

Listing 5.10. Source code for the LST05_10.CPP program.

```
/*
    simple C++ program that implements a one-time,
    four-function calculator using the switch statement.
*/

#include <iostream.h>
#include "conio.h"

#define BOOLEAN char
#define TRUE 1
#define FALSE 0

main()
{

    BOOLEAN ok;
    char op;
```

```
    float operand1, operand2, result;

    cout << "Enter first operand : ";
    cin >> operand1;
    cout << "\nEnter operation [in +-/*] : ";
    cin >> op;
    cout << "\nEnter second operand : ";
    cin >> operand2;
    cout << "\n";

    ok = TRUE; // assign optimistic default

    switch (op) {

      case '+' :
           result = operand1 + operand2;
           break;
      case '-' :
           result = operand1 - operand2;
           break;
      case '*' :
           result = operand1 * operand2;
           break;
      case '/' :
           if (operand2 != 0.0)
               result = operand1 / operand2;
           else
           { // division by zero
               cout << "\n Error: Cannot divide by zero!";
               ok = FALSE;
           }
           break;

      default :  // bad operator
           cout << "\nYou typed an invalid operator";
           ok = FALSE;
    } // switch

    cout << "\n\n";
    if (ok)
       cout << "\n" << operand1 << ' '
                    << op << ' '
                    << operand2  << " = "
                    << result << "\n\n";

    return 0;

}
```

Listing 5.11 is a modified version of Listing 5.10. It contains the following features:

1. The use of the arithmetic assignment operators +=, -+, *=, and /=.

2. Placing the character input statement, op = getche(), in the placeholder for the switch expression:

```
switch ( op = getche() ) {
```

The preceding expression is unusual because it contains nested expressions. The program first executes op = getche(), which causes the keyboard to provide an input character. The program stores this character in the op variable. The value in op is then used as the switch expression. Listing 5.11 contains the source code for the LST05_11.CPP program. The new program prompts you for the two operands and the operator (this sequence makes it easier to code the program).

Listing 5.11. Source code for the LST05_11.CPP program.

```
/*
    simple C++ program that implements a one-time,
    four-function calculator using the switch statement.
    This modified program version illustrates how the
    op = getche() assignment may be used inside a switch
    expression.  In addition, assignment operators are
    used in calculating the results.
*/

#include <stdio.h>
#include "conio.h"

#define BOOLEAN char
#define TRUE 1
#define FALSE 0

main()
{

    BOOLEAN ok;
    char op;
    float operand1, operand2, result;

    printf("Enter first operand : ");
    scanf("%f", &operand1);
    printf("\nEnter second operand : ");
    scanf("%f", &operand2);
    printf("\n");
```

```
ok = TRUE; // assign optimistic default
result = operand1; // initialize result with value of operand1

printf("Enter operation [in +-*/] : ");

switch ( op = getche() ) {

  case '+' :
      result += operand2;
      break;
  case '-' :
      result -= operand2;
      break;
  case '*' :
      result *= operand2;
      break;
  case '/' :
      if (operand2 != 0.0)
          result /= operand2;
      else
      { // division by zero
          printf("\n Error: Cannot divide by zero!");
          ok = FALSE;
      }
      break;

  default :  // bad operator
      printf("\nYou entered a bad operator");
      ok = FALSE;
} // switch

printf("\n\n");
if (ok)
   printf("\n %f %c %f = %f\n\n",
          operand1, op, operand2, result);

return 0;

}
```

The next example contains case labels that manage ranges of values. The program prompts you for the following information:

1. A month number (the program displays the quarter into which the specified month falls).

131

2. A character (the program tells you whether your input is an uppercase character, a lowercase character, a digit, an arithmetic operator, or something else).

Listing 5.12 contains the source code for the LST05_12.PAS program. The Pascal listing uses the ranges of values in its CASE statements. Listing 5.13 shows the source code for the LST05_13.CPP program. The Turbo C++ program demonstrates that the switch statement is adequate to handle small ranges of values, such as those for month numbers. The switch statement seems unsuitable for handling large ranges of values, such as the uppercase and lowercase characters. In fact, many of the uppercase and lowercase values were excluded to keep the program short.

Listing 5.14 shows the LST05_14.CPP program that uses the multiple-alternative if-else statement to translate the Turbo Pascal program in Listing 5.12. Notice that the if-else statement is able to match the Pascal CASE statement with a minimum of coding.

Listing 5.12. Source code for the LST05_12.PAS program.

```
PROGRAM Decision_Making_6;

Uses CRT;

{ Turbo Pascal program that demonstrates using the CASE statement
  containing CASE clauses made up of:

    1) Sets of discrete values.
    2) Ranges of values.

}

VAR month : INTEGER;
    ch : CHAR;

BEGIN

        { test numeric values for the CASE statement }
        WRITE('Type month number : ');
        READLN(month); WRITELN;

        WRITE('Month number ',month,' is in ');

        CASE month OF

            { set of discrete values }
            1,2,3    : WRITE('the first');
            { range of values }
```

```
    4..6       : WRITE('the second');
    { range of values }
    7..9       : WRITE('the third');
    { one discrete value and a range of values }
    10, 11..12 : WRITE('the fourth');
    ELSE         WRITE('an unknown');

END; { CASE }

WRITELN(' quarter');
WRITELN; WRITELN;

{ test character values for the CASE statement }
WRITE('Type a letter : ');
ch := ReadKey;  WRITELN(ch); WRITELN;
WRITE(ch,' is a');

CASE ch OF

    'A'..'Z' : WRITELN('n uppercase letter');
    'a'..'z' : WRITELN(' lowercase letter');
    '0'..'9' : WRITELN(' digit');
    '+','-','*','/' : WRITELN(' math operator');
    ELSE WRITELN(' something strange!');

END; { CASE }

END.
```

Listing 5.13. Source code for the LST05_13.CPP program.

```
/*
   C++ program that demonstrates using the switch statement
   containing case clauses made up of:

   1) Sets of discrete values.
   2) Ranges of values.

*/

#include <iostream.h>
#include "conio.h"

#define BOOLEAN char
```

continues

Listing 5.13. continued

```
#define TRUE 1
#define FALSE 0

main()
{

    int month;
    char ch;

    // test numeric values for the switch statement
    cout << "Enter month number : ";
    cin >> month;
    cout << "\n";

    cout << "Month number " << month << " is in ";

    switch (month) {

        case 1:
        case 2:
        case 3:
            cout << "the first";
            break;
        case 4 :
        case 5 :
        case 6 :
            cout << "the second";
            break;
        case 7 :
        case 8 :
        case 9 :
            cout << "the third";
            break;
        case 10 :
        case 11 :
        case 12 :
            cout << "the fourth";
            break;
        default :
            cout << "an unknown";
    }

    cout << " quarter\n\n\n";
```

```
// test character values for the switch statement
cout << "Enter a letter : ";
cin >> ch;
cout << "\n" << ch << " is a";

switch (ch) {

    case 'A' :
    case 'B' :
    case 'C' :
    case 'D' :
    // other case clauses for 'E' to 'Y' here
    case 'Z' :
       cout << "n uppercase letter\n";
       break;
    case 'a' :
    case 'b' :
    case 'c' :
    case 'd' :
    // other case clauses for 'e' to 'y' here
    case 'z' :
       cout << " lowercase letter\n";
       break;
    case '0' :
    // other case clauses for '1' to '8' here
    case '9' :
       cout << " digit\n";
       break;
    case '+' :
    case '-' :
    case '*' :
    case '/' :
       cout << " math operator\n";
       break;
    default :
       cout << " something strange!\n";

}

return 0;

}
```

Listing 5.14. Source code for the LST05_14.CPP program.

```
/*
    C++ program that demonstrates using the if-else statement
    instead of the switch statement to eliminate the long
    list of 'case' clauses.
*/

#include <iostream.h>
#include "conio.h"

#define BOOLEAN char
#define TRUE 1
#define FALSE 0

//define macro similar to Pascal's <var> IN [<low>..<high>]
#define in_range(var,low,high) (var >= low && var <= high)

main()
{
    int month;
    char ch;

    // test numeric values for the switch statement
    cout << "Enter month number : ";
    cin >> month; cout << "\n";

    cout << "Month number " << month << " is in ";
    // use if-else without the in_range macro
    if (month >= 1 && month < 4)
        cout << "the first";
    else if (month >= 4 && month < 7)
        cout << "the second";
    else if (month >= 7 && month < 10)
        cout << "the third";
    else if (month >= 10 && month < 13)
        cout << "the fourth";
    else
        cout << "an unknown";

    cout << " quarter\n\n\n";

    // test character values for the switch statement
    cout << "Enter a letter : ";
    cin >> ch;
    cout << "\n" << ch << " is a";

    // use the if-else with the in_range macro
```

```
if in_range(ch,'A','Z')
      cout << "n uppercase letter\n";
else if in_range(ch,'a','z')
      cout << " lowercase letter\n";
else if in_range(ch,'0','9')
      cout << " digit\n";
else if (ch == '+' || ch == '-' || ch == '*' || ch =='/')
      cout << " math operator\n";
else
      cout << " something strange!\n";

return 0;

}
```

Summary

This chapter presented the decision-making constructs in C++. These constructs include:

1. The single-alternative `if` statement:

```
if (tested_condition)
    statement; | { <sequence of statements> }
```

2. The dual-alternative `if`-`else` statement:

```
if (tested_condition)
    statement1; { <sequence #1 of statements> }
else
    statement1; { <sequence #1 of statements> }
```

3. The multiple-alternative `if`-`else` statement:

```
if (tested_condition1)
    statement1; | { <sequence #1 of statement> }
else if (tested_condition2)
    statement2; | { <sequence #2 of statement> }
else if (tested_condition3)
    statement3; | { <sequence #3 of statement> }
...
else if (tested_conditionN)
    statementN; | { <sequence #N of statement> }
[else
    statementN+1; | { <sequence #N+1 of statement> }]
```

137

if statements are governed by the following conditions:

- C++ contains no equivalent to the Pascal keyword THEN.

- The tested condition must be enclosed in parentheses.

- Blocks of statements are enclosed in curly braces.

4. The multiple-alternative switch statement:

```
switch (caseVar) {
    case constant1_1:
    case constant1_2:
    <other case labels>
        <one or more statements>
        break;
    case constant2_1:
    case constant2_2:
    <other case labels>
        <one or more statements>
        break;
    ...
    case constantN_1:
    case constantN_2:
    <other case labels>
        <one or more statements>
        break;

    default:
        <one or more statements>
        break;
}
```

C++ requires that the following conditions are observed when using a switch statement:

- The switch expression must be integer-compatible. The expression may be a constant, variable, expression, or function.

- The case labels must contain only constants.

- The switch statement requires one case label for each tested value.

- A break statement is required at the end of each set of statements so that program execution resumes at the end of the switch statement. If the break statement is omitted, the program execution resumes at the next case label.

- Each set of statements need not be enclosed in curly braces.

Loops

L oops are powerful language constructs that enable computers to perform repetitive tasks easily. This chapter focuses on loops and presents the following topics:

- the `for` loop statement
- exiting loops
- the `do-while` loop statement
- the `while` loop statement
- nested loops

Overview

Loops are essential in performing repetitive and iterative tasks such as accessing arrays and executing a sequence of statements. The three kinds of general loops are fixed, conditional, and infinite. Fixed loops iterate for a preset number of times. Conditional loops iterate as long as or until a tested condition is true. Infinite loops (also called open loops) iterate indefinitely—although this may seem like a dangerous prospect, a majority of open loops have a mechanism for exiting the loop. In a few applications, an open loop is a must. A good example is MS-DOS. The DOS processor is an infinite loop depicted by the following pseudocode:

```
Repeat
     display the DOS prompt
     wait for user input
     process the input
     if there is no error then
          execute command
     else
          display error message
     end
Until FALSE
```

If MS-DOS iterated for a fixed number of times or conditionally and then stopped, it could not function as an operating system.

The *for* Loop

The for loop in C++ resembles the FOR-NEXT loop in Pascal. The general syntax for the for loop statement is:

```
for (<initialization of loop control variables>;
     <loop continuation test>;
     <increment/decrement of loop control variables>)
```

The for loop statement has three components, all of which are optional. The first component initializes the loop control variables. In C++ you can employ more than one loop control variable. The second part of the loop is the condition that determines whether the loop makes another iteration. The last part of the for loop is the clause that increments and decrements the loop control variables. Unlike Pascal, the for loop in C++ has no default increment. The three components of the C++ for loop indicate that its features are fairly different from the Pascal FOR-NEXT loop.

The general form for translating an upward-counting Turbo Pascal FOR-NEXT loop to the C++ for loop is:

Pascal:

```
          FOR loopVar := first TO last
```

```
C++:
          for (loopVar = first; loopVar <= last; loopVar++)
```

The general form for translating a downward-counting Turbo Pascal FOR-NEXT loop to the C++ for loop is:

```
Pascal:
          FOR loopVar := last DOWNTO first

C++:
          for (loopVar = last; loopVar >= first; loopVar--)
```

The following example illustrates the fixed loop. The program prompts you to enter an integer in the range of 1 to 30 and calculates the factorial number for that integer. The program uses a fixed loop to obtain the factorial. If you enter a number outside the given range, the program displays an error message. Listing 6.1 contains the source code for the LST06_01.PAS program.

Listing 6.1. Source code for the LST06_01.PAS program.

```
PROGRAM For_Loop_1;

{
  Turbo Pascal program that calculates a
  factorial using a FOR loop
}

VAR factorial : REAL;
    i, n : BYTE;

BEGIN
    WRITE('Enter the factorial of [1..30] : ');
    READLN(n); WRITELN;

    IF (n > 0) AND (n <= 30) THEN BEGIN

       factorial := 1.0;

       FOR i := 1 TO n DO
           factorial := factorial * i;
```

continues

Listing 6.1. continued

```
        WRITELN(n,'! = ',factorial);
    END
    ELSE
        WRITELN('Sorry! Factorial is out of range');

END.
```

Listing 6.2 contains the source code for the LST06_02.CPP program.

Listing 6.2. Source code for the LST06_02.CPP program.

```
// C++ program that calculates a factorial using a for loop

#include <iostream.h>

#define BYTE short

main()
{
    // factorial is declared and also initialized
    double factorial = 1.0;
    BYTE i, n;

    cout << "Enter the factorial of [1..30] : ";
    cin >> n;
    cout << "\n";

    if (n > 0 && n <= 30) {
        for (i = 1; i <= n; i++)
          /* ----- ------ ---
               ^       ^     ^
               ¦       ¦     ¦
               ¦       ¦     ¦
               ¦       ¦     increment i by 1
               ¦       ¦
               ¦       test loop continuation condition
               ¦
              initialize loop counter
          */

            factorial *= (double) i;
```

```
        cout << n << "! = " << factorial << "\n";
    }
    else
        cout << "Sorry! factorial is out of range\n";

    return 0;
}
```

Notice the following differences between the Turbo Pascal and Turbo C++ listings:

1. The program initializes the loop control variable in the C++ `for` loop using the expression `i = 1`.

2. The loop continuation condition is `i <= n` (the equal sign ensures that the iteration for `i` equals `n` takes place). In other words, the loop iterates if `i` is less than or equal to `n`.

3. The loop increments its `i` control variable by 1 using the expression `i++`.

4. The C++ program declares and initializes the variable factorial in the same statement.

5. The loop updates the value of the variable factorial using a typecast of the `i` loop control variable.

C++, unlike C, its parent language, enables you to declare the loop control variables in the `for` loop. For example, the `for` loop in Listing 6.2 can be written as follows:

```
for (BYTE i = 1; i <= n; i++)
```

The `i` variable, of course, must be removed from the declaration statement at the beginning of function `main`.

The preceding program shows you how to declare a single loop control variable. The next program illustrates a `for` loop with multiple loop control variables. The program prompts you to enter the first and last numbers in a range of integers. It then calculates the mean value and the standard deviation for the range you specify. For the sake of demonstration, this program uses a downward-counting loop. Listing 6.3 contains the source code for the LST06_03.PAS program. Compile and run the Turbo Pascal program. A sample session follows:

```
[BEGIN SESSION]
Enter lower range : 10

Enter upper range : 20
```

```
Average        =   1.5000000000E+01

Std. deviation =   3.3166247904E+00
[END SESSION]
```

Listing 6.3. Source code for the LST06_03.PAS program.

```pascal
PROGRAM For_Loop_2;

{
  Turbo Pascal program that calculates the statistical average
  and standard deviation using a decremented FOR loop
}

VAR sum, sumX, sumXsqr,
    average, stdev    : REAL;
    i, low, high      : INTEGER;

BEGIN
    WRITE('Enter lower range : '); READLN(low);  WRITELN;
    WRITE('Enter upper range : '); READLN(high); WRITELN;

    { initialize statistical summations }
    sum := 0.0;
    sumX := 0.0;
    sumXsqr := 0.0;
    FOR i := high DOWNTO low DO BEGIN
        sum := sum + 1.0;
        sumX := sumX + i;
        sumXsqr := sumXsqr + SQR(i)
    END; { FOR }

    { calculate statistics }
    average := sumX / sum;
    stdev := SQRT((sumXsqr - SQR(sumX) / sum) / (sum - 1.0));

    WRITELN('Average        = ', average); WRITELN;
    WRITELN('Std. deviation = ', stdev); WRITELN;

END.
```

Listing 6.4 contains the source code for the LST06_04.CPP program. Compile and run the program and note the following sample session:

```
[BEGIN SESSION]
Enter lower range : 10

Enter upper range : 20

Average       = 15

Std. deviation = 3.316625
[END SESSION]
```

Listing 6.4. Source code for the LST06_04.CPP program.

```cpp
/*
  C++ program that calculates the statistical average
  and standard deviation using a decremented for loop
*/

#include <iostream.h>
#include <math.h>

// define square pseudo-function
#define SQR(x) ((x) * (x))

main()
{

    double sum, sumX, sumXsqr;
    double average, sdev;
    unsigned i, low, high;

    cout << "Enter lower range : ";
    cin >> low;
    cout << "\nEnter upper range : ";
    cin >> high;
    cout << "\n";

    for (i = high, sum = 0.0,
        // initialize counter & summations
        sumX = 0.0, sumXsqr = 0.0;
        // check loop termination condition
        i >= low;
        // decrement counter and increment data count
        i--) {
        // update summations using assignment
        // operators & type casting
        sumX += (double) i;
```

continues

Listing 6.4. continued

```
        sumXsqr += (double) SQR(i);
        sum++;
    }

    // calculate statistics
    average = sumX / sum;
    sdev = sqrt((sumXsqr - SQR(sumX) / sum) / (sum - 1.0));

    cout << "Average        = " << average << "\n\n";
    cout << "Std. deviation = " << sdev << "\n\n";

    return 0;

}
```

Examine the Turbo Pascal and Turbo C++ listings and notice the following aspects of the Turbo C++ program:

1. The for loop statement initializes the variable i and the statistical summation variables. The initial variable of variable i is the upper range limit.

2. The for loop statement uses the condition i >= low to test the loop continuation condition.

3. The third part of the for loop statement decrements the variable i and increments the variable sum.

4. The loop body increments the variables sumX and sumXsqr using the arithmetic assignment operators and typecasting.

Nested Loops

The preceding examples of for loops employed single loops. This next section presents an example that uses nested loops to draw a V-shape on the screen using the + character. The program also shows you how to skip the remaining part of a loop and resume with the next iteration. Note the finished product (I trimmed a few columns from the right side of the V-shape to make it fit on the printed page):

```
[BEGIN SESSION]
                                          :
                                          :
                                          :
                                          :
++                                        :
++++                                      :
++++++                                    :
++++++++                                  :
++++++++++                                :
++++++++++++                              :                    ++
++++++++++++++                            :                  ++++
++++++++++++++++                          :                ++++++
++++++++++++++++++                        :              ++++++++
++++++++++++++++++++                      :            ++++++++++
++++++++++++++++++++++                    :          ++++++++++++
++++++++++++++++++++++++                  :        ++++++++++++++
++++++++++++++++++++++++++                :      ++++++++++++++++
++++++++++++++++++++++++++++              :    ++++++++++++++++++
++++++++++++++++++++++++++++++            :  ++++++++++++++++++++
++++++++++++++++++++++++++++++++          :  ++++++++++++++++++++++
++++++++++++++++++++++++++++++++++        :  ++++++++++++++++++++++++
++++++++++++++++++++++++++++++++++++      :  ++++++++++++++++++++++++++
++++++++++++++++++++++++++++++++++++++    :  ++++++++++++++++++++++++++
++++++++++++++++++++++++++++++++++++++++++:++++++++++++++++++++++++++++++
                                          :
[END SESSION]
```

The program creates the V-shape one column at a time. To display each column, press the space bar. Listing 6.5 contains the source code for the LST06_05.PAS program. Listing 6.6 contains the source code for the LST06_06.CPP program.

Listing 6.5. Source code for the LST06_05.PAS program.

```pascal
Program For_Loop3;

Uses CRT;

{
  Turbo Pascal program that uses multiple loops to draw a simple
  histogram. The program also demonstrates the use of the GOTO
  statement.
}

LABEL 999, 998;
```

continues

147

Listing 6.5. continued

```pascal
CONST MAX_COL = 80;
      MID_COL = 40;
      MAX_ROW = 24;

{$DEFINE  DEBUG}  { debugging switch }

VAR i, x, xtransform, y : INTEGER;
    ch : CHAR;

BEGIN
    ClrScr;
    { draw X-axis }
    GotoXY(1,24);
    FOR x := 1 TO MAX_COL DO
        WRITE('_');

    { draw Y-axis }
    FOR y := 1 TO MAX_ROW DO BEGIN
        GotoXY(MID_COL,y);
        WRITE(':');
    END;

    FOR x := 1 TO MAX_COL-1 DO BEGIN
        {$IFDEF DEBUG}
            ch := ReadKey;
            IF ch IN ['Q','q'] THEN GOTO 999; { end program }
        {$ENDIF}

        { skip over median screen column }
        IF x = MID_COL THEN GOTO 998;

        xtransform := ABS(x - MID_COL) div 2;
        y := MAX_ROW - xtransform;

        IF y >= MAX_ROW THEN y := MAX_ROW - 1;

        { draw histogram bar }
        FOR i := y TO MAX_ROW-1 DO BEGIN
            GotoXY(x,i);
            WRITE('+');
        END; { FOR }

        998:

    END; { FOR }
```

```
    REPEAT
    UNTIL KeyPressed;

    999:

END.
```

Listing 6.6. Source code for the LST06_06.CPP program.

```cpp
/*
  C++ program that uses multiple loops to draw a simple histogram.
*/

#include <stdio.h>
#include <conio.h>
#include <math.h>

// define empty debugging macro
#define DEBUG

main()
{

    const int MAX_COL = 80;
    const int MID_COL = 40;
    const int MAX_ROW = 24;

    int i, x, xtransform, y;
    char ch = ' ';

    clrscr();
    // draw X-axis
    gotoxy(1,MAX_ROW);
    for (x = 1; x <= MAX_COL; x++)
        putchar('_');

    // draw Y-axis
    for (y = 1; y <= MAX_ROW; y++)  {
        gotoxy(MID_COL,y);
        putchar(':');
    }

    for (x = 1; x < MAX_COL; x++)  {
```

continues

Listing 6.6. continued

```
#ifdef DEBUG
      ch = getch();
      if (ch == 'Q' || ch == 'q')
        break; // break out of outer loop
#endif
      // skip over median screen column
      if (x == MID_COL)
        continue; // resume at next the iteration of outer loop

      xtransform = abs(x - MID_COL) / 2;
      y = MAX_ROW - xtransform;

      if (y >= MAX_ROW)
        y = MAX_ROW - 1;

      // draw histogram bar
      for (i = y; i < MAX_ROW; i++)  {
          gotoxy(x,i);
          putchar('+');
      }

  }

  if (ch == 'q')
    ch = 'Q';

  do {
    // nothing
  } while (ch != 'Q' && !getch() );

  return 0;
}
```

Each loop iteration draws a column of + characters (except at the MID_COL column). When the program reaches that column, it must skip the rest of the loop statement and resume at the next iteration. Compare the way in which Turbo Pascal and Turbo C++ programs implement this feature.

The Turbo Pascal program implements the jump using the following IF statement:

```
{ skip over median screen column }
IF x = MID_COL THEN GOTO 998;
```

The GOTO statement directs the program execution to the end of the current FOR loop. The Turbo C++ program has a better mechanism that uses the `continue` keyword to automatically jump to the end of the current loop:

```
// skip over median screen column
if (x == MID_COL)
    continue; // resume at next the iteration of outer loop
```

The Turbo C++ `continue` statement needs no labels. Most Pascal and C++ programmers prefer to avoid GOTO statements and labels. C++ also supports the `goto` statement and labels that are similar to Pascal labels (except that you do not need to declare them).

Open Loops Using *for* Loops

At the beginning of this chapter, I mentioned that the three components of the `for` loop are optional. In fact, C++ enables you to leave these three components empty. The result is an open loop. This feature highlights the difference between the C++ `for` loop and the Pascal FOR-NEXT loop. Other languages, such as Ada, Modula-2, and C, support formal open loops and mechanisms to exit these loops. C++ enables you to exit a loop in the two following ways:

1. The `break` statement causes program execution to resume after the end of the current loop. Use the `break` statement when you want to exit a `for` loop and resume with the remaining parts of the program. Turbo Pascal has no construct that resembles the `break` statement.

2. The `exit` function, declared in the stdlib.h header file, enables you to exit a program. The `exit` function is similar to the Turbo Pascal HALT intrinsic. Use `exit` if you want to stop iterating and exit the program.

The following program uses an open loop to repeatedly prompt you for a number. Input is displayed along with its square value. The program then asks whether you want to calculate the square of another number. If you enter the letter Y (or y), the program performs another iteration. If not, it stops. If you continue entering Y at the second prompt, the program keeps running. Listing 6.7 contains the source code for the LST06_07.PAS program. Compile and run the Turbo Pascal program and note the following sample session:

```
[BEGIN SESSION]
Enter a number : 5

( 5.0000000000E+00)^2 =  2.5000000000E+01
```

151

```
More calculations? (Y/N) y
Enter a number : 7

( 7.0000000000E+00)^2 =  4.9000000000E+01

More calculations? (Y/N) y

Enter a number : 9

( 9.0000000000E+00)^2 =  8.1000000000E+01

More calculations? (Y/N) n
[END SESSION]
```

Listing 6.7. Source code for the LST06_07.PAS program.

```pascal
Program Open_Loop;

{
  Turbo Pascal program that demonstrates using the
  WHILE loop to emulate an infinite loop.
}

Uses CRT;

VAR ch : CHAR;
    x, y : REAL;

BEGIN

    { WHILE loop with empty parts }
    WHILE TRUE DO BEGIN
       WRITELN;
       WRITE('Enter a number : ');
       READLN(x);
       WRITELN;
       y := x * x;
       WRITELN('(',x,')^2 = ',y); WRITELN;
       WRITE('More calculations? (Y/N) ');
       ch := ReadKey;
       WRITELN(ch);
       IF (ch <> 'y') AND (ch <> 'Y') THEN
           HALT(0);
    END;

END.
```

Listing 6.8 contains the source code for the LST06_08.CPP program. Compile and run the Turbo C++ program and note the following sample session:

```
[BEGIN SESSION]
Enter a number : 5

(5)^2 = 25
More calculations? (Y/N) y

Enter a number : 7

(7)^2 = 49

More calculations? (Y/N) y

Enter a number : 9

(9)^2 = 81

More calculations? (Y/N) n
[END SESSION]
```

Listing 6.8. Source code for the LST06_08.CPP program.

```
/*
    C++ program that demonstrates using the
    for loop to emulate an infinite loop.
*/

#include <iostream.h>
#include <stdlib.h>
#include <conio.h>

main()
{

    char ch;
    double x, y;

    // for loop with empty parts
    for (;;) {
        cout << "\n\nEnter a number : ";
        cin >> x;
        y = x * x;
        cout << "(" << x << ")^2 = " << y << "\n\n";
        cout << "More calculations? (Y/N) ";
```

continues

153

Listing 6.8. continued

```
    ch = getche();
    if (ch != 'y' && ch != 'Y')
        exit(0);
}

return 0;

}
```

Skipping Loop Iterations

C++ enables you to skip to the end of a loop and resume the next iteration using the continue statement, which is employed in Listing 6.6. The general form for using the continue statement is

```
for(iniExpression; condition; loopVarIncrement) {
    // sequence #1 of statements
    if (skipCondition)
        continue;
    // sequence #2 of statements
}
```

In the preceding form, the execution of the first sequence of statements in the for loop creates a condition that is tested in the if statement. If that condition is true, the if statement invokes the continue statement to skip the second sequence of statements in the for loop.

Exiting Loops

C++ supports the break statement to exit loops (including the for loop). The break statement causes the program to resume at the end of the current loop. The general form for using the break statement in a for loop is

```
for(iniExpression; condition; loopVarIncrement) {
    // sequence #1 of statements
    if (exitLoopCondition)
```

```
        break;
    // sequence #2 of statements
}
    // sequence #3 of statements
```

In the preceding form, the execution of the first sequence of statements in the for loop creates a condition that is tested in the if statement. If that condition is true, the if statement invokes the break statement to exit the loop altogether. Program execution resumes at the third sequence of statements.

The following Turbo C++ program, Listing 6.9, employs break and continue statements. The program contains two for loop statements. The first loop iterates for values in the range of –2 to 10. Each loop iteration calculates the square root value of the loop control variable. Because the square root function does not accept negative values, the loop uses an if statement to skip to the end of the loop if the variable x (a double-typed typecast of the loop control variable i) is negative. The if statement executes the continue statement when this condition is true.

The second for loop is an open loop that prompts you to enter a number, calculates the square root of your input, and displays both your input and the square root. To exit this open loop you must enter a negative number. The loop uses an if statement to detect a negative input and execute a break statement. The break statement enables the program to resume at the last program statement. Listing 6.9 contains the source code for the LST06_09.CPP program.

Listing 6.9. Source code for the LST06_09.CPP program.

```
/*
   C++ program that demonstrates the use of break and continue
*/

#include <iostream.h>
#include <math.h>

main()
{
   int i;
   double x, result;

   for (i = -2; i <= 10; i++) {
      x = (double) i;
      if (x < 0.0) continue;
      result = sqrt(x);
```

continues

155

Listing 6.9. continued

```
    cout << "SQRT(" << x << ") = " << result << "\n";
  }

  for (;;) {
    cout << "Enter a positive number "
         << "(exit using a negative number) : ";
    cin >> x;
    if (x < 0.0) break;
    result = sqrt(x);
    cout << "SQRT(" << x << ") = " << result << "\n";
  }

  return 0;
}
```

The *do-while* Loop

The do-while loop in C++ is a conditional loop that resembles the Pascal REPEAT-UNTIL loop. The do-while loop, however, iterates as long as a condition is true. The REPEAT-UNTIL loop iterates until a condition is true. The Boolean value of a tested condition in the do-while loop is the negated Boolean value of the tested condition in the REPEAT-UNTIL loop. The general syntax for the do-while loop is

```
do {
    sequence of statements
} while (condition);
```

To translate the Pascal REPEAT-UNTIL loop into the C++ do-while loop, employ the following form:

Pascal:

```
        REPEAT

            sequence of statements

        UNTIL condition;
```

```
C++:

        do {

                sequence of statements

        while (!(condition));
```

The following example uses the do-while loop. The Turbo Pascal version uses two nested REPEAT-UNTIL loops to perform the following tasks:

- The outer loop prompts you to enter a positive number.

- The inner loop calculates iteratively the square root of the entered number. The inner loop implements Newton's algorithm for calculating a square root.

- The entered number and its square root are displayed.

The outer loop iterates until you enter a non-positive number. If you enter a positive number the first time the program prompts you, the outer loop iterates only once. The inner loop iterates as many times as necessary to obtain a close approximation of the desired square root. Listing 6.10 contains the source code for the LST06_10.PAS program.

Listing 6.10. Source code for the LST06_10.PAS program.

```
PROGRAM Repeat_it;

{
  Turbo Pascal program that calculates the square root of a
  number by using Newton's root-seeking algorithm and a
  REPEAT-UNTIL loop.

  The program contains two REPEAT loops:

     1) The outer loop is used to reprompt the user for a
        positive number.

     2) The inner loop is used to iterate the refinement of the
        value for the sought square root.

}

CONST ACCURACY = 0.00001; { predefined accuracy }
```

continues

Listing 6.10. continued

```pascal
VAR number, sqroot : REAL;
    done : BOOLEAN;

BEGIN
    REPEAT
        WRITE('Enter a positive number ');
        READLN(number); WRITELN;

        IF (number > 0.0) THEN BEGIN
            { calculate initial number for the square root }
            sqroot := number / 2.0;
            { refine number }
            REPEAT
                sqroot := (number / sqroot + sqroot) / 2.0;
            UNTIL ABS(number - sqroot * sqroot) < ACCURACY;

            WRITELN('SQR(',number:10:5,') = ',sqroot:10:5);
            done := TRUE

        END
        ELSE BEGIN
            WRITELN('Please enter a positive number!');
            done := FALSE;
        END;

        WRITELN;

    UNTIL done;

END.
```

Listing 6.11 contains the source code for the LST06_11.CPP program. Examine the Pascal and C++ listings and note the following differences:

1. The condition in the UNTIL clause of the Pascal program translates into a C++ condition that is negated using the ! operator.

2. The C++ program includes the math.h header file to import the fabs function. This function returns the absolute value for the double data type.

3. The BOOLEAN type done in the Pascal program translates into the BOOLEAN alias for the char type (an integer-compatible type).

Listing 6.11. Source code for the LST06_11.CPP program.

```
/*
  C++ program that calculates the square root of a number
  by using Newton's root-seeking algorithm and a do-while loop.

  The program contains two do-while loops:

    1) The outer loop is used to reprompt the user for a
       positive number.
    2) The inner loop is used to iterate the refinement of the
       value for the sought square root.

*/

#include <iostream.h>
// import the fabs() function from math.h
#include <math.h>

#define BOOLEAN char

// predefined accuracy
#define ACCURACY  0.00001
#define TRUE 1
#define FALSE 0

main()
{

    float number, sqroot;
    BOOLEAN done;

    do {
        cout << "Enter a positive number : ";
        cin >> number;
        cout << "\n";

        if (number > 0.0)  {
            /* calculate initial guess for the square root */
            sqroot = number / 2.0;
            /* refine guess */
            do {

                sqroot = (number / sqroot + sqroot) / 2.0;

            } while
              ( !((fabs(number - sqroot * sqroot)) < ACCURACY) );
```

continues

159

Listing 6.11. continued

```
        cout << "SQRT(" << number << ") = " << sqroot << "\n";
        done = TRUE;

    }
    else {
        cout << "Please enter a positive number!\n";
        done = FALSE;
    }

    cout << "\n";

} while (!done);

return 0;
}
```

The next example uses the do-while loop to implement an improved version of the four-function calculator presented in Chapter 5, "Decision-Making." The earlier version performed a single calculation and ended the program—it was necessary to invoke the program from the DOS prompt each time you wanted to perform a calculation. The new version solves this frustrating feature by using a conditional loop. This loop contains statements that perform the following tasks:

- prompts you for the operands and operator

- performs the requested operation, if valid

- displays the operands, operator, and the result

- prompts you for another operation (press *Y* or *N* to answer this prompt)

Listing 6.12 contains the source code for the LST06_12.PAS program. Listing 6.13 contains the source code for the LST06_13.CPP program.

Listing 6.12. Source code for the LST06_12.PAS program.

```
PROGRAM Repeat_it2;

Uses CRT;
```

```
{

   This program is a modified version of an earlier simple
   calculator program.  The REPEAT loop is used as:

      1) An outer loop to enable the user to perform as many
         operations as desired.

      2) An inner loop to ensure that the user's input to
         Yes/No prompt is either an 'N' or a 'Y' (in both
         upper- and lowercase)

}

VAR ok : BOOLEAN;
    ans, op : CHAR;
    operand1, operand2, result : REAL;

BEGIN

   REPEAT

      WRITE('Type first operand : '); READLN(operand1); WRITELN;
      WRITE('Type operation [in +-/*] : '); op := ReadKey;
      WRITELN(op); WRITELN;
      WRITE('Type second operand : '); READLN(operand2); WRITELN;

      ok := TRUE; { assign optimistic default }

      CASE op OF

         '+' : result := operand1 + operand2;
         '-' : result := operand1 - operand2;
         '*' : result := operand1 * operand2;
         '/' : BEGIN
                  IF operand2 <> 0.0 THEN
                     result := operand1 / operand2
                  ELSE BEGIN { division by zero }
                     WRITELN('Error: Cannot divide by zero!');
                     ok := FALSE
                  END
               END

      ELSE BEGIN { bad operator }
        WRITELN('You typed an invalid operator');
        ok := FALSE
      END;
    END; { CASE }
```

continues

161

Listing 6.12. continued

```
      WRITELN; WRITELN;
      IF ok THEN BEGIN {display results if available }
         WRITELN(operand1, ' ', op, ' ', operand2, ' = ', result);
         WRITELN; WRITELN
      END;

      REPEAT
         WRITE('Want to perform more operations ? (Y/N) ');
         ans := ReadKey;
         WRITELN(ans);
         WRITELN;
         ans := Upcase(ans);
      UNTIL ans IN ['Y','N'];

   UNTIL ans = 'N';

END.
```

Listing 6.13. Source code for the LST06_13.CPP program.

```
/*
  This program is a modified version of an earlier simple
  calculator program.  The do loop is used as:

    1) An outer loop to enable the user to perform as many
       operations as desired.

    2) An inner loop to ensure that the user's input to
       Yes/No prompt is either an 'N' or a 'Y' (in both
       upper- and lowercase).
*/


#include <iostream.h>
#include <conio.h>

#define BOOLEAN char
#define TRUE 1
#define FALSE 0
#define Upcase(c += 'A' - 'a')
#define is_yes_no(var) (var == 'Y' || var == 'N')
```

```
main()
{
    BOOLEAN ok;
    char ans, op;
    double operand1, operand2, result;

    do {

        cout << "Type first operand : ";
        cin >> operand1;
        cout << "\nType operation [in +-/*] : ";
        op = getche();
        cout << "\n\nType second operand : ";
        cin >> operand2;
        cout << "\n";

        ok = TRUE; // assign optimistic default

        switch (op) {

          case '+' :
             result = operand1 + operand2;
             break;
          case '-' :
             result = operand1 - operand2;
             break;
          case '*' :
             result = operand1 * operand2;
             break;
          case '/' :
             if (operand2 != 0.0)
                  result = operand1 / operand2;
             else { // division by zero
                  cout << "Error: Cannot divide by zero!";
                  ok = FALSE;
             }
             break;

         default : { // bad operator
           cout << "You typed an invalid operator";
           ok = FALSE;
         }
        }

        cout << "\n";
        if (ok)   // display results if available
           cout << operand1 << " " << op << " " << operand2
```

continues

163

Listing 6.13. continued

```
                << " = " << result << "\n";
    do {
        cout << "Want to perform more operations ? (Y/N) ";
        ans = getche();
        cout << "\n\n";
        if (ans > 'Z') // character is a lower case ?
            ans = Upcase(ans);
    } while ( !(is_yes_no(ans)) );

  } while ( !(ans == 'N') );

  return 0;

}
```

Note the following differences between the Pascal and the C++ programs:

1. The Turbo Pascal statement ans := Upcase(ans) is translated into the following Turbo C++ statement:

```
if (ans > 'Z') // character is a lower case ?
    ans = Upcase(ans);
```

The Upcase identifier is a macro-based pseudofunction that converts the lower-case character into uppercase. The if statement is used to filter out the uppercase character arguments for the Upcase macro.

2. The Pascal program uses the following UNTIL clause:

```
UNTIL ans IN ['Y','N'];
```

The C++ program uses the following while clause:

```
} while ( !(is_yes_no(ans)) );
```

The is_yes_no identifier is a macro-based pseudofunction defined as:

```
#define is_yes_no(var) (var == 'Y' || var == 'N')
```

Compile and run the Turbo C++ program and note the following sample session:

```
[BEGIN SESSION]
Type first operand : 56

Type operation [in +-/*] : /
Type second operand : 45
```

```
56 / 45 = 1.244444

Want to perform more operations ? (Y/N) y

Type first operand : 144

Type operation [in +-/*] : /

Type second operand : 14


144 / 14 = 10.285714

Want to perform more operations ? (Y/N) n
[END SESSION]
```

The *while* Loop

The C++ while loop is another conditional loop that works like the Pascal WHILE loop. The general syntax for the while loop is

```
while (condition)
    statement; ¦ { sequence of statements }
```

Note that the tested condition of the while loop must be enclosed in parentheses. The while loop examines the tested condition before it iterates—if the tested condition is initially false, the while loop does not iterate. This contrasts with the do-while loop, which must iterate at least one time.

Following are two examples of the while loop. The first example modifies the preceding example (in Listing 6.13) to take advantage of the while loop's feature of testing its condition before iterating. The program performs the following tasks:

- prompts you to enter the operation you wish to execute (press *Q* to exit the program)

- if the input for the operation is not *Q*, it performs the next task

- prompts you to enter the two operands separated by a space

- performs the requested operation, if valid

- displays the operands, the operator, and the result

165

- prompts you to enter the operation you wish to execute or Q to exit the program

- resumes at the second task

Listing 6.14 contains the source code for the LST06_14.PAS program.

Listing 6.14. Source code for the LST06_14.PAS program.

```pascal
PROGRAM Do_While_1;

Uses CRT;

{
  Turbo Pascal program that uses a WHILE loop to enable the
  user to perform several basic math operations.
}

VAR ok : BOOLEAN;
    op : CHAR;
    operand1, operand2, result : REAL;

BEGIN
    WRITE('Type operation [+-/* or Q to quit] ');
    op := ReadKey;
    WRITELN(op); WRITELN;

    WHILE op <> 'Q' DO BEGIN

        WRITE('Type two numbers separated by a space : ');
        READLN(operand1,operand2); WRITELN;

        ok := TRUE;

        CASE op OF
            '+' : result := operand1 + operand2;
            '-' : result := operand1 - operand2;
            '*' : result := operand1 * operand2;
            '/' : BEGIN
                    IF operand2 <> 0.0 THEN
                        result := operand1 / operand2
                    ELSE BEGIN
                        WRITELN('Cannot divide by zero');
                        WRITELN;
                        ok := NOT ok;
                    END
```

```
                END
            ELSE BEGIN
                WRITELN('Bad operator');
                WRITELN;
                ok := NOT ok;
            END;
        END; { CASE }

        IF ok THEN WRITELN(operand1, ' ', op, ' ',
                            operand2, ' = ', result);

        WRITELN; WRITELN;

        WRITE('Type operation [+-/* or Q to quit] ');
        op := ReadKey;
        WRITELN(op); WRITELN;

    END; { WHILE }

END.
```

Listing 6.15 contains the source code for the LST06_15.CPP program. Compile and run the program and note the following sample session with the Turbo C++ program:

```
[BEGIN SESSION]
Type operation [+-/* or Q to quit] /
Type two numbers separated by a space : 355 113

355 / 113 = 3.141593

Type operation [+-/* or Q to quit] *
Type two numbers separated by a space : 12 23

12 * 23 = 276

Type operation [+-/* or Q to quit] Q
[END SESSION]
```

The WHILE loop condition in the Turbo Pascal program is

```
WHILE op <> 'Q' DO BEGIN
```

This condition is translated into the similar C++ code:

```
while (op != 'Q') {
```

Listing 6.15. Source code for the LST06_15.CPP program.

```
/*
  C++ program that uses a while loop to enable the
  user to perform several basic math operations.
*/

#include <iostream.h>
#include <conio.h>

#define BOOLEAN char
#define TRUE 1
#define FALSE 0

main()
{
    BOOLEAN ok;
    char op;
    float operand1, operand2, result;


    cout << "Type operation [+-/* or Q to quit] ";
    op = getche();

    while (op != 'Q') {

        cout << "\n";
        cout << "Type two numbers separated by a space : ";
        cin >> operand1 >> operand2;
        cout << "\n";

        ok = TRUE;

        switch (op) {
            case '+' :
                result = operand1 + operand2;
                break;
            case '-' :
                result = operand1 - operand2;
                break;
            case '*' :
                result = operand1 * operand2;
                break;
            case '/' :
                if (operand2 != 0.0)
                    result = operand1 / operand2;
                else {
```

```
                  cout << "Cannot divide by zero\n\n";
                  ok = !ok;
              }
            break;
        default :
            cout << "Bad operator\n\n";
            ok = ! ok;
    }

    if (ok)
        cout << operand1 << " " << op << " "
             << operand2 << " = " << result;

    cout << "\n\n";
    cout << "Type operation [+-/* or Q to quit] ";
    op = getche();

  }

  return 0;
}
```

The preceding Turbo C++ program presents an equivalent translation of its Turbo Pascal counterpart but does not take advantage of some of the special syntax features of C++. These syntax features enable you to combine the statement that reads the operator from the keyboard and the `while` loop condition. The result is the following new code fragment:

```
while ( (op = getche()) != 'Q') {
```

This kind of code seems strange for most novice C++ programmers. The compiled code first executes the `op = getche()` statement and tests whether the `op` variable is not the character *Q*. Listing 6.16 contains the source code for the LST06_16.CPP program, which contains the modified code. This feature, which also exists in C, demonstrates that you can produce terse code in both C++ and C.

Listing 6.16. Source code for the LST06_16.CPP program.

```
/*
  C++ program that uses a while loop to enable the
  user to perform several basic math operations.
*/
```

continues

169

Listing 6.16. continued

```
#include <iostream.h>
#include <conio.h>

#define BOOLEAN char
#define TRUE 1
#define FALSE 0

main()
{
    BOOLEAN ok;
    char op;
    float operand1, operand2, result;

    cout << "Enter operation [+-/* or Q to quit] ";

    while ( (op = getche()) != 'Q') {

        cout << "\n";
        cout << "Enter two numbers separated by a space : ";
        cin >> operand1 >> operand2;
        cout << "\n";

        ok = TRUE;

        switch (op) {
            case '+' :
                result = operand1 + operand2;
                break;
            case '-' :
                result = operand1 - operand2;
                break;
            case '*' :
                result = operand1 * operand2;
                break;
            case '/' :
                if (operand2 != 0.0)
                    result = operand1 / operand2;
                else {
                    cout << "Cannot divide by zero\n\n";
                    ok = !ok;
                }
                break;
            default :
                cout << "Bad operator\n\n";
                ok = ! ok;

        }
```

```
        if (ok)
           cout << operand1 << " " << op << " "
                << operand2 << " = " << result;
        cout << "\n\n";
        cout << "Enter operation [+-/* or Q to quit] ";

   }

   return 0;
}
```

The following example illustrates nested conditional loops used in a program that calculates one or more factorials. An outer loop enables you to obtain another factorial. The program uses two inner conditional loops. The first inner loop calculates the factorial, and the second loop iterates until you press *Y* or *N* in response to a Yes/No prompt.

The general scheme for the loops of the Turbo Pascal program is

```
REPEAT
WHILE number is greater than 1
         calculate factorial
     END

     REPEAT
         prompt for more calculations
     UNTIL answer is Y or N
UNTIL answer is no
```

Listing 6.17 contains the source code for the LST06_17.PAS program.

Listing 6.17. Source code for the LST06_17.PAS program.

```
PROGRAM Do_While_2;

Uses CRT;

{
  Turbo Pascal program that uses a WHILE loop to enable the
  user to calculate several factorials.
}

VAR ans : CHAR;
    i, number : BYTE;
    factorial : REAL;
```

continues

171

Listing 6.17. continued

```
BEGIN
    REPEAT
        WRITE('Enter the factorial number : ');
        READLN(number); WRITELN;

        IF number IN [1..30] THEN BEGIN
            factorial := 1.0;
            i := number;
            WHILE i > 1 DO BEGIN
                factorial := factorial * i;
                DEC(i)
            END; { WHILE }

            WRITELN(number,'! = ',factorial);
        END
        ELSE
            WRITELN('Number is out of range');

        WRITELN;
        REPEAT
            WRITE('Enter another factorial? (Y/N) ');
            ans := ReadKey; WRITELN(ans); WRITELN;
            ans := Upcase(ans);
        UNTIL ans IN ['Y','N'];

    UNTIL ans = 'N';

END.
```

The general scheme for the loops of the Turbo C++ program is

```
do
    while number is greater than 1
            calculate factorial

    do
            prompt for more calculations
    while answer is neither Y nor N
while answer is not No
```

Listing 6.18 contains the source code for the LST06_18.CPP program.

Listing 6.18. Source code for the LST06_18.CPP program.

```cpp
/*
  C++ program that uses a while loop to enable the
  user to calculate several factorials.
*/

#include <iostream.h>
#include <conio.h>

#define BYTE short
#define touppercase (c += 'A' - 'a')

main()
{
    char ans;
    BYTE i, number;
    double factorial;

    do {
        cout << "Enter the factorial number : ";
        cin >> number;
        cout << "\n";

        if (number >= 1 && number <= 30) {
            factorial = 1.0;
            i = number;
            while (i > 1)
                factorial *= (double) i--;

            cout << number << "! = " << factorial << "\n";
        }
        else
            cout << "Number is out of range\n";

        cout << "\n\n";

        do {
            cout << "Enter another factorial? (Y/N) ";
            ans = getche();
            cout << "\n\n";
            if (ans > 'Z')
                touppercase(ans);
        } while ( !(ans == 'Y' || ans == 'N') );

    } while (ans != 'N');

}
```

Compare the code for the Turbo Pascal and the Turbo C++ programs. Notice that the WHILE loop, which calculates the factorial in the Pascal program:

```
WHILE i > 1 DO BEGIN
    factorial := factorial * i;
    DEC(i)
END; { WHILE }
```

is translated into the following loop in the C++ program:

```
while (i > 1)
    factorial *= (double) i--;
```

The C++ loop applies the decrement operator to the i variable. Placing this operator in the arithmetic assignment statement enables the while loop to perform its task in a single statement.

Summary

This chapter covered C++ loops and topics related to loops:

- The for loop in C++, which has the following general syntax:

  ```
  for (<initialization of loop control variables>;
       <loop continuation test>;
       <increment/decrement of loop control variables>)
  ```

  The for loop contains three components: the loop initialization, loop continuation condition, and the increment/decrement of the loop variables.

- Open loops, which are for loops with empty components. The break statement enables you to exit the current loop and resume program execution at the first statement following the loop. The exit function (prototyped in stdlib.h) enables you to make a critical loop exit by halting the C++ program.

- The continue statement enables you to jump to the end of the loop and resume with the next iteration. The advantage of the continue statement is that it uses no labels to direct jumps.

- The conditional do-while loop, which has the following general syntax:

  ```
  do {
      sequence of statements
  } while (condition);
  ```

The do-while loop iterates at least once.

- The conditional while loop, which has the following general syntax:

```
while (condition)
     statement; ¦ { sequence of statements }
```

The while loop may not iterate if its tested condition is initially false.

- Nested loops enable you to nest all kinds of loops.

SIMPLE FUNCTIONS

Functions are the basic building blocks that conceptually extend the C++ language to fit your custom applications. C is more function-oriented than C++ because of class support, inheritance, and other object-oriented programming features. Nevertheless, functions still play an important role in C++. This chapter focuses on the following aspects of simple C++ functions:

- C++ function syntax
- function parameters
- returning function values
- inline functions
- local variables
- void functions used as procedures
- recursive functions
- exiting functions
- function parameter default arguments
- overloading functions

C++ Functions

C++ functions are different from Pascal functions in both syntax and operation. The general form for the ANSI C style of declaring functions, to which C++ adheres, is:

```
returnType functionName(typedParameterList)
```

The differences between C++ and Pascal functions are:

1. The return type of C++ functions appears before the function name.

2. C++ has no equivalent to the Pascal FUNCTION keyword because all routines in C++ are functions. C++ has no formal Pascal-like procedures.

3. If the parameter list is empty, use empty parentheses. C++ provides you with the option of using the void keyword to state explicitly that the parameter list is void.

4. The typed parameter list consists of typed parameters that use the following general format:

    ```
    type1 parameter1, type2 parameter2, ...
    ```

    The preceding general format shows that an individual parameter is declared in the same way as a variable—first state the type and then the parameter's identifier. The list of parameters in C++ is comma-delimited. Also, you cannot group (as you can in Pascal) a sequence of parameters that have the same data type. You must explicitly declare each parameter.

5. The body of a C++ function is enclosed in curly braces. The closing brace is not followed by a semicolon.

6. C++ (unlike C) supports passing parameters by value and by reference. This feature is good news for readers like you because it facilitates translation of Pascal code.

7. C++ supports local constants, data types, and variables. Although these data items can appear in nested block statements, C++ does not support nested functions.

8. The return keyword returns a function's value.

To translate a simple Pascal function into a C++ function, use the following form:

Pascal:

```
FUNCTION functionName(parameterList) : returnType;
<declaration of data items>
BEGIN
    <function body>
    functionName := returnValue;
END;
```

C++:

```
returnType functionName(parameterList)
{
    <declarations of data items>

    <function body>
    return returnValue;
}
```

The semicolon-delimited list of Pascal parameters

```
parameter1 : type1; VAR parameter2 : type2
```

translates into the following comma-delimited list:

```
type1 parameter1, type2& parameter2
```

The & operator tells the C++ compiler that the parameter is passed by reference, not by value.

Look at the following simple C++ function. The program prompts you to enter an integer and returns its square value. Listing 7.1 contains the source code for the LST07_01.PAS program.

Listing 7.1. Source code for the LST07_01.PAS program.

```
PROGRAM Use_function_1;

{
  Turbo Pascal program to implement a function to square integers
}

VAR i, j : INTEGER;
```

continues

Listing 7.1. continued

```
FUNCTION square(X : INTEGER) : INTEGER;

BEGIN
    square := X * X
END;

BEGIN
    WRITE('Enter a number : '); READLN(i); WRITELN;
    j := square(i);
    WRITELN(i,'^2 = ',j);
    WRITELN; WRITELN;
END.
```

The C++ program actually contains two versions of the square function: square1 and square2. Note that the first version has the keyword inline before the function's return type. The inline keyword tells the C++ compiler to replace function calls with the function's statements. Macro-based pseudofunctions have not gained favor with the designers of C++. These scientists complain about the lack of type-checking in macro-based pseudofunctions. They also dislike the fact that most pseudofunctions produce errors in specific cases. The answer to C's macro-based pseudofunction is the C++ inline function. Inline functions work as normal functions do except for their contribution to the compiled code. I will be using inline functions throughout the remainder of this book.

Listing 7.2. Source code for the LST07_02.CPP program.

```
/*
    C++ program to implement a function to square integers
*/

#include <iostream.h>

// inline function version
inline int square1(int x)
{
    return x * x;
}
```

```
// normal function version
int square2(int x)
{
    return x * x;
}

main()
{

    int i, j;

    cout << "Enter a number : ";
    cin >> i;
    j = square1(i);
    cout << "\n" << i << "^2 = "
        << j << " using inline function\n";
    j = square2(i);
    cout << "\n" << i << "^2 = "
        << j << " using normal function\n";

    return 0;
}
```

Compare the Pascal square function with the C++ square2 function and note the following differences:

1. The Pascal declaration of the square function is

   ```
   FUNCTION square(X : INTEGER) : INTEGER;
   ```

2. The C++ declaration of the square2 function is

   ```
   int square2(int x)
   ```

Notice the following differences between the two function declarations:

- there is no FUNCTION keyword in the C++ declaration

- the INTEGER return type of function square appears before the square2 function name

- the parameter X : INTEGER translates to int x (the data type and parameter name are swapped and the delimiting colon disappears)

- the parameter list of function square2 does not end with a semicolon

181

The following example solves for the root of a mathematical function, f(x). The root is the value of *x* that makes f(x) equal to zero. The functions involved in this example return the double type. Using Newton's iterative method, the program solves for the root of a nonlinear user-defined function. The program declares the root function to obtain iteratively the root of the fx function. The current code of the program solves for the root of the following mathematical function:

$$f(X) = X3{-}2X2 + 5X + 5$$

The root function has three parameters that define the guess for the root, the desired accuracy, and the maximum number of iterations. A global constant supplies the argument for the parameter that holds the maximum number of iterations. The root function yields the value of the root. If the number of iterations exceeds the maximum limit, the function returns the last refined guess for the root. The program prompts you for the initial guess and the required accuracy.

Listing 7.3 contains the source code for the LST07_03.PAS program. Listing 7.4 contains the source code for the LST07_04.CPP program. Compile and run the Turbo C++ program and note the following sample session that supplies an initial guess of 2 and an accuracy of 1.E-7:

```
[BEGIN SESSION]
Enter guess and accuracy : 2 1.0e-7

Root = -0.718935
[END SESSION]
```

Listing 7.3. Source code for the LST07_03.PAS program.

```
PROGRAM Use_function_2;

{ Turbo Pascal program to solve for the root of a function }

CONST MAX_ITERATIONS = 30;

VAR tolerance, rootGuess : REAL;

FUNCTION fx(x : REAL) : REAL;
{ the nonlinear function whose root is sought }
BEGIN
    fx := x * x * x - 2 * x * x + 5 * x + 5.0
END;

FUNCTION root(rootGuess, tolerance : REAL; max_iter : INTEGER) : REAL;

{ function to solve for the sought root }
```

```
CONST EPSILON = 1.0E-10;
      MAX_TOLERANCE = 0.01;

VAR numIter : INTEGER;
    deltaX, incrX : REAL;

BEGIN

    IF tolerance > MAX_TOLERANCE THEN tolerance := MAX_TOLERANCE
    ELSE IF tolerance < EPSILON THEN tolerance := EPSILON;

    numIter := 0; { initialize iteration counter }

    REPEAT
      { calculate differential increment }
      IF ABS(rootGuess) > 1.0 THEN incrX := 0.01 * rootGuess
                        ELSE incrX := 0.01;
      { calculate improvement in rootGuess }
      deltaX := 2.0 * incrX * fx(rootGuess) /
                     (fx(rootGuess+incrX) - fx(rootGuess-incrX));
      { update rootGuess }
      rootGuess := rootGuess - deltaX;
      { increment loop counter and test for divergence }
      INC(numIter);
      IF numIter > MAX_ITERATIONS THEN deltaX := 0.0;

    UNTIL ABS(deltaX) < tolerance;

    root := rootGuess;
END;

BEGIN
    WRITE('Enter guess and accuracy : ');
    READLN(rootGuess, tolerance); WRITELN;
    WRITELN('Root = ',root(rootGuess, tolerance, MAX_ITERATIONS));
    WRITELN; WRITELN;
END.
```

Listing 7.4. Source code for the LST07_04.CPP program.

```
/*
   C++ program to solve for the root of a function
*/
```

Listing 7.4. continued

```
#include <iostream.h>
#include <math.h>

// need to declare prototype of functions
double root(double, double, int);

main()
{
    const int MAX_ITERATION = 30;

    double tolerance, rootGuess;

    cout << "Enter guess and accuracy : ";
    cin >> rootGuess >> tolerance;
    cout << "\nRoot = "
         <<   root(rootGuess, tolerance, MAX_ITERATION)
         << "\n\n";

    return 0;
}

double fx(double x)
// the nonlinear function whose root is sought
{
    return (x * x * x - 2 * x * x + 5 * x + 5.0);
}

double root(double rootGuess, double tolerance, int maxIter)
// function to solve for the sought root
{
    // declare local constants
    const double EPSILON = 1.0E-10;
    const double MAX_TOLERANCE = 0.01L;

    // declare local variables
    int numIter = 0;
    double deltaX, h;

    if (tolerance > MAX_TOLERANCE)
       tolerance = MAX_TOLERANCE;
    else if (tolerance < EPSILON)
       tolerance = EPSILON;

    do {
      // calculate differential increment
```

```
    if (fabs(rootGuess) > 1.0)
       h = 0.01 * rootGuess;
    else
       h = 0.01;
    // calculate improvement in rootGuess
    deltaX = 2.0 * h * fx(rootGuess) /
                  (fx(rootGuess+h) - fx(rootGuess-h));
    // update rootGuess
    rootGuess -= deltaX;
    // increment loop counter and test for divergence
    if (++numIter > maxIter)
       deltaX = 0.0;

  } while ( !((fabs(deltaX) <  tolerance)) );
   // OR use (fabs(deltaX) >= tolerance)

  return rootGuess;
}
```

Compare the Turbo Pascal and the Turbo C++ versions and note the following program aspects:

1. The Turbo C++ program makes a forward declaration of the root function. This kind of declaration in C++ is called a *prototype*. The prototype is necessary because the root function comes after function main, which calls function root. Notice also that there is no prototype for function fx because it is defined before function root, the only routine that calls function fx.

> The prototype of a function must list the data type of the parameters and must end with a semicolon. The prototype does not require you to specify parameter names.

2. The declaration of function root is:

```
double root(double rootGuess, double tolerance, int maxIter)
```

C++ function declaration differs from Pascal in that each parameter appears by specifying first its data type and then its name. As the preceding declaration shows, C++ does not enable you to group the first two parameters that have the same data type. Thus, the following declaration is illegal:

```
double root(double rootGuess, tolerance; int maxIter) // Error!!!!
```

You can place each parameter on a separate line and optionally include a clarifying comment, as shown here:

```
double root(double rootGuess,    // guess for root
            double tolerance,    // root accuracy
            int maxIter)         // maximum number of iterations
```

3. Both program versions declare local constants and variables inside the root function. The Turbo C++ version has the following declarations:

```
// declare local constants
const double EPSILON = 1.0E-10;
const double MAX_TOLERANCE = 0.01L;

// declare local variables
int numIter = 0;
double deltaX, h;
```

Inline Functions

In the preceding section I mentioned C++ inline functions, and in Chapter 4, "The Preprocessor and Compiler Directives," I presented a Turbo C++ program that uses macro-based pseudofunctions. The following example presents a Turbo C++ program that contains both macro-based and inline functions. In this section I take a more detailed look at inline functions. Listing 7.5 contains the source code for the LST07_05.CPP program. The program performs the same set of tasks twice: once using the macro-based pseudofunction and once using the inline functions. The names of inline functions in the program are derived by adding the prefix fn_ to the name of the corresponding pseudofunction.

Compile and run the Turbo C++ program and note the following sample session:

```
[BEGIN SESSION]
Enter an integer : 10

10 squared = 100

1 / 0.100000 = 10.000000

The lowercase of B is b

The uppercase of f is F

press any key to continue <any key>
```

```
Type a letter or a digit : h

          character is uppercase : FALSE
          character is lowercase : TRUE
          character is a letter  : TRUE
          character is a digit   : FALSE

Enter two integers (delimited by a space) : 41 55


The largest of the two numbers is 55

The smallest of the two numbers is 41

ABS(41) = 41

press any key to continue <any key>

Performing the same tasks using C functions


Enter an integer : 10

10 squared = 100

1 / 0.100000 = 10.000000

The lowercase of B is b

The uppercase of f is F

press any key to continue <any key>

Type a letter or a digit : h

          character is uppercase : FALSE
          character is lowercase : TRUE
          character is a letter  : TRUE
          character is a digit   : FALSE

Enter two integers (delimited by a space) : 41 55


The largest of the two numbers is 55

The smallest of the two numbers is 41

ABS(41) = 41
[END SESSION]
```

Listing 7.5. Source code for the LST07_05.CPP program.

```c
/*
   C++ program to compare macro-based pseudofunctions
   with inline functions.
*/

#include <stdio.h>
#include <conio.h>
#include "screen.h"

// define data type macros
#define BOOLEAN char
#define BYTE unsigned char

// define boolean constants
#define FALSE 0
#define TRUE 1

// macros that define pseudo one-line functions
#define boolean(x) ((x) ? "TRUE" : "FALSE")
#define abs(x) (((x) >= 0) ? (x) : -(x))
#define max(x,y) (((x) > (y)) ? (x) : (y))
#define min(x,y) (((x) > (y)) ? (y) : (x))
#define sqr(x) ((x) * (x))
#define cube(x) ((x) * (x) * (x))
#define reciprocal(x) (1 / (x))
#define XOR(test1,test2) (((test1 + test2) == TRUE) ? TRUE : FALSE)

// macros used for character testing
#define islower (c >= 'a' && c <= 'z')
#define isupper (c >= 'A' && c <= 'Z')
#define isdigit (c >= '0' && c <= '9')
#define isletter ((c >= 'A' && c <= 'Z') || (c >= 'a' && c <= 'z'))

// macros used in character case conversions
#define tolowercase (c - 'A' + 'a')
#define touppercase (c - 'a' + 'A')

// declare inline functions that perform same tasks as macros

inline int fn_abs(int x)
{
   if (x < 0)
      return (-x);
   else
      return x;
}
```

```
inline int fn_max(int x, int y)
{
    return (x > y) ? x : y;
}

inline int fn_min(int x, int y)
{
    return (x > y) ? y : x;
}

inline int fn_sqr(int x)
{
    return x * x;
}

inline int fn_cube(int x)
{
    return x * x * x;
}

inline double fn_reciprocal(double x)
{
    return 1 / x;
}

inline BOOLEAN fn_XOR(BOOLEAN test1, BOOLEAN test2)

{
    return ((test1 + test2) != TRUE) ? FALSE : !FALSE;
}

inline BOOLEAN fn_islower(char c)
{
    return (c >= 'a' && c <= 'z') ? !FALSE : FALSE;
}

inline BOOLEAN fn_isupper(char c)
{
    return (c >= 'A' && c <= 'Z') ? !FALSE : FALSE;
}

inline BOOLEAN fn_isdigit(char c)
{
    return (c >= '0' && c <= '9') ? !FALSE : FALSE;
}
```

continues

Listing 7.5. continued

```c
inline BOOLEAN fn_isletter(char c)
{
    return ((c >= 'A' && c <= 'Z') || (c >= 'a' && c <= 'z')) ?
        !FALSE : FALSE;
}

inline char fn_tolowercase(char c)
{
    return (c >= 'A' && c <= 'Z') ? (c - 'A' + 'a') : c;
}

inline char fn_touppercase(char c)
{
    return (c >= 'a' && c <= 'z') ? (c - 'a' + 'A') : c;
}

main()
{

    BOOLEAN bool;
    BYTE i, j;
    int k, m;
    char ch, akey;
    double x = 0.10;


    printf("Enter an integer : "); scanf("%d", &k);
    printf("\n");
    printf("%d squared = %d ", k, sqr(k));
    printf("\n\n");

    printf("1 / %f = %f", x, reciprocal(x));
    printf("\n\n");

    ch = 'B';
    printf("The lowercase of %c is %c", ch, tolowercase(ch));
    printf("\n\n");
    ch = 'f';
    printf("The uppercase of %c is %c", ch, touppercase(ch));

    printf("\n\npress any key to continue");
    akey = getch();
    clrscr;

    printf("\n\nType a letter or a digit : "); ch = getche();
    bool = isupper(ch);
```

```
gotoxy(10,5);
printf("character is uppercase : %s\n",boolean(bool));
bool = islower(ch);
gotoxy(10,6);
printf("character is lowercase : %s\n",boolean(bool));
bool = isletter(ch);
gotoxy(10,7);
printf("character is a letter  : %s\n",boolean(bool));
bool = isdigit(ch);
gotoxy(10,8);
printf("character is a digit   : %s\n",boolean(bool));
printf("\n");
printf("Enter two integers (delimited by a space) : ");
scanf("%d %d", &k, &m);
printf("\n\n");
printf("The largest of the two numbers is %d\n\n", max(k,m));
printf("The smallest of the two numbers is %d\n\n", min(k,m));
printf("ABS(%d) = %d\n\n", k, abs(k));

printf("\npress any key to continue");
akey = getch();

// do same tasks using functions

clrscr;
printf("Performing the same tasks using C functions\n\n\n");

printf("Enter an integer : "); scanf("%d", &k);
printf("\n");
printf("%d squared = %d ", k, fn_sqr(k));
printf("\n\n");

printf("1 / %f = %f", x, fn_reciprocal(x));
printf("\n\n");

ch = 'B';
printf("The lowercase of %c is %c", ch, fn_tolowercase(ch));
printf("\n\n");

ch = 'f';
printf("The uppercase of %c is %c", ch, fn_touppercase(ch));
printf("\n\npress any key to continue");
akey = getch();
clrscr;

printf("\n\nType a letter or a digit : "); ch = getche();
bool = fn_isupper(ch);
```

continues

191

Listing 7.5. continued

```
    gotoxy(10,5);
    printf("character is uppercase : %s\n",boolean(bool));
    bool = fn_islower(ch);
    gotoxy(10,6);
    printf("character is lowercase : %s\n",boolean(bool));
    bool = fn_isletter(ch);
    gotoxy(10,7);
    printf("character is a letter  : %s\n",boolean(bool));
    bool = fn_isdigit(ch);
    gotoxy(10,8);
    printf("character is a digit   : %s\n",boolean(bool));
    printf("\n");
    printf("Enter two integers (delimited by a space) : ");
    scanf("%d %d", &k, &m);
    printf("\n\n");
    printf("The largest of the two numbers is %d\n\n",fn_max(k,m));
    printf("The smallest of the two numbers is %d\n\n",fn_min(k,m));
    printf("ABS(%d) = %d\n\n", k, fn_abs(k));

    return 0;
}
```

Void Functions as Procedures

ANSI C standard recognizes the void type as typeless. Consequently, the void type facilitates stating that a function that returns a void type is a form of procedure. C++ has adopted the ANSI C standard in supporting and using the void type. Before the advent of the void type in C, programmers declared the return type as int and simply discarded the function result by placing the function call in a statement by itself. Some C programmers use the #define directive to create void as an alias of int.

In the preceding example I included the screen.h header file, which declares several macros that implement pseudofunctions to clear the screen, clear to the end of a line, move the cursor, or wait for a key. The following program uses void-typed functions instead of the screen.h file to perform these tasks. The program has no macro-based pseudofunctions and declares all of its functions as non-inline. Listing 7.6 contains the source code for the LST07_06.CPP program. The listing declares the following void-typed functions:

```
void clrscr()
void gotoxy(int col,int row)
void clreol()
void wait_key()
```

Listing 7.6. Source code for the LST07_06.CPP program.

```
/*
   C++ program to use void functions as procedures.
*/

#include <stdio.h>
#include <conio.h>

// define data type macros
#define BOOLEAN char
#define BYTE unsigned char

// define boolean constants
#define FALSE 0
#define TRUE 1
#define boolean(x) ((x) ? "TRUE" : "FALSE")

int fn_abs(int x)
{
   return (x < 0) ? -x : x;
}

int fn_max(int x, int y)
{
   return (x > y) ? x : y;
}

int fn_min(int x, int y)
{
   return (x > y) ? y : x;
}

int fn_sqr(int x)
{
   return x * x;
}

int fn_cube(int x)
{
   return x * x * x;
```

continues

Listing 7.6. continued

```
}
double fn_reciprocal(double x)
{
    return 1 / x;
}

BOOLEAN fn_XOR(BOOLEAN test1, BOOLEAN test2)

{
    return ((test1 + test2) != TRUE) ? FALSE : !FALSE;
}

BOOLEAN fn_islower(char c)
{
    return (c >= 'a' && c <= 'z') ? !FALSE : FALSE;
}

BOOLEAN fn_isupper(char c)
{
    return (c >= 'A' && c <= 'Z') ? !FALSE : FALSE;
}

BOOLEAN fn_isdigit(char c)
{
    return (c >= '0' && c <= '9') ? !FALSE : FALSE;
}

BOOLEAN fn_isletter(char c)
{
    return ((c >= 'A' && c <= 'Z') || (c >= 'a' && c <= 'z')) ?
        !FALSE : FALSE;
}

char fn_tolowercase(char c)
{
    return (c - 'A' + 'a');
}

char fn_touppercase(char c)
{
    return (c - 'a' + 'A');
}

// set of void functions (i.e. procedures) to perform screen
// management and waiting for a key to be pressed
```

```
void clrscr()
{
   printf("\x1b[2J");
}

void gotoxy(int col,int row)
{
   printf("\x1b[%d;%dH", row, col);
}

void clreol()
{
   printf("\x1b[K");
}

void wait_key()
{
  char akey;

   printf("\n\npress any key to continue");
   akey = getch();
}

main()
{

   BOOLEAN bool;
   BYTE i, j;
   int k, m;
   char ch;
   double x = 0.10;

   printf("Enter an integer : "); scanf("%d", &k);
   printf("\n");
   printf("%d squared = %d ", k, fn_sqr(k));
   printf("\n\n");

   printf("1 / %f = %f", x, fn_reciprocal(x));
   printf("\n\n");

   ch = 'B';
   printf("The lowercase of %c is %c", ch, fn_tolowercase(ch));
   printf("\n\n");

   ch = 'f';
   printf("The uppercase of %c is %c", ch, fn_touppercase(ch));
```

continues

195

Listing 7.6. continued

```
wait_key();
clrscr();

printf("\n\nType a letter or a digit : "); ch = getche();
bool = fn_isupper(ch);
gotoxy(10,5);
printf("character is uppercase : %s\n",boolean(bool));
bool = fn_islower(ch);
gotoxy(10,6);
printf("character is lowercase : %s\n",boolean(bool));
bool = fn_isletter(ch);
gotoxy(10,7);
printf("character is a letter  : %s\n",boolean(bool));
bool = fn_isdigit(ch);
gotoxy(10,8);
printf("character is a digit   : %s\n",boolean(bool));
printf("\n");
printf("Enter two integers (delimited by a space) : ");
scanf("%d %d", &k, &m);
printf("\n\n");
printf("The largest of the two numbers is %d\n\n",fn_max(k,m));
printf("The smallest of the two numbers is %d\n\n",fn_min(k,m));
printf("ABS(%d) = %d\n\n", k, fn_abs(k));

return 0;
}
```

Recursive Functions

Like Pascal, C++ supports recursive functions and does not require a special syntax to indicate that the function is recursive.

The following example calculates a factorial using recursion. The `factorial` function returns the factorial by recursively calling itself. Listing 7.7 contains the source code for the LST07_07.PAS program. Listing 7.8 contains the source code for the LST07_08.CPP program.

Compare the two versions and note the following:

1. The recursive function in Turbo C++ is similar to the recursive function in Turbo Pascal.

2. The Turbo C++ version returns the recursive values using a typecast to the double data type:

```
return (double) x * factorial(x - 1);
```

Listing 7.7. Source code for the LST07_07.PAS program.

```
PROGRAM Recursive_Factorials;

{ Turbo Pascal program that calculates factorials recursively }

VAR n : BYTE;

FUNCTION factorial(x : BYTE) : REAL;
{ recursive factorial function }
BEGIN
    IF x > 1 THEN factorial := x * factorial(x - 1)
            ELSE factorial := 1.0
END;

BEGIN
    WRITE('Enter factorial number : ');
    READLN(n); WRITELN;
    WRITELN(n,'! = ',factorial(n));
    WRITELN; WRITELN;
END.
```

Listing 7.8. Source code for the LST07_08.CPP program.

```
/*
   C++ program that calculates factorials recursively
*/

#include <stdio.h>

#define BYTE unsigned char

main()
{

    BYTE n;
    double factorial(BYTE);
```

continues

Listing 7.8. continued

```
    printf("Enter factorial number : ");
    scanf("%d", &n);
    printf("\n%d! = %lf\n\n\n", n, factorial(n));
}

double factorial(BYTE x)
// recursive factorial function
{
    if (x > 1)
      return (double) x * factorial(x - 1);
    else
      return 1.0L;
}
```

Exiting Functions

Sometimes conditions make it impossible to continue executing the statements in a routine, and you must exit. Turbo Pascal offers the EXIT statement for this purpose. C++ provides the return statement to exit from a function. If a function has the void type, employ the return statement and omit the expression after the return. If you exit a nonvoid function, the return statement should yield a value that indicates the reason for exiting the function.

Default Arguments

The default argument is a new language feature that has no parallel in C or Pascal. This new feature is quite simple and very powerful. C++ enables you to assign default arguments to the parameters of a function. When you omit the argument of a parameter that has a default argument, the default argument is used automatically. Using default arguments requires that you follow these rules:

1. If you assign a default argument to a parameter, you must do so for all subsequent parameters in the same parameter list. You cannot randomly assign default arguments to parameters. This rule means that the parameter list can be divided into two groups. The leading parameters have no default arguments, and the trailing parameters have.

2. You must supply an argument for each parameter that has no default argument.

3. You may omit the argument for a parameter that has a default argument.

4. If you omit the argument for a parameter with a default argument, the arguments for all subsequent parameters must be omitted.

The best way to list parameters with default arguments is to place them in reverse order of their likelihood of using their default arguments. Place those least likely to use their default arguments first and those most likely to use their arguments last.

A simple example, showing the default argument, follows. This program declares the power function to raise a number to a power. The parameters of the function are base, exponent, and errorValue. The base parameter represents the base number and has no default argument. The exponent parameter represents the power to which the base number is raised. The exponent parameter has a default argument of 2. The errorValue parameter represents the numeric code for an error that results from using a nonpositive argument for the base number. The default argument for the errorValue parameter is -1.E + 30, a large negative number.

Function main in the following program makes these calls to function power:

1. The first call supplies the arguments for all parameters:

   ```
   << power(x, y, -1.0E+300)
   ```

2. The second call omits the argument for the last parameter:

   ```
   << power(x, y)
   ```

3. The third call uses the default arguments for the second and third parameters.

   ```
   << power(x)
   ```

   The preceding call returns the square of the value stored in variable x.

4. The last call passes arguments to all parameters:

   ```
   << power(z, y, -1.0E+50)
   ```

   The preceding call generates an error and yields the value -1.0E + 50 because the value stored in variable z is negative.

Listing 7.9 shows the source code for the LST07_09.CPP program.

Moving from Turbo Pascal to Turbo C++

Listing 7.9. Source code for the LST07_09.CPP program.

```
/*
   C++ program demonstrates default arguments
*/

#include <iostream.h>
#include <math.h>

double power(double base,
             double exponent = 2,
             double errorValue = -1.E+30)
{
  return (base > 0) ? exp(exponent * log(base)) : errorValue;
}

main()
{
    double x = 5;
    double y = 2;
    double z= -5;
    cout << x << "^" << y << " = "
         << power(x, y, -1.0E+300)
         << " using full-argument list call\n";
    cout << x << "^" << y << " = "
         << power(x, y)
         << " using a two-argument list call\n";
    cout << x << "^" << 2 << " = "
         << power(x)
         << " using all of the default arguments\n";
    cout << z << "^" << y << " = "
         << power(z, y, -1.0E+50)
         << " using full-argument list call\n";

    return 0;

}
```

Function Overloading

Function overloading is a new language feature in C++ that has no parallel in C or Pascal. This new feature enables you to declare multiple functions that have the same name but different parameter lists (also called the function signature). The function's return type is

200

not part of the function signature because C++ enables you to discard the result. Consequently, if return types are omitted, the compiler is not able to distinguish between two functions with the same parameters and different return types.

Assigning default arguments to overloaded functions can cause duplicate signatures for some functions (when the default arguments are used). The C++ compiler detects this ambiguity and generates a compile-time error.

The next example shows three overloaded power functions. The program declares the following power functions:

```
double power(double base, double exponent)
double power(double base, int exponent)
long power(int base, int exponent)
```

The first overloaded function raises a double-typed base number to a double-typed exponent and yields a double-typed return. The second overloaded function raises a double-typed base number to an int-typed exponent and yields a double-typed return. The third overloaded function raises an int-typed base number to an int-typed exponent and yields a long-typed return. The overloaded functions are distinctly coded. Each version takes advantage of the parameter types.

Function main calls the various overloaded functions. The compiler is able to select the appropriate function by examining the data types of the supplied arguments.

Use default arguments to reduce the number of overloaded functions.

Listing 7.10 contains the source code for the LST07_10.CPP program.

Listing 7.10. Source code for the LST07_10.CPP program.

```
/*
    C++ program demonstrates function overloading
*/

#include <iostream.h>
#include <math.h>
```

continues

201

Listing 7.10. continued

```
double power(double base, double exponent)
{
  return (base > 0) ? exp(exponent * log(base)) : -1.E+30;
}

double power(double base, int exponent)
{
  double product = 1;
  if (exponent > 0)
    for (unsigned i = 1; i <= exponent; i++)
        product *= base;
  else
    for (unsigned i = -1; i >= exponent; i--)
        product /= base;
  return product;
}

long power(int base, int exponent)
{
  long product = 1;
  if (base > 0 && exponent > 0)
    for (unsigned i = 1; i <= exponent; i++)
        product *= base;
  else
    product = -0xffffffff;
  return product;
}

main()
{
    double x = 2;
    double y = 8;
    int m = 2;
    int n = 8;

    cout << x << "^" << y << " = "
        << power(x, y)
        << " using power(double, double)\n";
    cout << x << "^" << n << " = "
        << power(x, n)
        << " using power(double, int)\n";
    cout << m << "^" << n << " = "
        << power(m, n)
        << " using power(int, int)\n";
```

```
    return 0;

}
```

Summary

This chapter presented simple C++ functions and focused on the following topics:

- The general form for defining functions is:

```
returnType functionName(parameterList)
{
    <declarations of data items>

    <function body>
    return returnValue;
}
```

- `Inline` functions, like macro-based pseudofunctions, enable you to expand their statements in place. Unlike these pseudofunctions, however, `inline` functions perform type-checking.

- `Void` functions are routines that perform a task and return no result. These functions are similar to Pascal procedures.

- `Recursive` functions perform a task by calling themselves.

- Exiting C++ functions is accomplished by using the `return` statement. `Void` functions need not include an expression after the `return` keyword.

- Default arguments enable you to assign default values to the parameters of a function. When you omit the argument of a parameter that has a default argument, the default argument is used automatically.

- Function overloading enables you to declare multiple functions that have the same name but different parameter lists (also called the function signature). The function's return type is not part of the function signature because C++ enables you to discard the `result`.

8

POINTERS, ARRAYS, AND STRINGS

This chapter examines data types that go beyond the trivial and simple predefined types. The aim of this chapter is to give you a feel for the importance of pointers in C++. Although pointers exist in Pascal, C++ uses them more effectively. This chapter focuses on the following topics:

- storage classes

- the scope of variables

- pointers to predefined data types

- single and multidimensional arrays

- pointers used to access arrays in C++

- strings in C++

Storage Classes

Like C, its parent language, C++ supports several storage classes (or categories, if you prefer to avoid confusing them with formal C++ classes). This means that not all variables in C++ have the same life span.

Automatic

The automatic storage category includes the local variables, which the runtime system creates when their host function is called. When the function terminates, the runtime system automatically removes these variables. Automatic variables in C++ greatly resemble local variables in Pascal. C++ variables are automatic by default.

Static

The variables in the static storage category are more permanent. The compiler assigns fixed memory locations to store the static variables of various functions. Consequently, static variables exist between calls to their host functions and retain their information. This feature enables a function to preserve information generated by previous calls. To declare a variable as static, you must place the keyword static before the data type of the variable. You need not declare global variables as static because they exist during the entire program execution.

> Although Turbo Pascal doesn't formally support static variables, you can easily emulate them using local typed constants. The next program repeatedly prompts you to enter a floating-point number or 0 to exit. When you enter a nonzero number, the program displays the average of the numbers thus far entered.

Listing 8.1 contains the source code for the LST08_01.PAS program.

Listing 8.1. Source code for the LST08_01.PAS program.

```
PROGRAM Emulate_Static_Variables;

Uses CRT;
```

```
{
  Turbo Pascal program that emulates static variables by using
  local typed constants.
}

VAR x : REAL;

FUNCTION average(x : REAL) : REAL;

{ function to return the statistical average }

{ declare and initialize the typed constants }
CONST sum : REAL = 0.0;
      sumX : REAL = 0.0 ;
      sumX2 : REAL = 0.0;

BEGIN
    { update the statistical summations }
    sum := sum + 1.0;
    sumX := sumX + x;
    sumX2 := sumX2 + x * x;

    { calculate the average }
    average := sumX / sum;

END;

BEGIN
    clrscr;

    WRITE('Enter number [0 to exit] : ');
    READLN(x); WRITELN;
    WHILE x <> 0.0 DO BEGIN
        WRITELN('Current average = ',average(x));
        WRITELN;
        WRITE('Enter number [0 to exit] : ');
        READLN(x); WRITELN;
      END; { WHILE }

END.
```

Listing 8.2 shows the source code for the LST08_02.CPP program. Compile and run
the Turbo C++ program. Here is a sample session:

```
Enter number [0 to exit] : 1

Current average = 1
Enter number [0 to exit] : 2
```

```
Current average = 1.50

Enter number [0 to exit] : 3

Current average = 2

Enter number [0 to exit] : 0
```

Listing 8.2. Source code for the LST08_02.CPP program.

```cpp
/*
   C++ program that uses static variables in a routine.
*/

#include <iostream.h>
#include <conio.h>

double average(double); // declare function prototype

main()
{

    double x;

    clrscr();

    cout << "Enter number [0 to exit] : ";
    cin >> x; cout << "\n";

    while (x != 0.0)  {
        cout << "Current average = "
             << average(x) << "\n\n"
             << "Enter number [0 to exit] : ";
        cin >> x;
        cout << "\n";
    }

    return 0;
}

double average(double x)

// function to return the statistical average

{
    // declare and initialize local static variables
```

```
    static double sum = 0.0L, sumX = 0.0L, sumX2 = 0.0L;

    // update the statistical summations
    sum++;
    sumX += x;
    sumX2 += x * x;

    // calculate the average
    return sumX / sum;

}
```

Compare the Turbo Pascal and Turbo C++ program versions. Notice that the `static` variables sum, sumX, and sumX2 are declared in the C++ function average as:

```
static double sum = 0.0L, sumX = 0.0L, sumX2 = 0.0L;
```

Static variables in the Turbo Pascal program are emulated by local typed constants. The Turbo C++ function main has no access to the static variables. Similarly, the Turbo Pascal main program section has no access to the typed constants.

> Static variables enable you to implement functions that are heuristic (able to earn) and therefore more efficient.

The following code fragment demonstrates a C++ function that calculates factorials. To speed up function execution, it uses a static array that stores the factorials for the numbers 1 through 30, perhaps the most frequent arguments. The first time you invoke this factorial function, it calculates and stores the first 30 factorials. In subsequent calls, the function examines your argument to determine if it is less than 31. If so, the function simply returns the value stored in the static array. If not, the function must calculate the requested factorial. However, the function can start from the factorial of 30 and proceed to the requested number. Examine the following code for this function:

```
double factorial(unsigned n)
{
  static flag = 0;
  static data[31];
  double product = 1;

  // calculate the factorials for 1 to 30
  if (flag == 0) {
    data[0] = 1.0;
```

```
    data[1] = 1.0;
    for (unsigned i = 2; i < 31; i++)
      data[i = (double) i * data[i-1];
  }

  if (n < 31)
    product = data[n];
  else {
    product = data[30];
    for (unsigned i = 31; i <= n; i++)
      product *= (double) i;
  }
  return product;
}
```

Extern

The extern storage category is used to resolve problems that might occur from accessing data declared in external source code files. This situation arises when you are working on a large software program that involves numerous files. The extern declaration informs the compiler to resolve the address allocation during the linking phase. Such a phase involves the other files.

The following example uses two source code files. The matSize and missingCode variables, along with the mat matrix, are common to both source code files. To prevent the compiler from allocating two sets of addresses for these variables, I employed the extern class storage indicator in the second source file. Examine the source code for the first file:

```
#include <iostream.h>
int matSize;
double missingData;
double mat[20][20];

main()
{
  cout << "Enter the size of the matrix : ";
  cin >> matSize;
  cout << "\n\nEnter the numeric code for missing data : ";
  cin >> missingData;

  // statements to enter and process matrix mat

  return 0;
}
```

Now examine the source code for the second file:

```
extern int matSize;
extern double missingData;
extern double mat[20][20];

double calcDeterminant()
{
  double determinant;

  // statements to calculate the determinant of matrix mat
  return determinant;
}
```

Register

To make C++ suitable for systems programs, the language offers the `register` storage category to significantly speed up program execution. The `register` storage category tells the compiler to use a CPU register instead of a memory location. This storage scheme saves time that would be used accessing the memory location while retrieving and saving data. You can employ this storage scheme with characters, integers, and pointers. You can use a `register` variable as the index of an array or as an initialization variable used to set up the values of an array.

> Do not use the `register` storage class until you become a proficient C++ programmer.

Scope of Variables

C++, like C, supports only one level of functions. You cannot declare nested functions as you can in Pascal. However, unlike Pascal, both C++ and C enable you to declare local variables in nested scopes. Each scope is defined by curly braces. Statement blocks used in looping and decision-making constructs automatically define a nested scope. C++ and C enable you to define a statement block that is not associated with looping and decision-making constructs. Think of such a block as an autonomous BEGIN-END block in Pascal.

As a Pascal programmer, you learned to place the declarations of constants, types, and variables immediately after the routine's declaration and before the main BEGIN-END block in that routine. You cannot declare any nondynamic data inside the main BEGIN-END block of a routine. Consequently, the scope of the local variables extends throughout the routine, regardless of how many statements actually use the local variables. This Pascal storage scheme can easily result in maintaining local variables in a routine long after their role has ended.

C++ empowers you to remedy the Pascal storage scheme and can render large programs more memory efficient than their Pascal counterparts. As I stated earlier, C++ enables you to define a new block of statements, inside which you declare new automatic variables. When program execution passes the beginning of the block, the variables declared in that block come into being. Similarly, when program execution reaches the end of a block, the runtime system removes all variables defined in that block.

The following example demonstrates how the C++ storage scheme works. The program calculates the average and standard deviation of data you enter. It first prompts you to enter the number of data points and then asks you to key in the numeric data. The Turbo Pascal version illustrates how such a program declares its variable in the manner dictated by the language. Listing 8.3 shows the source code for the LST08_03.PAS program.

Listing 8.3. Source code for the LST08_03.PAS program.

```
PROGRAM Basic_stat;

Uses CRT;

{
   This Turbo Pascal program calculates the basic statistics for
   a given set of data.  This program is translated into two C++
   versions.  The first is close to a mirror image of the Pascal
   code.  The second version illustrates the feature in C++ that
   permits the declaration of variables in the middle of the
   code.
}

VAR x, sum, sumX, sumX2 : REAL;
    mean, sdev : REAL;
    i, count : INTEGER;

BEGIN
    clrscr;

    REPEAT
```

```
      WRITE('Enter number of data (> 1) : ');
      READLN(count); WRITELN;
   UNTIL count > 1;

   { initialize statistical summations }
   sum := count;
   sumX := 0.0;
   sumX2 := 0.0;

   FOR i := 1 TO count DO BEGIN
      WRITE('Enter a number : ');
      READLN(x); WRITELN;
      sumX := sumX + x;
      sumX2 := sumX2 + x * x
   END; { FOR }

   { calculate the mean and std. deviation }
   mean := sumX/ sum;
   sdev := SQRT((sumX2 - sumX * sumX / sum) / (sum - 1.0));

   WRITELN('Mean          = ',mean); WRITELN;
   WRITELN('Std. deviation = ',sdev); WRITELN;

END.
```

The Turbo C++ version shown in Listing 8.4 is a straightforward translation of the Turbo Pascal version. The function main declares all local variables before any executable statements.

Listing 8.4. Source code for the LST08_04.CPP program.

```
/*
  C++ program that is a translation of the Pascal program that
  calculates the basic statistics for a given set of data.  This
  version shows the usual fashion for which all of the variables
  are declared at the beginning of the code in main().  All of
  the variables are visible (and accessible) throughout the
  code of main().
*/

#include <iostream.h>
#include <math.h>
#include <conio.h>
```

continues

Listing 8.4. continued

```
main()
{
    double x, sum, sumX, sumX2;
    double mean, sdev;
    int i, count;

    clrscr();

    do {
        cout << "Enter number of data (> 1) : ";
        cin >> count;
        cout << "\n";
    } while ( !(count > 1) );

    // initialize statistical summations
    sum = count;
    sumX = 0.0;
    sumX2 = 0.0;

    for (i = 1; i <= count; i++)  {
        cout << "Enter a number : ";
        cin >> x;
        cout << "\n";
        sumX += x;
        sumX2 +=  x * x;
    }

    // calculate mean and std. deviation
    mean = sumX/ sum;
    sdev = sqrt((sumX2 - sumX * sumX / sum) / (sum - 1.0));

    cout << "Mean            = " << mean << "\n\n"
         << "Std. deviation = " << sdev << "\n\n";

    return 0;
}
```

Now look at a modified version of the Turbo C++ program that uses statement blocks to declare nested variables. Such variables have a tailored life span. I divided the program into the following blocks:

1. The do-while loop that prompts you to enter the number of data points.

2. The sequence of statements that initializes the statistical summations.

3. The for loop that prompts you for the data.

4. The sequence of statements that calculates and displays the results.

Listing 8.5 shows the source code for the LST08_05.CPP program.

Listing 8.5. Source code for the LST08_05.CPP program.

```
/*
   This C++ program is a modified version of the last one.
   It uses multiple scope variables, a feature not supported
   by Pascal.  This feature enables you to save memory by
   declaring large arrays and matrices that store temporary
   data inside new sub-levels of code.  The memory space of
   these arrays is reclaimed once the end of the sub-level
   block is reached.
*/


#include <iostream.h>
#include <math.h>
#include <conio.h>

/*------------- outline for program level blocks -------------

main()
{                                  SCOPE OF VARIABLES
                          -----------------------------------------
  <declarations>          count
                            |
  <do-while loop>           |
                            |
  { sub-level #1            |    sum,sumX,sumX2
    { sub-level #2          |          |         i,x
      <for loop>            |          |          |
                            |          |          |
    } end of #2             |          |          V
                            |          |
    {sub-level #2           |          |               mean,sdev
     <calculations>         |          |                  |
     <output>               |          |                  |
    } end of #2             |          |                  V
  }  end of #1              |          V
                            |
                            V
} end of main()
```

continues

Listing 8.5. continued

```
*/

main()
{
    // only variable 'count' is visible throughout main
    int count;

    clrscr;

    do {
        cout << "Enter number of data (> 1) : ";
        cin >> count;
        cout << "\n";
    } while ( !(count > 1) );

    { // declare sub-level #1: the variables declared below
      // are visible within this code block.
      double sum = count, sumX = 0.0L, sumX2 = 0.0L;
      { // declare sub-level #2: all the variables from the
        // previous levels plus 'i' and 'x' are visible
        // within this code block.
        double x;
        int i;

        for (i = 1; i <= count; i++)  {
            cout << "Enter a number : ";
            cin >> x;
            cout << "\n";
            sumX += x;
            sumX2 +=  x * x;
        }
        // end of sub-level #2, variable 'i' is no longer
        // accessible
      }

      { // declare a second sub-level #2
        double mean, sdev;

        // calculate mean and std. deviation
        mean = sumX/ sum;
        sdev = sqrt((sumX2 - sumX * sumX / sum) / (sum - 1.0));

        cout << "Mean            = " << mean << "\n\n"
             << "Std. deviation = " << sdev << "\n\n";
```

```
        // end of second sub-level #2
      }
      // end of sub-level #1
    }

    return 0;
}
```

The preceding example shows four different scopes of variables:

1. The variable `count` exists in all statements of function `main`.

2. The summation variables `sum`, `sumX`, and `sumX2` exist in the first nested block. The runtime system creates them after the `do-while` loop ends its iteration.

3. The `for` loop control variable `i` and the input variable `x` exist only in the block that encloses the for loop. The program doesn't need them anywhere else.

4. The variables `mean` and `sdev` appear in the latter parts of function `main`.

Pointers to Predefined Data

In general terms, a pointer is a variable that stores the address of another item, such as a variable, function, or procedure. C++ requires that you associate a data type (including void) with a declared pointer. The associated data type may be a predefined type or a user-defined structure, as with Pascal pointers. Unlike Turbo Pascal, C++ and C facilitate the use of pointers.

Declaring pointers in C++ is similar to declaring ordinary variables. The difference is that you need to place an asterisk before the name of a pointer. Pointers are declared in the following way:

```
int *intPtr; // pointer to an int
double *realPtr; // pointer to a double
char *aString; // pointer to a character
```

You can also declare pointers and nonpointers in the same lines, as shown below:

```
int *intPtr, anInt;
double *realPtr, x;
char *aString, aKey;
```

C++ enables you to place the asterisk character right after the associated type. You shouldn't interpret this syntax to mean that every identifier in the declaration is a pointer:

```
int* intPtr; // pointer to an int
double* realPtr; // pointer to a double
char* aString; // pointer to a character
int *intP, j; // intP is a pointer to int, j is an int
double *realPtr, *doublePtr;  // both identifiers
                              // are pointers to a double
```

As with ordinary variables, you must initialize a pointer before you use it. In fact, the need to initialize pointers is more pressing—using uninitialized pointers can cause unpredictable program behavior or even a system hang.

The designers of C++ chose to introduce new operators to handle the dynamic allocation and deallocation of memory. These C++ operators, not present in C, are `new` and `delete`. Although the C dynamic memory functions `malloc`, `calloc`, and `free` are still available, you should use the `new` and `delete` operators. (Somehow I think this recommendation may be an easy sell for a Turbo Pascal programmer like you.)

The general syntax for using the `new` and `delete` operators in creating dynamic scalar variables is:

```
pointer = new type;
delete pointer;
```

The `new` operator returns the address of the dynamically allocated variable. The `delete` operator removes the dynamically allocated memory accessed by a pointer. To allocate and deallocate a dynamic array, use the following general syntax:

```
arrayPointer = new type[arraySize];
delete [] arrayPointer;
```

If the dynamic allocation of operator `new` fails, it returns a `NULL` pointer. Therefore, you should test for a `NULL` pointer if you suspect potential trouble after using the `new` operator.

To assign the address of a variable to a compatible pointer you need to use the address-of operator &:

```
pointer = &variable;
```

To access the contents of the memory location indicated by a pointer, you must use the * reference operator:

```
variable = *pointer;
```

The declaration of pointers is translated using the following general form:

Pascal:

```
pointer : ^type;
```

C++:

```
type *pointer;
```

The translation of the Pascal NEW intrinsic into the C++ new operator uses the following general form:

Pascal:

```
NEW(pointer);
```

C++:

```
pointer = new type;
```

The translation of the Pascal DISPOSE intrinsic into the C++ delete operator uses the following general form:

Pascal:

```
DISPOSE(pointer);
```

C++:

```
delete pointer;
```

To save the address of an existing variable in a pointer, use the following general form:

Pascal:

```
pointer = @variable;
```

continues

---

continued

C++:

```
pointer = &variable;
```

To translate an initialized pointer, use the following general form:

Pascal:

```
pointer^ = expression;
```

and

```
variable = pointer^;
```

C++:

```
*pointer = expression;
```

and

```
variable = *pointer;
```

The following example illustrates the two main kinds of pointers: those used to allocate dynamic memory and those that point to existing variables. The Turbo Pascal and Turbo C++ versions of the program use the pointers intPtr1, longPtr1, and charPtr1 to allocate and access dynamic memory at runtime. These pointers, as their names suggest, point to int, long, and char types, respectively. By contrast, the pointers intPtr2, longPtr2, and charPtr2 point to the variables i, j, and c. The two program versions assign values to the variables i, j, and c before passing their addresses to the pointers intPtr2, longPtr2, and charPtr2, respectively. Neither version performs any meaningful task other than illustrating the two kinds of pointers. Listing 8.6 shows the source code for the LST08_06.PAS program.

Listing 8.6. Source code for the LST08_06.PAS program.

```
PROGRAM Simple_Pointers;

Uses CRT;

{
  Turbo Pascal program that illustrates using pointers to access
  simple data types in Pascal.
}

VAR intPtr1, intPtr2  : ^INTEGER; { pointers to integers }
    longPtr1, longPtr2 : ^LONGINT; { pointers to long integers }
```

```
        charPtr1, charPtr2 : ^CHAR;      { pointers to characters }
        i : INTEGER;
        j : LONGINT;
        c : CHAR;

BEGIN

    { create dynamic space associated with pointers }
    NEW(intPtr1);
    NEW(longPtr1);
    NEW(charPtr1);

    { assign values to variables }
    i := 9;
    j := 41;
    c := 'X';

    { obtain pointers of variables }
    intPtr2 := @i;
    longPtr2 := @j;
    charPtr2 := @c;

    REPEAT
        WRITE('Enter a positive number : ');
        READLN(intPtr1^); WRITELN;
    UNTIL intPtr1^ > 0;

    INC(intPtr1^);
    longPtr1^ := SQR(intPtr1^ + intPtr2^);
    WRITELN(intPtr1^ + intPtr2^,' squared = ',longPtr1^);
    WRITELN;

    WRITELN(longPtr2^,' squared = ',longPtr2^ * longPtr2^);
    WRITELN;

    DEC(intPtr1^, 3);
    charPtr1^ := CHR(intPtr1^);
    WRITELN(charPtr1^,' has the ASCII code of ',intPtr1^);
    WRITELN(charPtr2^,' has the ASCII code of ',ORD(charPtr2^));
    WRITELN; WRITELN;

    WRITELN; WRITELN;

    { dispose of the dynamic space associated with pointers }
    DISPOSE(intPtr1);
    DISPOSE(longPtr1);
    DISPOSE(charPtr1);

END.
```

Compile and run the Turbo Pascal version. Examine the following sample session:

```
Enter a positive number : 55

65 squared = 4225

41 squared = 1681

5 has the ASCII code of 53
X has the ASCII code of 88
```

Listing 8.7 shows the source code for the LST08_07.CPP program. The two program versions demonstrate the translation rules presented earlier in this section. The translations deal with predefined data types in both languages.

Listing 8.7. Source code for the LST08_07.CPP program.

```
/*
  C++ program that illustrates using pointers to access
  simple data types in C++.
*/

#include <iostream.h>
#include <stdlib.h>

// define square function

int square(int x)

{
  return x * x;
}

main()
{
      int *intPtr1, *intPtr2; // pointers to integers */
      long *longPtr1, *longPtr2; // pointers to long integers
      char *charPtr1, *charPtr2; // pointers to characters
      int i = 9;
      long j = 41;
      char c = 'X';

      // create dynamic space associated with pointers
```

```
intPtr1 = new int;
longPtr1 = new long;
charPtr1 = new char;

intPtr2 = &i;
longPtr2 = &j;
charPtr2 = &c;

do {
    cout << "Enter a positive number : ";
    // note that intPtr1 needs the * operator in cin
    cin >> *intPtr1;
    cout << "\n";
 } while (*intPtr1 <= 0);

(*intPtr1)++; // () are used to increment the number
             // pointed to and not the address of the pointer
*longPtr1 = square(*intPtr1 + *intPtr2);
cout << (*intPtr1 + *intPtr2)
     << " squared = "
     << *longPtr1 << "\n\n"
     << *longPtr2
     << " squared = "
     << ((*longPtr2) * (*longPtr2))
     << "\n\n";

*intPtr1 -= 3;
*charPtr1 = *intPtr1;
cout << *charPtr1
     << " has the ASCII code of "
     << *intPtr1 << "\n\n";
cout << *charPtr2
     << " has the ASCII code of "
     << int(*charPtr2) << "\n\n";

// dispose of the dynamic space associated with pointers
delete intPtr1;
delete longPtr1;
delete charPtr1;

return 0;

}
```

Arrays: An Overview

Arrays are important and popular data structures. They enable you to manipulate a collection of data items that share the same basic data type. C++ supports arrays of different dimensions and requires that you observe the following rules:

1. The lower bound of any dimension in a C++ array is set at zero. You can't override or alter this lower bound.

2. Declaring a C++ array entails specifying the number of members in each dimension. Keep in mind that this number is always equal to the upper bound plus one.

3. You must enclose array indices in brackets.

4. In the case of multidimensional arrays, you must enclose the size or indices of each dimension in a separate pair of brackets.

Examine the following example of declaring and using arrays in C++:

```
long m[10], n[15];
double x[5, 200], y[5];

m[0] = 4;
m[9] = 12;
x[2][199] = 123.3;
y[4] = y[3] + 12.3;
```

One-Dimensional Arrays

The simplest kind of arrays are one-dimensional. The general syntax for declaring a one-dimensional array is:

```
type arrayName[numberOfElements];
```

The indices of the preceding general form range from 0 to numberOfElements − 1.

To translate a one-dimensional array from Pascal to C++, use the following rules:

Pascal:

```
AnArray : ARRAY[LOW..HIGH] OF dataType;
```

> C++:
>
> ```
> dataType AnArray[HIGH - LOW + 1];
> ```

Listing 8.8 contains the source code for the LST08_08.PAS program, which uses a 30-element numeric array to calculate the average of the data in the array. The program prompts you to enter the actual number of data and then validates your input. The program then calculates the average of the data in the array and displays the result.

Listing 8.8. Source code for the LST08_08.PAS program.

```
Program Simple_Arrays;

Uses CRT;

{
  Turbo Pascal program that demonstrates the use of
  one-dimensional arrays.  The average value of the array
  is calculated.
}

CONST MAX = 30;

VAR x : ARRAY [1..MAX] OF REAL;
    sum, sumX, mean : REAL;
    i, n : INTEGER;

BEGIN
    ClrScr;

    REPEAT { obtain number of data points }
        WRITE('Enter number of data points [2 to ',MAX,'] : ');
        READLN(n); WRITELN;
    UNTIL n IN [2..MAX];

    { prompt user for data }
    FOR i := 1 TO n DO BEGIN
        WRITE('X[',i,'] : ');
        READLN(x[i]); WRITELN;
    END;

    { initialize summations }
    sum := n;
    sumX := 0.0;
```

continues

225

Listing 8.8. continued

```
{ calculate sum of observations }
FOR i := 1 TO n DO
    sumX := sumX + x[i];

mean := sumX / sum; { calculate the mean value }

WRITELN; WRITELN;
WRITELN('Mean = ',mean); WRITELN; WRITELN;

END.
```

Listing 8.9 shows the source code for the LST08_09.CPP program.

Listing 8.9. Source code for the LST08_09.CPP program.

```
/*
  C++ program that demonstrates the use of one-dimensional
  arrays.  The average value of the array is calculated.
*/

#include <iostream.h>
#include <conio.h>

const int MAX = 30;

main()
{

    double x[MAX];
    double sum, sumX = 0.0, mean;
    int i, n;

    clrscr();

    do { // obtain number of data points
        cout << "Enter number of data points [2 to "
             << MAX << "] : ";
        cin >> n;
        cout << "\n";
    } while (n < 2 || n > MAX);

    // prompt user for data
    for (i = 0; i < n; i++) {
```

```
        cout << "X[" << i << "] : ";
        cin >> x[i];
        cout << "\n";
    }

    // initialize summations
    sum = n;

    // calculate sum of observations
    for (i = 0; i < n; i++)
        sumX += x[i];

    mean = sumX / sum; /* calculate the mean value */

    cout << "\n\nMean = " << mean << "\n\n";

    return 0;
}
```

Because C++ fixes the lower bound of an array at zero, I made a few adjustments when I translated the Pascal version to C++. These adjustments affect the two `for` loops in the C++ version. The two Pascal `FOR-NEXT` loops have the following loop setup:

```
FOR i := 1 TO n DO BEGIN
```

The loop control `i` variable has values that vary between 1 and `n`, the number of data points. In the Turbo C++ version, the two corresponding `for` loops have the following setup:

```
for (i = 0; i < n; i++) {
```

The loop control `i` variable iterates between `0` and `n - 1`, so the loop continuation test is `i < n` and not `i <= n`.

The `cout` statement, which displays the contents of the loop control variable in the first `for` loop, emits values that range from `0` to `n - 1`. Therefore, the prompting indices in the Turbo C++ program are one less than the corresponding indices in the Turbo Pascal version.

With C++ you can easily initialize arrays. You must enclose the list of initializing values in curly braces. The list is comma-delimited and can span multiple lines. If the number of items in the initializing list is fewer than the number of array elements, the compiler assigns zeros to balance array elements. Because of this flexibility, you can more easily initialize arrays in C++ than arrays of typed constants in Turbo Pascal. What happens if the list of initializing values has more items than the number of array elements? The compiler flags a compile-time error.

The LST08_10.CPP program, shown in Listing 8.10, modifies the preceding Turbo C++ program to supply data internally. Consequently, I eliminated the step that prompts you for the number of data and the data itself. The program displays the average value of the data in the initializing list. Although this program does not interact with the user, it stores data in the source code. You can periodically edit the program to add, edit, and delete data before recalculating a new average value.

Listing 8.10. Source code for the LST08_10.CPP program.

```
/*
   C++ program that demonstrates the use of one-dimensional
   arrays.  The average value of the array is calculated.
   The array has its values preassigned internally.
*/

#include <iostream.h>
#include <conio.h>

const int MAX = 10;

main()
{

    double x[MAX] = { 12.2, 45.4, 67.2, 12.2, 34.6, 87.4,
                      83.6, 12.3, 14.8, 55.5 };
    double sum = MAX, sumX = 0.0, mean;
    int i, n = MAX;

    clrscr();

    // calculate sum of observations
    for (i = 0; i < n; i++)
        sumX += x[i];

    mean = sumX / sum; // calculate the mean value

    cout << "\n\nMean = " << mean << "\n\n";

    return 0;
}
```

If you use Turbo Pascal arrays that are typed constants, you may be frustrated by having to count the exact number of initializing values. C++ provides a solution to this problem.

It enables you to automatically size an array using the number of items in the corresponding initializing list. Consequently, you need not place a number in the brackets of the array; the compiler does the work for you.

LST08_11.CPP, shown in Listing 8.11, is a modified version of LST08_10.CPP and uses the automatic array-sizing feature.

Listing 8.11. Source code for the LST08_11.CPP program.

```
/*
  C++ program that demonstrates the use of one-dimensional
  arrays.  The average value of the array is calculated.
  The array has its values preassigned internally.
*/

#include <iostream.h>
main()
{

    double x[] = { 12.2, 45.4, 67.2, 12.2, 34.6, 87.4,
                   83.6, 12.3, 14.8, 55.5 };
    double sum,  sumx = 0.0, mean;
    int i, n;

    n = sizeof(x) / sizeof(double);
    sum = n;

    // calculate sum of observations
    for (i = 0; i < n; i++)
        sumx += x[i];

    mean = sumx / sum; // calculate the mean value

    cout << "\n\n"
         << "Number of data points = " << n << "\n"
         << "Mean = " << mean << "\n\n";

    return 0;
}
```

Notice that the preceding program does not declare the MAX constant that appears in the previous version, shown in Listing 8.10. How does the program determine the number of array elements? The code shows that the number of elements in array x is calculated by dividing the size of array x by the size of its basic data type. You can use this method to obtain the size of any array of any data type.

229

Multidimensional Arrays

Multidimensional arrays are supersets of one-dimensional arrays. Each dimension provides you with an additional access attribute. Two-dimensional arrays, or matrices, are the most popular kind of multidimensional arrays. Three-dimensional arrays are used less frequently than matrices. The general syntax for declaring two-dimensional and three-dimensional arrays is as follows:

```
type array [size1][size2];
type array [size1][size2][size3];
```

As with simple arrays, each dimension has a lower bound index of 0, and the declaration defines the number of elements in each dimension.

> To translate a two-dimensional array from Pascal to C++, use the following guide-line:
>
> Pascal:
>
> ```
> AnArray : ARRAY[LOW1..HIGH1, LOW2..HIGH2] OF dataType;
> ```
>
> C++:
>
> ```
> dataType AnArray[HIGH1 - LOW1 + 1][HIGH2 - LOW2 + 1];
> ```

It is important to understand how C++ stores the elements of multidimensional arrays. The reasons for learning about this storage scheme will become apparent later on in this chapter. Most compilers store the elements of a multidimensional array in a contiguous fashion. The runtime code calculates where a given element is located in that long array. With Turbo Pascal, you need not worry about the storage scheme for multidimensional arrays. However, the reverse is true in C++.

To explain the storage scheme of multidimensional arrays, I employ a convention for referencing the indices of the different dimensions. The following schema specifies the dimension numbering and the concept of high- and low-order dimensions. As an extreme example, note the following six-dimensional array.

```
      1    2    3    4    5    6   <— dimension number
M [20]  [2]  [4]  [3]  [2]  [4]
    higher dimension order —>
```

The first element of the M array is M[0][0][0][0][0][0] and it is stored at the first memory location of array M. The M array is stored in a contiguous block of 3,840 elements. The

second location in that contiguous block stores the element at index 1 in the highest dimension number, dimension 6 (M[0][0][0][0][0][1]). The locations of the subsequent elements in the contiguous block store the subsequent elements in dimension 6 until the upper limit, index 3, of dimension 6 is reached. Reaching this limit bumps the index of dimension 5 by 1 and resets the index of dimension 6 to 0. This process is repeated until every element in a multidimensional array is accessed. You can imagine this storage scheme as a gasoline pump meter: the rightmost digits turn fastest, and the leftmost digits turn slowest.

The following example that uses a three-dimensional array, M[3][2][2], shows the sequence of storing the elements of array M:

```
M[0][0][0]      <-- the starting memory address
M[0][0][1]      <-- 3rd dimension is filled
M[0][1][0]
M[0][1][1]      <-- 2nd and 3rd dimensions are filled
M[1][0][0]
M[1][0][1]      <-- 3rd dimension is filled
M[1][1][0]
M[1][1][1]      <-- 2nd and 3rd dimensions are filled
M[2][0][0]
M[2][0][1]      <-- 3rd dimension is filled
M[2][1][0]
M[2][1][1]      <-- all dimensions are filled
```

The next program example illustrates basic matrix manipulation. The program manages a matrix that contains up to 10 columns and 30 rows. It performs the following tasks:

- prompts you to enter the number of rows (the program validates your input)

- prompts you to enter the number of columns (the program validates your input)

- prompts you to enter the matrix elements

- calculates and displays the average for each column in the matrix

Listing 8.12 shows the source code for the LST08_12.PAS program.

Listing 8.12. Source code for the LST08_12.PAS program.

```
Program Two_Dim_Arrays;

Uses CRT;

{
```

continues

Listing 8.12. continued

```pascal
  Turbo Pascal program that demonstrates the use of
  two-dimensional arrays.  The average value of each matrix
  column is calculated.
}

CONST MAX_COL = 10;
      MAX_ROW = 30;

VAR x : ARRAY [1..MAX_ROW,1..MAX_COL] OF REAL;
    sum, sumX, mean : REAL;
    i, j, rows, columns : INTEGER;

BEGIN
    ClrScr;
    REPEAT
        WRITE('Enter number of rows [2 to ',MAX_ROW,'] : ');
        READLN(rows); WRITELN;
    UNTIL rows IN [2..MAX_ROW];

    REPEAT
        WRITE('Enter number of columns [1 to ',MAX_COL,'] : ');
        READLN(columns); WRITELN;
    UNTIL columns IN [1..MAX_COL];

    FOR i := 1 TO rows DO BEGIN
        FOR j := 1 TO columns DO BEGIN
            WRITE('X[',i,',',j,'] : ');
            READLN(x[i,j]); WRITELN;
        END;
        WRITELN;
    END;

    FOR j := 1 TO columns DO BEGIN
        sum := rows;
        sumx := 0.0;

        FOR i := 1 TO rows DO
            sumx := sumx + x[i,j];

        mean := sumx / sum;

        WRITELN; WRITELN;
        WRITELN('Mean for column ',j,' = ',mean);
```

```
END; { FOR j }

WRITELN; WRITELN;

END.
```

Listing 8.13 shows the source code for the LST08_13.CPP program.

Listing 8.13. Source code for the LST08_13.CPP program.

```cpp
/*
  C++ program that demonstrates the use of two-dimensional arrays.
  The average value of each matrix column is calculated.
*/

#include <iostream.h>
#include <conio.h>

const int MAX_COL = 10;
const int MAX_ROW = 30;

main()
{

    double x[MAX_ROW][MAX_COL];
    double sum, sumx, mean;
    int rows, columns;

    clrscr();

    do {
        cout << "Enter number of rows [2 to "
             << MAX_ROW << "] : ";
        cin >> rows;
        cout << "\n";
    } while (rows < 2 || rows > MAX_ROW);

    do {
        cout << "Enter number of columns [1 to "
             << MAX_COL << "] : ";
        cin >> columns;
        cout << "\n";
    } while (columns < 1 || columns > MAX_COL);
```

continues

233

Listing 8.13. continued

```
for (int i = 0; i < rows; i++)  {
    for (int j = 0; j < columns; j++)  {
        cout << "X[" << i << "][" << j << "] : ";
        cin >> x[i][j];
        cout << "\n";
    }
    cout << "\n";
}


for (int j = 0; j < columns; j++)  {
    sum = rows;
    sumx = 0.0;

    for (i = 0; i < rows; i++)
        sumx += x[i][j];

    mean = sumx / sum;

    cout << "\n\nMean for column " << j
         << " = " << mean << "\n";

}

cout << "\n\n";

return 0;
}
```

In translating the Turbo Pascal version to the Turbo C++ version, I decremented the indices of matrix x by 1. This change affects the translation of the Turbo Pascal FOR-NEXT loops:

```
FOR i := 1 TO rows DO BEGIN
    FOR j := 1 TO columns DO BEGIN
```

which I translated into the C++ for loops:

```
for (i = 0; i < rows; i++) {
    for (j = 0; j < columns; j++) {
```

The ranges of values for the loop control variables i and j are shifted downward by 1.

C++ enables you to initialize multidimensional arrays in a manner similar to the initialization of one-dimensional arrays. You must use a list of values that appears in the same sequence in which the elements of the initialized multidimensional array are stored. This is why it is important to understand how C++ stores the elements of a multidimensional array.

The following listing is a modified version of the preceding C++ program that uses an initializing list to internally supply the program with data. Consequently, the program doesn't prompt you for data. Listing 8.14 shows the source code for the LST08_14.CPP program.

Listing 8.14. Source code for the LST08_14.CPP program.

```
/*
  C++ program that demonstrates the initialization of a
  two-dimensional array. The average value of each matrix
  column is calculated.
*/

#include <iostream.h>
#include <conio.h>

const int MAX_COL = 5;
const int MAX_ROW = 3;

main()
{

    double x[MAX_ROW][MAX_COL] = { /* --- data for row 1 --- */
                                   { 1.1, 2.1, 3.1, 4.2, 5.5 },
                                   /* --- data for row 2 --- */
                                   { 6.6, 7.7, 8.8, 6.4, 1.2 },
                                   /* --- data for row 3 --- */
                                   { 9.8, 2.3, 4.5, 7.8, 4.3 }
                                 };
    double sum, sumX, mean;
    int rows = MAX_ROW, columns = MAX_COL;

    clrscr();

    for (int j = 0; j < columns; j++)  {
```

continues

Listing 8.14. continued

```
    sum = rows;
    sumX = 0.0;

    for (int i = 0; i < rows; i++)
        sumX += x[i][j];

    mean = sumX / sum;

    cout << "\n\nMean for column "
         << j << " = " << mean << "\n";

    }

    cout << "\n\n";

    return 0;
}
```

Accessing Arrays with Pointers

A program variable is a label that tags a memory address. Using a variable in a program means accessing the associated memory location by specifying its name, or tag. In this sense, a variable becomes a name that points to a memory location or a pointer. C++ and C support a special use for the names of arrays. The compiler interprets the bare name of an array as the address of its first element. Therefore, if x is an array, the expressions &x[0] and x are equivalent. In the case of a matrix named mat, the expressions &mat[0][0] and mat are also equivalent. This aspect of C++ and C empowers them to work as high-level assembly languages. If you have the address of a data item, you've got its number, so to speak. Knowing the memory address of a variable or array enables you to manipulate its contents using pointers.

With C++ you can use a pointer to access the various elements of an array. When you access element x[i] of array x, the compiled code performs two tasks. First, it obtains the base address of array x (that is, where the first array element is located). Second, the compiled code uses index i to calculate the offset from the base address of the array. This offset equals i multiplied by the size of the basic array type:

address of element x[i] = address of x + i * sizeof(basicType)

Assuming that pointer `ptr` points to the base address of array x,

ptr = x; // pointer ptr points to address of x[0]

I can now substitute `ptr` for x in the preceding equation and come up with the following result:

address of element x[i] = ptr + i * sizeof(basicType)

C++ and C absolve you from having to explicitly state the size of the basic array type, thus simplifying the preceding equation. In this manner, they become high-level assemblers. You can now write:

address of element x[i] = p + i

The new equation states that the address of element `x[i]` is the expression `(p + i)`.

The next program illustrates the use of pointers to access one-dimensional arrays. This program is a modified version of the Turbo C++ program that calculates the average value of data in an array. The new version alters its parent program in the following ways:

1. The program uses the name of the array to store data in the array itself. In this case, the bare name of the array acts as a pointer.

2. The program uses the `realPtr` double-typed pointer to illustrate accessing the elements of an array using a distinct pointer.

Listing 8.15 shows the source code for the LST08_15.CPP program.

Listing 8.15. Source code for the LST08_15.CPP program.

```
/*
   C++ program that demonstrates the use of pointers with
   one-dimensional arrays.  Program calculates the average
   value of the data found in the array.
*/

#include <iostream.h>
#include <conio.h>

const int MAX = 30;

main()
{
```

continues

Listing 8.15. continued

```
double x[MAX];
// declare pointer and initialize with base
// address of array x
double *realPtr = x; // same as = &x[0]
double sum, sumx = 0.0, mean;
int i, n;

clrscr();

do {
    cout << "Enter number of data points [2 to "
        << MAX << "] : ";
    cin >> n;
    cout << "\n";
} while (n < 2 || n > MAX);

for (i = 0; i < n; i++) {
    cout << "X[" << i << "] : ";
    // use the reference form *(x+i) to store data in x[i]
    cin >> *(x + i);
    cout << "\n";
}

sum = n;

for (i = 0; i < n; i++)
/* use the pointer form *(realPtr + i) to access x[i] */
    sumx += *(realPtr + i);

mean = sumx / sum;

cout << "\n\nMean = " << mean << "\n\n";

return 0;
}
```

Notice the following features of the preceding source code:

1. The cin >> input statement appears as:

   cin >> *(x + i);

   instead of the equivalent form:

   cin >> x[i];

   because the expressions *(x + i) and x[i] are equivalent.

2. The program simultaneously declares and initializes the realPtr pointer using the following statement:

```
double *realPtr = x;
```

The pointer stores the basic address of array x. Consequently, the expressions *(realPtr + i) and x[i] access the same array element. This equivalence is based on the following steps:

1. The expressions x[i] and *(x + i) are equivalent.

2. The realPtr pointer has the base address of array x.

3. Therefore, the expressions x[i] and *(realPtr + i) are equivalent.

The preceding Turbo C++ program maintains the same address in the realPtr pointer. Employing pointer arithmetic with the for loop index i, I can write a new program version that increments the offset to access the elements of array x. C++ provides you with another choice that enables you to sequentially access the elements of an array without the help of an explicit offset value. The method merely involves using the increment or decrement operator with a pointer. You still need to initialize the pointer to the base address of an array and then use the ++ operator to access the next array element. Listing 8.16 shows the source code for the LST08_16.CPP program, which uses the pointer increment method.

Listing 8.16. Source code for the LST08_16.CPP program.

```
/*
  C++ program that demonstrates the use of pointers with
  one-dimensional arrays.  The average value of the array
  is calculated.  This program modifies the previous version
  in the following way:  the realPtr is used to access the
  array without any help from any loop control variable.
  This is accomplished by 'incrementing' the pointer, and
  consequently incrementing its address.  This program
  illustrates pointer arithmetic that alters the pointer's
  address.

*/
#include <iostream.h>
#include <conio.h>

const int MAX = 30;
```

continues

239

Listing 8.16. continued

```
main()
{
    double x[MAX];
    double *realPtr = x;
    double sum, sumx = 0.0, mean;
    int i, n;

    clrscr();

    do {
        cout << "Enter number of data points [2 to "
            << MAX << "] : ";
        cin >> n;
        cout << "\n";
    } while (n < 2 || n > MAX);

    // loop variable i is not directly involved in accessing
    //  the elements of array x
    for (i = 0; i < n; i++) {
        cout << "X[" << i << "] : ";
    // increment pointer realPtr after taking its reference
        cin >> *realPtr++;
        cout << "\n";
    }

    // restore original address by using pointer arithmetic
    realPtr -= n;

    sum = n;

    // loop variable i serves as a simple counter
    for (i = 0; i < n; i++)
    // increment pointer realPtr after taking a reference
        sumx += *(realPtr++);

    mean = sumx / sum;

    cout << "\n\nMean = " << mean << "\n\n";

    return 0;

}
```

The preceding Turbo C++ program first initializes the `realPtr` pointer to the base address of array x. The program uses the `realPtr` pointer in the keyboard input statement:

```
cin >> *realPtr++;
```

When the input loop terminates, the `realPtr` pointer points to the tail of array x. To reset the pointer to the base address of array x, the program uses the following assignment:

```
realPtr -= n;
```

The preceding statement causes the `realPtr` pointer to access the array element x[0]. The program uses the same incrementing method to calculate the sum of data in the second `for` loop:

```
sum += *(realPtr++);
```

Because the preceding statement uses neither the name of the array nor a typical index, it may look strange to a Turbo Pascal programmer.

Accessing Matrices with Pointers

Using pointers to access the elements of a matrix is a bit more elaborate than using them to access the elements of a simple array. To access a simple array, you need the base address of that array along with a single offset (index) to the targeted element. In the case of multidimensional arrays, you need an offset value for each dimension. The two-dimensional array is presented here as a study case. First, think of the matrix as an array of arrays. To access a matrix element, you first need a pointer to the array that represents the targeted row. You then need a second pointer to access the exact element in the targeted row. This process involves using a pointer to a pointer, a feature supported in C++.

The LST08_17.CPP program, shown in Listing 8.17, uses pointers to access the elements of a matrix (it is a modified version of Listing 8.13).

Listing 8.17. Source code for the LST08_17.CPP program.

```
/*
  C++ program that demonstrates the use of pointers to access
  two-dimensional arrays. The average value of each matrix column
  is calculated.
*/
```

continues

Listing 8.17. continued

```cpp
#include <iostream.h>
#include <conio.h>

const int MAX_COL = 10;
const int MAX_ROW = 30;

main()
{

    double x[MAX_ROW][MAX_COL];
    double sum, sumX, mean;
    int rows, columns;

    clrscr();

    do {
        cout << "Enter number of rows [2 to "
            << MAX_ROW << "] : ";
        cin >> rows;
        cout << "\n";
    } while (rows < 2 || rows > MAX_ROW);

    do {
        cout << "Enter number of columns [1 to "
            << MAX_COL << "] : ";
        cin >> columns;
        cout << "\n";
    } while (columns < 1 || columns > MAX_COL);

    for (int i = 0; i < rows; i++)  {
        for (int j = 0; j < columns; j++)  {
            cout << "X[" << i << "][" << j << "] : ";
            cin >> *(*(x+i)+j);
            cout << "\n";
        }
        cout << "\n";
    }

    for (int j = 0; j < columns; j++)  {
        sum = rows;
        sumX = 0.0;

        for (i = 0; i < rows; i++)
            sumX += *(*(x+i)+j);

        mean = sumX / sum;
```

```
        cout << "\n\nMean for column "
             << (j + 1) << " = " << mean << "\n\n";

    }

    cout << "\n\n";

    return 0;

}
```

The ordinary access to row i and column j uses the reference, x[i][j]. You can regard x[i][j] as the element j of the one-dimensional array x[i]. Using concepts developed earlier in this chapter, you can say that x[i] is equivalent to *(x + i). Consequently, the element x[i][j] is equivalent to *(x + i)[j], an intermediate form. Expanding this intermediate form, you can say that the expressions x[i][j] and *(*(x + i) + j) are equivalent.

The general form for accessing a multidimensional array using pointers is:

x[i][j]...[n][m]

which is equivalent to:

*(*(... *(*(x + i) + j) ... + n) + m)

The dimensions with a lower order are nested more deeply than the dimensions with a higher order.

Strings in C++

With the exception of a few programs that performed character manipulation, the examples presented so far have been numerical. You have perhaps noticed the absence of string-based examples. I have deliberately postponed mentioning strings because C++ and C regard them as arrays of characters that end with the special null character (ASCII 0). This character is also called the null terminator. When you declare a string variable as an array of characters, be sure to reserve an extra space for the null terminator. The advantage of using the null terminator is that it enables you to create strings that exceed the 255-character limit of Turbo Pascal strings.

When it comes to managing strings, C++ and C use an approach that deviates significantly from that of Turbo Pascal. First, you can't assign null-terminated strings to each other by using the = operator. Second, you can't concatenate strings with other strings or other characters using the + operator. In addition, manipulating null-terminated strings often involves using pointers.

C programmers have developed the standard string library string.h that contains the most frequently used string-manipulation functions. The stdio.h header file prototype functions also support string I/O.

The next example carries out simple character translation in a string. The program prompts you to enter a string, the character to be replaced, and the replacement character. Listing 8.18 shows the source code for the LST08_18.PAS program. The Pascal program looks trivial.

Listing 8.18. Source code for the LST08_18.PAS program.

```
Program Translate_String_Characters;

Uses CRT;

{
  Turbo Pascal program that demonstrates how a string is
  sometimes treated as an array of characters.   Program
  examines the characters of a string and translates those
  that match.
}

VAR aString : STRING[80];
    oldChar, newChar : CHAR;
    i : BYTE;

BEGIN
    ClrScr;
    WRITELN('Enter a string');
    READLN(aString); WRITELN; WRITELN;
    WRITE('Enter character to replace : ');
    READLN(oldChar); WRITELN;
    WRITE('Enter new character : ');
    READLN(newChar); WRITELN;

    FOR i := 1 TO Length(aString) DO
```

```
        IF aString[i] = oldChar THEN
            aString[i] := newChar;

    WRITELN;
    WRITELN('The translated string is');
    WRITELN(aString); WRITELN; WRITELN;

END.
```

Listing 8.19 contains the source code for the LST08_19.CPP program. The Turbo C++ program version uses the gets and puts functions to enter and display strings. These functions are prototyped in the stdio.h header file and are specialized in basic string I/O.

Listing 8.19. Source code for the LST08_19.CPP program.

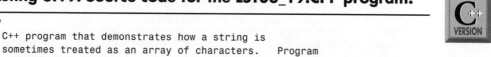

```
/*
  C++ program that demonstrates how a string is
  sometimes treated as an array of characters.   Program
  examines the characters of a string and translates those
  that match.
*/

#include <stdio.h>
#include <conio.h>

#define BYTE unsigned char

main()
{

    char aString[81];
    char oldChar, newChar;
    BYTE i;

    clrscr();
    printf("Enter a string\n");
    gets(aString); printf("\n\n");
    printf("Enter character to replace : ");
    oldChar = getche(); printf("\n");
    printf("Enter new character : ");
    newChar = getche(); printf("\n");

    /* string index starts at zero */
    for (i = 0; aString[i] != '\0'; i++)
```

continues

245

Listing 8.19. continued

```
        if (aString[i] == oldChar)
            aString[i] = newChar;

    printf("\nThe translated string is\n");
    puts(aString); printf("\n\n");

    return 0;
}
```

Compare the Turbo Pascal and Turbo C++ program versions and notice the following differences:

1. The C++ string variable aString has 81 characters—one more than 80, the size of the string variable in the Turbo Pascal version. This extra character is needed to store the null terminator.

2. Processing the characters in the Turbo Pascal strings uses the Length intrinsic to define the iteration range of the following loop:

   `FOR i := 1 TO Length(aString) DO`

   The Turbo C++ version detects the null character to determine when to stop the for loop:

   `for (i = 0; aString[i] != '\0'; i++)`

   I could have written the Turbo C++ version using the strlen function, which is prototyped in the string.h header file and is similar to the Length function in Turbo Pascal. However, the preceding version is more efficient because it skips calling the string-length function.

3. Accessing individual characters in Turbo Pascal and Turbo C++ is similar.

4. The arguments for the string I/O functions, gets and puts, are pointers to strings. Therefore, the program uses the bare name of the string variable as the required pointer.

As you become more proficient at manipulating null-terminated strings in C++, you realize the functions prototyped in string.h header files (and other header files) rely heavily on pointers. The gets and puts functions are good examples. The following program, which uses an explicit pointer to manipulate the string, is a modified version of the LST08_19.CPP program Listing 8.20 shows the source code for the LST08_20.CPP program.

Listing 8.20. Source code for the LST08_20.CPP program.

```c
/*
   C++ program that demonstrates how a string is
   accessed using a character pointer.  The program
   examines the characters of a string and translates those
   that match.
*/

#include <stdio.h>
#include <conio.h>

#define BYTE unsigned char

main()
{

    char aString[81];
    char *ptr = aString;
    char oldChar, newChar;
    BYTE i;

    clrscr();
    printf("Enter a string\n");
    gets(aString); printf("\n\n");
    printf("Enter character to replace : ");
    oldChar = getche(); printf("\n");
    printf("Enter new character : ");
    newChar = getche(); printf("\n");

    for (/* no initialization is needed */; *ptr != '\0'; ptr++) {
        if (*ptr == oldChar)
            *ptr = newChar;
    }

/* -------------- OR USE THE FOLLOWING FORM --------------

    while (*ptr != '\0') {
        if (*ptr == oldChar)
            *ptr = newChar;
        ptr++;
    }

*/

/* -------------- OR USE THE FOLLOWING FORM --------------
    for (i = 0; *(ptr+i) != '\0'; i++)
```

continues

Listing 8.20. continued

```
        if (*(ptr+i) == oldChar)
            *(ptr+i) = newChar;
*/

    printf("\nThe translated string is\n");
    puts(aString); printf("\n\n");

    return 0;
}
```

The preceding Turbo C++ program applies the increment operator to the ptr pointer in order to access the various characters in the input string. Notice that the first for loop, which uses the ptr pointer as a loop control, needs no initialization section because the pointer is initialized when declared. The program contains two alternate loops that are commented out. The first loop is a while loop that tests the expression (*ptr != '\0'). The second loop is a for loop that uses the i loop control variable. This variable provides an offset used to access character number i using the expression *(ptr + i).

Compile and run the program. Enter the string "Joseph Shammas" and enter the search and replace characters m and n. The program session follows:

```
Enter a string
Joseph Shammas


Enter character to replace : m
Enter new character : n

The translated string is
Joseph Shannas
```

The preceding examples serve to introduce you to basic string-handling methods. Turbo Pascal offers a collection of predefined string-handling intrinsics, such as the frequently employed Pos, Delete, and Insert. The next Turbo Pascal program uses these functions to perform the following:

1. Display the string "I am a Turbo Pascal Programmer"

2. Replace the word "Pascal" with "C++"

3. Insert the words "very good" before the word "Turbo"

4. Replace "I am" with "You are"

Listing 8.21 shows the source code for the LST08_21.PAS program.

Listing 8.21. Source code for the LST08_21.PAS program.

```pascal
Program String_Test1;

Uses CRT;

{
  Turbo Pascal program that uses predefined string functions and
  procedures to manipulate strings.  Program also uses string
  constants, typed string constants and string variables.
}

CONST TITLE = 'STRING TEST PROGRAM';
      PHRASE : STRING[40] = 'I am a Turbo Pascal Programmer.';

VAR strlen, charPos, charCount : BYTE;
    aString : STRING[80];

BEGIN
    ClrScr;
    strlen := Length(TITLE);
    GotoXY(40 - strlen div 2, 1);
    WRITELN(TITLE);
    WRITELN; WRITELN;
    WRITELN(PHRASE); WRITELN;

    aString := PHRASE;
    charPos := Pos('Pascal',PHRASE);
    charCount := Length('Pascal');
    Delete(aString, charPos, charCount);
    Insert('C',aString,charPos);
    WRITELN(aString); WRITELN;
    charPos := Pos('Turbo',aString);
    Insert('very good ',aString,charPos);
    WRITELN(aString); WRITELN;

    { manipulate the typed constant string as a variable }
    PHRASE := aString;
    Delete(PHRASE, 1, 4);
    PHRASE := 'You are' + PHRASE;
    WRITELN(PHRASE); WRITELN;

END.
```

Listing 8.22 shows the source code for the LST08_22.CPP program. The C++ program contains functions that emulate the Turbo Pascal intrinsics Pos, Delete, and Insert.

Listing 8.22. Source code for the LST08_22.CPP program.

```
/*
  C++ program that uses predefined string functions and
  procedures to manipulate strings.  Program also uses string
  constants, typed string constants and string variables.
*/

#include <stdio.h>
#include <string.h>
#include <conio.h>

#define BYTE unsigned char

main()
{

    const char *TITLE = "STRING TEST PROGRAM";
    const char PHRASE[40] = "I am a Turbo Pascal Programmer.";

    BYTE strlen_, charPos, charCount;
    char* aString;
    // declare prototype for Pos, Delete() and Insert() functions
    int Pos(char* str, char* substr);
    void Delete(char*, int, int);
    void Insert(char*, char*, int);

    clrscr();
    strlen_ = strlen(TITLE);
    gotoxy(40 - strlen_ / 2, 1);
    puts(TITLE);
    printf("\n\n");
    printf("%s\n\n", PHRASE);

    strcpy(aString, PHRASE);
    charPos = Pos(aString,"Pascal");
    charCount = strlen("Pascal ");

    Delete(aString, charPos, charCount);
    Insert("C++ ", aString, charPos);
    puts(aString); printf("\n");
    charPos = Pos(aString,"Turbo");
    Insert("very good ", aString, charPos);
    puts(aString); printf("\n");

    Delete(aString, 0, 4);
    Insert("You are", aString, 0);
    puts(aString); printf("\n");
```

```
      return 0;
}

/*--------------- string operation routines ----------------

These routines mimic frequently used Turbo Pascal string routines.

----------------------------------------------------------*/

int Pos(char* str, char* substr)

{
  int i = 0, j, k;

  while (*str != '\0') {
    for (j = i, k = 0; *str == *substr; j++, k++) {
        substr++;
        str++;
        if (*substr == '\0') return i;
    }
    str++;
    i++;
  }
  /* no match found */
  return (-1);
}

void Delete(char* str, int first, int count)

{
  int length, last;
  int i, j, k;

  length = strlen(str);
  /* validity of parameters */
  if (first < length && first >= 0 &&
      count < length && count >= 0)   {
    last = first + count - 1;
    for (i = 0, k = 0; *(str + i) != '\0'; i++)
        if (i < first ¦¦ i > last)
          *(str + k++) = *(str + i);

      /* k is already pointing to the next character */
      *(str + k) = '\0';
  }
}
```

continues

Listing 8.22. continued

```
void Insert(char* substr, char* str, int index)

{
  int i, j, strlim;
  char tmpstr[101];

  strlim = strlen(str) - 1;
  if (index < 0) index = 0;

  if (index >= strlim) {
     i = 0;
     j = strlim + 1;
     while ( *(str + j++) == *(substr + i++) );
  }
  else {
     i = 0;
     if (index > 0) {
        for (; i < index; i++)
           *(tmpstr + i) = *(str + i);
     }
     for (j = 0; *(substr + j) != '\0'; i++, j++)
           *(tmpstr + i) = *(substr + j);


     for (j = index; *(str + j) != '\0'; i++, j++)
           *(tmpstr + i) = *(str + j);

     /* index i is already pointer to the end-of-string */
     *(tmpstr + i) = '\0';

     strcpy(str, tmpstr);
  }
}
```

The following output comes from the Turbo C++ program:

```
                    STRING TEST PROGRAM


I am a Turbo Pascal Programmer.

I am a Turbo C++ Programmer.

I am a very good Turbo C++ Programmer.

You are a very good Turbo C++ Programmer.
```

Notice the following aspects of the C++ program:

1. The program declares the identifier TITLE as a constant character-typed pointer. This pointer always accesses the base address of the memory location that stores the string "STRING TEST PROGRAM". This kind of pointer is indeed fixed:

```
const char *TITLE = "STRING TEST PROGRAM";
```

2. The PHRASE array is a constant that holds up to 40 characters, including the null terminator:

```
const char PHRASE[40] = "I am a Turbo Pascal Programmer.";
```

3. The prototypes of the string-handling functions are:

```
int Pos(char* str, char* substr);
void Delete(char*, int, int);
void Insert(char*, char*, int);
```

4. The program uses the strlen function to return the length of different strings. The prototype of function strlen is located in the string.h header file.

Summary

This chapter presents various topics that deal with arrays, pointers, and strings. You learned about the following:

- Storage classes—C++ contains four storage classes:

    1. Automatic: the local variables of a function are automatically allocated and deallocated at runtime when the host function is invoked or terminated.

    2. Static: the local variables of a function retain their values after the host function terminates.

    3. Extern: this storage class is used in multifile projects to avoid duplicating memory space for the same variables. The linker is involved in resolving the references to external variables.

    4. Register: this class uses the CPU registers, instead of memory location, to manipulate variables that are characters, integers, or pointers.

- Scope of variables—C++ enables you to declare variables between program statements and to enclose them in a statement block. The scope of these variables extends throughout the same block. At the end of the block, they can't be accessed because their memory space is reclaimed.

- Pointers to simple data types—pointers are declared in C++ using one of two forms:

```
type* pointer;
type *pointer;
```

The first form declares a pointer type and is able to define one or more pointers. In the second form, the identifier `pointer` is declared as the pointer to `type` and can be preceded or followed by the declaration of ordinary variables.

Pointers can take the address of a variable and consequently access its contents using the address-of operator &:

```
pointer = &variable;
```

You can also allocate dynamic memory and use a pointer to access the memory location using the `new` operator:

```
pointer = new type;
```

You can deallocate dynamic memory using the `delete` operator:

```
delete pointer;
```

- Single and multidimensional arrays—C++ supports arrays of a varying number of dimensions. The following rules are observed in declaring and using arrays:

  1. The lower bound of each dimension is fixed at 0.

  2. When declaring an array, you specify the number of elements in each dimension and not the upper bound limit.

  3. Square brackets are used to hold the indices of arrays.

  4. Declaring and using multidimensional arrays involves the use of separate sets of brackets for each dimension. Note the following example of declaring a matrix:

  ```
  double table[10][45];
  ```

  Also note the following example of accessing matrix elements:

  ```
  table [5][11] = 12.3;
  ```

  Multidimensional arrays are stored in a contiguous form so that the elements of the higher dimensions are closer to each other. By contrast, the elements of the lower dimensions are stored farther away from each other.

- Accessing arrays using pointers—accessing one-dimensional arrays involves the following rule:

The bare name of the array is a pointer to its first element, as shown in the following example:

```
int a[10], *ptr;

ptr = a;        /* or */
ptr = &a[0];
```

To access the i element of an array, you can substitute *(array + i) for the traditional form array[i]:

```
for (i = 0; i <= 10; i++)
a[i] = i;
```

which has the same net effect as:

```
for (i = 0; i <= 10; i++)
*(a+i) = i;
```

The array name can be replaced with a pointer to the base address of the array:

```
ptr = a;
for (i = 0; i <= 10; i++)
    *(ptr+i) = i;
```

Ultimately, you can access the element of an array in sequence by incrementing a pointer:

```
for (i = 0, ptr = a; i <= 10; i++, ptr++)
*ptr = i;
```

The handling of multidimensional arrays with pointers involves the use of pointers to other pointers. For example, the traditional reference to row i and column j of a matrix element is x[i][j]. This is replaced by *(*(x+i) +j) (or *(*(ptr+i) +j) if pointer ptr has the base address of matrix 'x').

- Strings in C++—C++ regards strings as arrays of characters that are terminated with the null character. C++ strings are not limited to 255 characters; they are limited by the memory model used or the availability of memory. When you declare an array, you must account for the extra space used by the null character.

- Character-typed pointers are frequently used to manipulate strings and are extensively used in string functions. C++ relies on libraries to provide a rich set of string-handling functions. You can't perform normal string assignments using the = operator nor can you concatenate strings using the + operator. All tasks related to string handling are performed using the library of string function STRING.H. Strings and their pointers can be initialized during declaration using the = operator.

TP 9
TC++

ENUMERATED AND STRUCTURED DATA TYPES

Creating user-defined data types is one of the features expected to be included in modern programming languages. This chapter builds on Chapter 8, "Pointers, Arrays, and Strings," and examines the enumerated data types and structures that enable you to better organize your data. In this chapter you will learn about the following:

- type definition using `typedef`
- enumerated data types
- structures
- pointers to structures
- unions
- pointers to unions
- `far` pointers

The enumerated types of Pascal and C++ are very similar. The same can be said of Pascal records and C++ structures, as well as Pascal variant records and C++ unions.

Type Definition in C++

In the main section of a Pascal routine, you define new data types in the TYPE sections. New types includes aliases of existing types, array types, pointer types, and records. C++ offers the typedef keyword that enables you to perform similar tasks. Note the following general syntax for using typedef:

```
typedef knownType newType;
```

The typedef statement defines a new type from a known one. You can use typedef to create aliases that shorten the names of existing data types. In the examples presented so far, I used macros to emulate the work of typedef. The advantage of typedef is that the compiler knows about both the old and new types. Consider the BOOLEAN macro-based pseudotype frequently used in preceding chapters:

```
#define BOOLEAN unsigned char
```

You can replace this macro with the following typedef statement:

```
typedef unsigned char BOOLEAN;
typedef unsigned char boolean;
```

Using the following general syntax, you can use typedef also to define the name of an array type:

```
typedef baseType arrayTypeName[arraySize];
```

The typedef statement defines the arrayTypeName, whose basic type and size are baseType and arraySize. For example, to define a string that stores 80 characters, excluding the null terminator, write the following C++ statement:

```
typedef char string80[81];
```

You can also define types that represent arrays and matrices:

```
typedef double realArray[10];
typedef double realMatrix[10][30];
```

> The role of `typedef` in C++ has evolved slightly from its role in C. Differences in the C and C++ languages, discussed in the next section, are responsible for this change.

Enumerated Data Types

The basic notion of enumerated data types is the same in both Pascal and C++. An enumerated type defines a list of unique identifiers and associates values with these identifiers. Although the enumerated identifiers must be unique, the values assigned to them are not.

The general syntax for declaring an enumerated type in C++ is:

```
enum enumType { <list of enumerated identifiers> };
```

Note the following example of declaring an enumerated type:

```
enum diskCapacity { disk360, disk720, disk1_2,
                    disk1_4, disk2_8 };
```

C++ associates integer values with enumerated identifiers. For example, in the preceding type, the compiler assigns 0 to disk360, 1 to disk720, and so on.

C++ is more flexible than Pascal in declaring enumerated types. First, the language enables you to explicitly assign a value to an enumerated identifier, as in the following example:

```
enum weekDay { Sun = 1, Mon, Tue, Wed, Thu, Fri, Sat };
```

This declaration explicitly assigns 1 to the enumerated identifier Sun. The compiler then assigns the next integer, 2, to the next identifier, Mon, and so on. You can explicitly assign a value to each member of the enumerated list. Moreover, these values need not be unique. Note the following examples of this flexibility in declaring enumerated types in C++:

```
// explicit value assignment for every list member
enum colors { black = 1, red = 2, blue = 3, green = 5,
              yellow = 7, white = 11 };

// intermittent value assignment
enum colors { black = 1, red, blue, green = 5,
              yellow = 7, white = 11 };

enum choiceType { false, true, dont_care = 0 };
```

259

The compiler associates the identifier `false` with 0 by default. However, the compiler also associates the value 0 with `dont_care` because of the explicit assignment.

With C++, you can declare variables that have enumerated types in the following ways:

1. The declaration of the enumerated type can include the declaration of the variables of that type. Note the general syntax:

```
enum enumType { <list of enumerated identifiers> }
               <list of variables>;
```

   Using the days of the week example, the declaration of variables of that type is

```
enum weekDay { Sun = 1, Mon, Tue, Wed, Thu, Fri, Sat }
              recycleDay, payDay, movieDay;
```

2. The enumerated type and its variables can be declared separately. This is the customary approach used in Pascal:

```
enum enumType { <list of enumerated identifiers> };
enumType var1, var2, ..., varN;
```

> C++ uses a different syntax than C to declare enumerated variables. C requires that the enum keyword appears in the declaration of such variables. The designers of C++ consider this feature an unnecessary redundancy. In addition, they consider an enumerated type to be a fully-defined, user-defined type known to the C++ compiler. If you look at C code, you will notice the enum keyword is also used in declaring variables of enumerated types.

The next Turbo Pascal program uses an enumerated type to model the days of the week. The program prompts you to enter a number that corresponds to a day of the week. It then displays one of the following messages:

1. If you enter 1 or 7 (to select Sunday or Saturday), the program displays the message `"Oh! The weekend!"`.

2. If you enter 6 (to select Friday), the program displays the string `"T.G.I.F.!!"`.

3. If you enter a number between 2 and 5, corresponding to Monday through Thursday, the program displays the message, `"Work, work, work!"`.

Listing 9.1. contains the source code for the LST09_01.PAS program.

Listing 9.1. Source code for the LST09_01.PAS program.

```pascal
Program Test_Enum;

{$V-}
Uses CRT;

{ Turbo Pascal program that demonstrates
  the use of enumerated types }


TYPE WeekDays = (NullDay, Sunday, Monday, Tuesday,
                 Wednesday, Thursday, Friday, Saturday);

VAR day  : WeekDays;
    akey : CHAR;
    more : BOOLEAN;
    j : WORD;


FUNCTION EnumVal(i : BYTE) : WeekDays;
{ function to return the i'th enumerated list member }
VAR aDay : WeekDays;

BEGIN
    aDay := NullDay;
    INC(aDay, i);
    EnumVal := aDay
END;

BEGIN
    ClrScr;

    REPEAT

        REPEAT
            WRITE('Enter a day number (Sun=1, Mon=2, etc) : ');
            READLN(j); WRITELN;
        UNTIL j IN [1..7];

        day := EnumVal(j); { use enumerated function }

        CASE day OF
            Sunday, Saturday : WRITELN('Oh! The weekend!');
            Friday : WRITELN('T.G.I.F.!!');
            Monday..Thursday : WRITELN('Work, work, work!');
        END;
```

continues

261

Listing 9.1. continued

```
        WRITELN; WRITELN;
        WRITE('more? (Y/N) '); akey := ReadKey;
        IF akey IN ['Y','y'] THEN more := TRUE
                             ELSE more := FALSE;

        WRITELN; WRITELN;

    UNTIL NOT more;

END.
```

Note the following sample session from the program:

```
Enter a day number (Sun=1, Mon=2, etc) : 2

Work, work, work!


more? (Y/N) y

Enter a day number (Sun=1, Mon=2, etc) : 1

Oh! The weekend!


more? (Y/N) y

Enter a day number (Sun=1, Mon=2, etc) : 6

T.G.I.F.!!


more? (Y/N) n
```

The Turbo Pascal program employs the EnumVal function to obtain the enumerated value of day number i. The program applies a simple program trick to obtain its result and keep the code short. Listing 9.2 contains the source code for the C++ program, LST09_02.CPP.

Listing 9.2. Source code for the LST09_02.CPP program.

```
// C++ program that demonstrates the use of enumerated types

#include <iostream.h>
#include <conio.h>
```

```
// make global enumerated definitions

enum WeekDays { NullDay, Sunday, Monday, Tuesday,
                Wednesday, Thursday, Friday, Saturday };

enum Boolean { false, true };

main()
{
    WeekDays day;
    Boolean more;
    char akey;
    unsigned j;
    // define prototype of enumerated function
    WeekDays enumVal(unsigned);

    clrscr();
    do {
        do {
          cout << "Enter a day number (Sun=1, Mon=2, etc) : ";
          cin >> j;
          cout << '\n';
        } while (j < 1 || j > 7);

        day = enumVal(j); // use enumerated function
        switch (day) {
            case Sunday:
            case Saturday:
              cout << "Oh! The weekend!";
              break;
            case Friday:
              cout << "T.G.I.F.!!";
              break;
            case Monday:
            case Tuesday:
            case Wednesday:
            case Thursday:
              cout << "Work, work, work!";
              break;
        }
        cout << "\n\n"
             << "more? (Y/N) ";
        akey = getche();
        more = (akey == 'Y' || akey == 'y') ? true : false;
        cout << "\n\n";

    } while (more == true);
```

continues

263

Listing 9.2. continued

```
    return 0;
}

WeekDays enumVal(unsigned  i)
// enumerated function to get the i'th enumerated element
{
  WeekDays aDay;

  aDay = NullDay;
  aDay += i;
  return aDay;
}
```

The Turbo C++ program uses the enumerated types WeekDays and Boolean. The latter emulates the predefined Turbo Pascal BOOLEAN type. The C++ program also prototypes the enumVal function as:

```
WeekDays enumVal(unsigned);
```

C++ applies the same trick found in the Pascal version of function enumVal. However, unless you choose the compiler option that enables you to treat enum types as ints, you get a compiler warning for mixing integers and enumerated types.

Structures

Structures enable you to define a new type that logically groups several fields or members. These members can be predefined types or other structures. Note the following general syntax for declaring a structure in C++:

```
struct structTage {
    < list of members >
};
```

Examine the following examples of declaring structures:

```
struct complex {
    double real;
    double imag;
};

struct personalType {
    char name[31];
```

```
    char title[21];
    char address[31];
    char city[16];
    char state[3];
    char zip[11];
    unsigned age;
    double weight;
};
```

Translating Pascal records into C++ structures employs the following general form:

Pascal:

```
recordType = RECORD
    field1 : type1;
    field2 : type2;
    ...
    fieldN : typeN;
END;
```

C++:

```
struct recordType {
    type1 field1;
    type2 field2;
    ...
    typeN fieldN;
};
```

After you define a struct type, you can use that type to declare variables such as:

```
complex c1, c2, c3;
personalType me, you, dawgNamedBoo;
```

You can also declare structured variables when you define the structure itself, as follows:

```
struct complex {
    double real;
    double imag;
} c1, c2, c3;
```

Interestingly, C++ enables you to declare untagged structures. With such declarations, you can declare structured variables without defining a name for their structure. For example, the following structure definition declares variables c1, c2, and c3, but omits the name of the structure:

```
struct {
     double real;
     double imag;
} c1, c2, c3;
```

> Note the syntactic differences between C and C++. C requires you to use the `struct` keyword to declare structured variables in the same way it requires you to use the `enum` keyword to declare enumerated variables. Again, C++ designers consider this to be redundant. They also consider the struct type, like enum, to be a fully-defined, user-defined type known to the compiler. If you look at C code, notice the `struct` keyword that is also used in declaring variables that are structures.

C++ enables you to declare and initialize a structured variable. The syntax is cleaner than that of Turbo Pascal:

```
complex c = { 1.0, -8.3 };
personalType me = { "Namir Shammas", "author", "4814 Mill Park",
                    "Biscaine", "MI", "48104", 38, 190.5 };
```

As in Pascal, accessing the members of a structure uses the dot operator:

```
c1.real = 12.45;
c1.imag = 34.56;
c2.real = 23.4 / c1.real;
c2.imag = 0.98 * c1.imag;

me.age = 38;
you.weight += 2; // gained 2 pounds!
```

What about using a pointer to a structure? In Pascal you must first use the ^ operator to access the structure as a whole and then apply the dot operator to access a specific field. In C++ the syntax is cleaner and uses the -> operator to access the sought member of a structure. The following code fragment compares the two languages:

```
{ Pascal }
TYPE PascalPtr = ^complex;

PascalPtr = @PascalComplexVar;
PascalPtr^.x := 10;

// C++
complex *cppPtr = &cppComplexVar;
cppPtr->x = 10;
```

The next program uses structures and their pointers and illustrates the following:

1. Using structures.

2. Using an array of structures.

3. Using pointers to individual structures.

4. Using pointers to an array of structures.

Listing 9.3 contains the source code for the LST09_03.PAS program, which prompts you to enter four coordinates. The first three coordinates are reference values, and the fourth is a search coordinate. The program calculates the closest and farthest reference coordinates from the search coordinate.

Listing 9.3. Source code for the LST09_03.PAS program.

```
Program Test_Records;

Uses Crt;

CONST
  MAX_POINTS = 3;

TYPE

  TCoord = RECORD
    X : REAL;
    Y : REAL;
  END;

  PCoord = ^TCoord;

  TPoints = ARRAY [1..MAX_POINTS] OF TCoord;
  PPoints = ^TPoints;

VAR
  Coord : TCoord;
  CoordPtr : PCoord;
  Points : TPoints;
  PointsPtr : PPoints;
  MinDistance, MaxDistance, Distance : REAL;
  i, Imax, Imin : INTEGER;

BEGIN
```

continues

267

Listing 9.3. continued

```
ClrScr;

FOR i := 1 TO MAX_POINTS DO BEGIN
  WRITE('Enter X coordinate for point # ', i, ' : ');
  READLN(Points[i].X);
  WRITE('Enter Y coordinate for point # ', i, ' : ');
  READLN(Points[i].Y);
  WRITELN;
END;
WRITELN;

WRITE('Enter X coordinate for search point : ');
READLN(Coord.X);
WRITE('Enter Y coordinate for search point : ');
READLN(Coord.Y);
WRITELN;

{ initialize the minimum distance variable with
  a very large value }
MinDistance := 1.0E+30;
{ initialize the maximum distance variable with
  a negative value }
MaxDistance := -1.0;

CoordPtr := @Coord;
PointsPtr := @Points;

FOR i := 1 TO MAX_POINTS DO BEGIN
  Distance := SQRT(SQR(CoordPtr^.X - PointsPtr^[i].X) +
                   SQR(CoordPtr^.Y - PointsPtr^[i].Y));
  { update minimum distance? }
  IF Distance < MinDistance THEN BEGIN
    Imin := i;
    MinDistance := Distance;
  END;
  { update maximum distance? }
  IF Distance > MaxDistance THEN BEGIN
    Imax := i;
    MaxDistance := Distance;
  END;
END;

WRITELN('Point number ', Imin,
        ' is the closest to the search point');
WRITELN('Point number ', Imax,
        ' is the farthest from the search point');
```

```
END.
```

Listing 9.4 shows the source code for the LST09_04.CPP program.

Listing 9.4. Source code for the LST09_04.CPP program.

```
// C++ program that demonstrates using a simple structure

#include <iostream.h>
#include <conio.h>
#include <math.h>

const int MAX_POINTS = 3;

struct TCoord {
    double X;
    double Y;
};

typedef TCoord TPoints[MAX_POINTS];

inline double sqr(double x)
{
  return x * x;
}

main()
{
  TCoord Coord, *CoordPtr = &Coord;
  TPoints Points, *PointsPtr = &Points;

  double MinDistance, MaxDistance, Distance;
  int i, Imax, Imin;

  clrscr();

  for (i = 0; i < MAX_POINTS; i++) {
    cout << "Enter X coordinate for point # " << i << " : ";
    cin >> Points[i].X;
    cout << "Enter Y coordinate for point # " << i << " : ";
    cin >> Points[i].Y;
    cout << '\n';
  }
  cout << '\n';

  cout << "Enter X coordinate for search point : ";
  cin >> Coord.X;
  cout << "Enter Y coordinate for search point : ";
```

continues

269

Listing 9.4. continued

```
cin >> Coord.Y;
cout << '\n';


// initialize the minimum distance variable with
// a very large value
MinDistance = 1.0E+30;
// initialize the maximum distance variable with
// a negative value
MaxDistance = -1.0;

for (i = 0; i < MAX_POINTS; i++) {
  Distance = sqrt(sqr(CoordPtr->X - PointsPtr[i]->X) +
                  sqr(CoordPtr->Y - PointsPtr[i]->Y));
  // update minimum distance?
  if (Distance < MinDistance) {
    Imin = i;
    MinDistance = Distance;
  }
  // update maximum distance?
  if (Distance > MaxDistance) {
    Imax = i;
    MaxDistance = Distance;
  }
}

cout << "Point number " << Imin <<
        " is the closest to the search point\n"
     << "Point number " << Imax <<
        " is the farthest from the search point\n";

return 0;
}
```

Compare the two versions, and notice the following differences in data type:

Pascal	C++	Purpose
TCoord	TCoord	models a coordinate
PCoord		pointer type to TCoord
TPoints	TPoints	array of TCoord
PPoints		pointer type to TPoints

The Pascal version declares variables that use the types TCoord, PCoord, TPoints, and PPoints. The C++ version declares variables and pointers that use the TCoord and TPoints types.

Both program versions access the X and Y members of structure TCoord using the Coord.X and Coord.Y expressions. Similarly, both versions access the X and Y members of array Points using the Points[i].X and Points[i].Y expressions.

When you use pointers to access members of structures, the syntax used is different. For example, to access the X member of variable Coord using pointer CoordPtr, the Turbo Pascal version uses CoordPtr^.X , and the C++ version uses CoordPtr->X. Similarly, to access the X member of the I'th element of Points using the pointer PointsPtr, the Turbo Pascal version uses PointsPtr^[i].X, and the Turbo C++ version uses PointsPtr[i]->X.

Unions

C++ unions resemble Pascal variant records without the fixed part. The general syntax for unions is:

```
union unionTag {
    type1 member1;
    type2 member2;
    ...
    typeN memberN;
};
```

The size of the unionTag type is equal to the size of the largest member in the union. An example of declaring a union follows:

```
union Long {
    unsigned mWord[2];
    long mLong;
};
```

The union Long has two members: the two-element array mWord and the long-typed mLong member. Unions offer an easy alternative for quick data conversion. Unions were more significant in past decades when the price of memory was much higher and using unions to consolidate memory was feasible.

The next program uses unions to add two complex numbers. You choose whether to use Cartesian or polar coordinates. You can enter the complex number, using either coordinate, and obtain the result in the corresponding coordinate system. Listing 9.5 shows the source code for the LST09_05.PAS program.

271

Listing 9.5. Source code for the LST09_05.PAS program.

```pascal
Program Test_Variant_Records;

{$V-}
Uses CRT;

{ Turbo Pascal program that demonstrates variant record types }

TYPE Complex = RECORD
          CASE BOOLEAN OF
              TRUE  : (xcoord, ycoord : REAL);
              FALSE : (angle, modulus : REAL);
          END;

VAR a, b, c : Complex;
    rectangular : BOOLEAN;
    ch : CHAR;

PROCEDURE AddComplex;

VAR x, y : REAL;

BEGIN
    IF rectangular THEN BEGIN
        c.xcoord := a.xcoord + b.xcoord;
        c.ycoord := a.ycoord + b.ycoord
    END
    ELSE BEGIN
        x := a.modulus * cos(a.angle) + b.modulus * cos(b.angle);
        y := a.modulus * sin(a.angle) + b.modulus * sin(b.angle);
        c.angle := arctan(y/x);
        c.modulus := SQRT(x*x + y*y);
    END;
END;

PROCEDURE GetInput;

BEGIN
    WRITE('Use Rectangular or Polar coordinates? (R/P) ');
    ch := Upcase(ReadKey); WRITELN(ch); WRITELN;
    IF ch <> 'P' THEN rectangular := TRUE
                 ELSE rectangular := FALSE;
    IF rectangular THEN BEGIN
        WRITE('Enter first complex number (x y coord) : ');
        READLN(a.xcoord, a.ycoord); WRITELN;
        WRITE('Enter second complex number (x y coord) : ');
        READLN(b.xcoord, b.ycoord); WRITELN;
```

```
        END
        ELSE BEGIN
            WRITE('Enter first complex number (modulus angle) : ');
            READLN(a.modulus, a.angle); WRITELN;
            WRITE('Enter second complex number (modulus angle) : ');
            READLN(b.modulus, b.angle); WRITELN;
        END;

END;


PROCEDURE ShowResults;

BEGIN
    IF rectangular THEN
        WRITELN('Result = (',c.xcoord,') + (',c.ycoord,')')
    ELSE
        WRITELN('Result = ',c.modulus,' @ ',c.angle,' radians');

END;


BEGIN
    ClrScr;
    WRITELN('PROGRAM TO ADD COMPLEX NUMBERS':50);
    WRITELN; WRITELN;

    REPEAT

        GetInput;
        AddComplex;
        ShowResults;

        WRITELN; WRITELN;
        WRITE('Add more numbers? Y/N ');
        ch := UpCase(ReadKey);
        WRITELN; WRITELN;

    UNTIL ch <> 'Y';

END.
```

The Turbo Pascal listing declares the Complex type as a variant record. The program also declares the AddComplex, GetInput, and ShowResults procedures. I use global variables to eliminate parameters from these procedures and simplify the code.

273

The following C++ program declares the TRect and TPolar structures and uses them in the declaration of union Complex. This version also declares the addComplex, getInput, and showResults functions.

The Turbo C++ program uses global variables that are of type Complex and pointers to these variables to illustrate the use of both variables and pointers in accessing members of unions. The getInput and showResults functions use the Complex-typed variables a, b, and c to access the union members. These variables use the dot operator to access union members rect and polar. The addComplex function uses pointers ap, bp, and cp to access union members rect and polar. Notice that accessing members of a union in C++ uses the same syntax as accessing members of structures.

Listing 9.6. Source code for the LST09_06.CPP program.

```
/* C++ program that demonstrates variant record types using
   the union structure                                      */

#include <iostream.h>
#include <conio.h>
#include <math.h>

struct TRect {
   double xcoord;
   double ycoord;
};

struct TPolar {
   double angle;
   double modulus;
};

union Complex {
   TRect rect;
   TPolar polar;
};

enum Boolean { true, false };

// declare global variables
Complex a, b, c;
Complex *ap = &a, *bp = &b, *cp = &c;
Boolean rectangular;
char ch;
```

```cpp
// declare prototype of user-defined functions
void getInput(), addComplex(), showResults();

main()
{

    clrscr();
    cout << "\t\tPROGRAM TO ADD COMPLEX NUMBERS\n\n\n";

    do {

        getInput();
        addComplex();
        showResults();

        cout << "\n\n";
        cout << "Add more numbers? Y/N ";
        ch = getche();
        if (ch >= 'a' && ch <= 'z') ch += 'A' - 'a';
        cout << "\n\n";

    } while (ch == 'Y');

    return 0;

}


void addComplex()
{

  double x, y;

  if (rectangular == true) {
      cp->rect.xcoord = ap->rect.xcoord + bp->rect.xcoord;
      cp->rect.ycoord = ap->rect.ycoord + bp->rect.ycoord;
  }
  else {
      x = ap->polar.modulus * cos(ap->polar.angle) +
          bp->polar.modulus * cos(bp->polar.angle);
      y = ap->polar.modulus * sin(ap->polar.angle) +
          bp->polar.modulus * sin(bp->polar.angle);
      cp->polar.angle = atan(y/x);
      cp->polar.modulus = sqrt(x*x + y*y);
  }
}
```

continues

275

Listing 9.6. continued

```
void getInput()
{
    cout << "Use Rectangular or Polar coordinates? (R/P) ";
    ch = getche();
    if (ch >= 'a' && ch <= 'z') ch += 'A' - 'a';
    cout << "\n\n";

    if (ch != 'P')
       rectangular = true;
    else
       rectangular = false;

    if (rectangular == true)  {
        cout << "Enter first complex number (x y coord) : ";
        cin >> a.rect.xcoord >> a.rect.ycoord;
        cout << "\n";
        cout << "Enter second complex number (x y coord) : ";
        cin >> b.rect.xcoord >> b.rect.ycoord;
        cout << "\n";
    }
    else {
        cout << "Enter first complex number (modulus angle) : ";
        cin >> a.polar.modulus >> a.polar.angle;
        cout << "\n";
        cout << "Enter second complex number (modulus angle) : ";
        cin >> b.polar.modulus >> b.polar.angle;
        cout << "\n";
    }

}

void showResults()
{
    if (rectangular == true)
        cout << "Result = (" << c.rect.xcoord << ", "
             << c.rect.ycoord << ")\n";
    else
        cout << "Result = " << c.polar.modulus << " @ "
             << c.polar.angle << " radians\n";

}
```

Far Pointers

The architecture of the Intel 80x86 processors uses 64K segments. This means that the pointers I have used so far store only the offset address to the currently used data segment. What happens when you want to access an address that lies outside the current data segment? You must use far pointers. Such pointers store both the segment and offset addresses of a memory location and consequently require more memory. This is the reason not every C++ and C pointer is a far pointer. Interestingly, all Turbo Pascal pointers are far pointers. Therefore, when you translate Turbo Pascal programs that tap into specific far addresses and move data between these addresses, take into account the difference in pointer types.

To declare a pointer as far, you must place the far keyword between the pointer's access type and its name:

```
type far *farPointer;
```

To use a far pointer, you must assign a long-typed address to it:

```
farPointer = (type far *) address;
```

The following program writes directly to the color video (assuming you have a color video adapter) and fills the screen with the letter you type. The program fills the screen with a different letter, using a different color, until you press the letter *Q*.

This C++ program declares the VIDEO_ADDR macro, which stores the long-typed address 0xB8000000, the base address of the color video adapter. The program declares the pointer screenPtr as follows:

```
int far *screenPtr;
```

Using the following statement, the program assigns the base address of the adapter to the screenPtr pointer:

```
screenPtr = (int far *) VIDEO_ADDR;
```

The following statement enables the screenPtr pointer to write directly to the screen:

```
*(screenPtr + i) = ch ¦ attr;
```

Listing 9.7 shows the source code for the LST09_07.CPP program.

Listing 9.7. Source code for the LST09_07.CPP program.

```cpp
/* C++ program that uses a far pointer to write directly to
   a color video screen.
*/

#include <iostream.h>
#include <conio.h>

#define VIDEO_ADDR 0xB8000000 // address of a color monitor
#define DISPLAY_ATTR 0x0100

main()
{
  int far *screenPtr;
  int i;
  long attr = DISPLAY_ATTR;
  const int BYTES = 2000;
  char ch;

  clrscr();
  cout << "Press any key (Q to exit)";

  while ((ch = getche()) != 'Q') {
    clrscr();
    screenPtr = (int far *) VIDEO_ADDR;
    for (i = 0; i < BYTES; i++)
      *(screenPtr + i) = ch ¦ attr;
    attr += 0x0100;
  }

}
```

Summary

This chapter introduced you to user-defined data types and covered the following topics:

- You can use typedef statements to create alias types of existing types and define array types. The general syntax for using typedef is:

  ```cpp
  typedef knownType newType;
  ```

- Enumerated data types enable you to declare unique identifiers that represent a collection of logically related constants. The general syntax for declaring an enumerated type in C++ is:

```
enum enumType { <list of enumerated identifiers> };
```

- Structures enable you to define a new type that logically groups several fields or members. These members can be predefined types or other structures. The general syntax for declaring a structure in C++ is:

```
struct structTage {
    < list of members >
};
```

- Unions are a form of variant structures. The general syntax for unions is:

```
union unionTag {
    type1 member1;
    type2 member2;
    ...
    typeN memberN;
};
```

- Far pointers store both the segment and offset address of a memory location. Therefore, far pointers access data outside the current data segment. To declare a pointer as far, you must place the far keyword between the pointer's access type and its name:

```
type far *farPointer;
```

To use a far pointer, you must assign a long-typed address to it:

```
farPointer = (type far *) address;
```

ADVANCED
FUNCTIONS

This chapter discusses advanced uses of functions (such as passing strings, pointers, arrays, and structures). More practical functions, such as those that sort data, also are covered. Also in this chapter, you'll learn about the following topics:

- passing arrays as function arguments

- passing strings as function arguments

- passing structures as function arguments

- passing reference parameters

- accessing command-line arguments

- pointers to functions

- functions with varying argument lists

Passing Arrays as Arguments

When you write a C++ function that passes an array parameter, you need to declare that parameter as a pointer to the basic type of the array. The general syntax for prototyping such a function is:

```
basicType array;
returnType function(basicType*, <other parameter types>);
```

The general syntax for defining the preceding function is:

```
returnType function(basicType arrParam*, <other parameters>)
```

or:

```
returnType function(basicType arrParam[], <other parameters>)
```

C++ enables you to declare the array parameter by using a pair of empty brackets. C++ programmers use this form less frequently than the explicit pointer form, even though the brackets actually enhance code readability.

The following program examples use a function with a parameter that accesses an array. These programs fill a 100-element array with random numbers that range between 0 and 999, inclusive. The median function searches the array for the largest and smallest values. Using these two results, the function calculates the median value. Listing 10.1 is the source code for the Pascal program. Listing 10.2 is the source code for the C++ program.

Listing 10.1. Source code for the LST10_01.PAS program.

```
Program Pass_Array;

{ Turbo Pascal program that passes an array to a function to
  calculate the median value of the array elements. The array
  itself is generated as random numbers.
}

CONST MAX = 100;

TYPE intArray = ARRAY [1..MAX] OF WORD;

VAR data : intArray;
    i : WORD;
```

```
FUNCTION median(x      : intArray;  { input }
                count : WORD        { input }) : WORD;

VAR big, small : WORD;
    j : WORD;

BEGIN
    big := x[1];
    small := x[1];

    FOR j := 2 TO MAX DO BEGIN
        IF big < x[j] THEN big := x[j];
        IF small > x[j] THEN small := x[j]
    END;

    median := small + (big - small) div 2;

END;

BEGIN
    randomize;
    { fill array with random values }
    FOR i := 1 TO MAX DO
        data[i] := Trunc(1000 * random);

    WRITELN;
    WRITE('The median of ',MAX,' random numbers = ');
    WRITELN(median(data, MAX));
    WRITELN; WRITELN;

END.
```

Listing 10.2. Source code for the LST10_02.CPP program.

```
/* C++ program that passes an array to a function to
   calculate the median value of the array elements. The array
   itself is generated as random numbers.
*/

#include <iostream.h>
#include <stdlib.h>

const unsigned MAX = 100;
```

continues

Listing 10.2. continued

```
typedef unsigned int word;
typedef word intArray[MAX];

main()
{

    intArray data;
    word i;
    word median(word*, word);

    randomize();
    // fill array with random values
    for (i = 0; i < MAX; i++)
        data[i] = random(1000);

    cout << "\nThe median of "
        << MAX
        << " random numbers = "
        << median(data, MAX);

    return 0;
}

word median(word x[], word count)

{
    word big = x[0], small = x[0];
    word j;

    for (j = 1; j < count; j++)  {
        if (big < x[j])  big = x[j];
        // use pointer form
        if (small > *(x+j))  small = *(x+j);
    }

        return (small + (big - small) / 2);

}
```

The Turbo C++ program declares the following prototype for function median in function main:

```
word median(word*, word);
```

in which word is a typedef'd alias for the predefined type unsigned. The program also declares the heading for the median function as follows:

```
word median(word x[]222, word count)
```

Using empty brackets absolves you from declaring a specific array size. This feature enables you to write functions that handle arrays of varying sizes. The new Borland Pascal 7.0 supports the open array feature that is similar to what you see in the C++ version of the median function. The older Turbo Pascal versions supported untyped parameters that enabled you to implement similar features. However, using untyped parameters requires that you be quite familiar with using pointers.

The median function initializes the big and small local variables to x[0]. The main function calls the median function in the following statement:

```
cout << "\nThe median of "
     << MAX
     << " random numbers = "
     << median(data, MAX);
```

The first argument of median is data, the name of the array (which is also the pointer to the array).

In the next program, I present a new Turbo C++ version that uses the following heading for median:

```
word median(word *x, word count)
```

In addition, the statements in median use and increment the x pointer to access the various elements of the array argument. Because main passes a copy of the address of the array to median, incrementing the pointer does not affect the address of the argument in main.

Listing 10.3. Source code for the LST10_03.CPP program.

```
/* C++ program that passes an array to a function to
   calculate the median value of the array elements.  The array
   itself is generated as random numbers.  This version makes
   better use of pointers in function median.
*/

#include <iostream.h>
#include <stdlib.h>

const unsigned MAX = 100;

typedef unsigned int word;
```

continues

Listing 10.3. continued

```
main()
{

    word data[MAX];
    word i;
    word median(word*, word);

    randomize();
    // fill array with random values
    for (i = 0; i < MAX; i++)
        data[i] = random(1000);

    cout << "\nThe median of "
         << MAX
         << " random numbers = "
         << median(data, MAX);

    return 0;

}

word median(word *x, word count)

{
    word big = *x, small = *x;
    word j;

    for (j = 1; j < count; j++)  {
        x++; // increment pointer address
        if (big < *x)  big = *x;
        if (small > *x)  small = *x;
    }

    return (small + (big - small) / 2);

}
```

Using Strings as Arguments

Because C++ treats strings as arrays of characters, the rules for passing arrays as arguments to functions also apply to strings. The following programs are simple examples for a string

function that converts the characters of its arguments to uppercase. Listing 10.4 contains the source code for the LST10_04.PAS program. Listing 10.5 shows the source code for the LST10_05.CPP program.

Listing 10.4. Source code for the LST10_04.PAS program.

```
Program Pass_String;

{$V-}

{ Turbo Pascal program that passes a string to a function to
  return the uppercase version of the string.
}

TYPE STRING80 = STRING[80];
     STRING255 = STRING[255];

VAR strng : STRING255;
    freq : WORD;

FUNCTION uppercase(strng : STRING80) : STRING80;

VAR i : BYTE;

BEGIN

    { loop to convert each character to uppercase }
    FOR i := 1 TO Length(strng) DO
        strng[i] := UpCase(strng[i]);

    uppercase := strng;

END;

BEGIN
    REPEAT
        WRITE('Enter string : ');
        READLN(strng);
        IF strng <> '' THEN BEGIN
            WRITELN(uppercase(strng));
            WRITELN;
        END;
    UNTIL strng = '';
    WRITELN; WRITELN;
END.
```

Listing 10.5. Source code for the LST10_05.CPP program.

```
/* C++ program that passes a string to a function to
   return the uppercase version of the string.
*/

#include <iostream.h>
typedef unsigned int word;

char* uppercase(char*);

main()
{
    char strng[256];
    word freq;

    do {
        cout << "Enter string : ";
        cin.getline(strng, 255);
        if (*strng != '\0')  {
            cout << uppercase(strng) << "\n";
        }
    } while (*strng != '\0');

    cout << "\n\n";
}


char* uppercase(char strng[])

{

    int count = 0;
    int ascii_shift = 'A' - 'a';
    char copystr[256];
    char* strptr = copystr;

    do {
        copystr[count++] = strng[count];
    } while (strng[count] != '\0');
    copystr[count] = '\0';

    count = 0; /* reset counter variable */
    /* loop to convert each character to uppercase */
    while ( *strptr != '\0') {
        if ((*strptr  >= 'A' && *strptr <= 'Z') ||
            (*strptr  >= 'a' && *strptr <= 'z'))
            *strptr += ascii_shift;
```

```
        count++;
        strptr++;
}

    strptr -= count;

    return strptr;

}
```

Notice the following in the Turbo C++ version:

1. The uppercase function needs no data type identifier that parallels the STRING80 type in the Turbo Pascal program version.

2. The prototype for the uppercase function is:

```
char* uppercase(char*);
```

The preceding prototype indicates the single parameter is a pointer to a character, needed to access a string. The prototype also shows that the function returns a pointer to a character. This pointer accesses the resulting string.

3. The two program versions invoke the uppercase function in a similar way, even though each program version declares the uppercase function differently. In the Turbo Pascal version, it is:

```
WRITELN(uppercase(strng));
```

and in the Turbo C++ version, it is:

```
cout << uppercase(strng) << "\n";
```

4. In the Turbo C++ program version, the uppercase function uses the strng identifier as a pointer to scroll through the characters of the string argument. When the pointer reaches the end of the string, you need to reset its address to the original value. The two ways to accomplish this task are as follows:

   • Use a local pointer to store the base address of the string argument. Then return that local pointer as the function's result.

   • Utilize a local variable to obtain the string length. After the while loop finishes iterating, decrement the pointer address by the string length. This operation resets the pointer address to the base address of the string argument. Return the pointer. I used this solution in the preceding Turbo C++ program.

Using Structures as Arguments

Like Pascal, C++ enables you to pass structures either by value or by reference. This section demonstrates passing structures by value. In the next section, I'll show you how to pass structures by reference. The structure's type appears in the function prototype and heading in a manner similar to that of predefined types.

Listing 10.6 is a simple example. This program calculates the distance between two points in space. The `coordinates` record structure assists in logically relating the three-dimensional coordinates of a point in space. The program calculates the distance by using the `distance` function. This function takes two coordinates-typed parameters and yields a floating-point result. Listing 10.6 is the source code for LST10_06.PAS, the Pascal version of the program. Listing 10.7 is the source code for LST10_07.CPP, the C++ version of the program.

Listing 10.6. Source code for the LST10_06.PAS program.

```
Program Pass_Structure;

Uses CRT;
{$V-}

{ Turbo Pascal program that passes a record to a function to
  calculate the distance between two space coordinates.
}

TYPE
  coordinates = RECORD
      X,
      Y,
      Z : REAL;
  END;

VAR coord1, coord2 : coordinates;


FUNCTION distance(coord1, coord2 : coordinates) : REAL;

VAR deltaX, deltaY, deltaZ : REAL;
BEGIN
```

```
    deltaX := coord1.X - coord2.X;
    deltaY := coord1.Y - coord2.Y;
    deltaZ := coord1.Z - coord2.Z;

    distance := SQRT(deltaX * deltaX +
                     deltaY * deltaY +
                     deltaZ * deltaZ);
END;

BEGIN

    ClrScr;

    WITH coord1 DO BEGIN
        WRITE('Enter X-Y-Z coordinates of first object : ');
        READLN(X,Y,Z);
    END;

    WITH coord2 DO BEGIN
        WRITE('Enter X-Y-Z coordinates of second object : ');
        READLN(X,Y,Z);
    END;

    WRITE('Distance between objects = ',distance(coord1,coord2));
    WRITELN; WRITELN

END.
```

Listing 10.7. Source code for the LST10_07.CPP program.

```
/* C++ program that passes a record to a function to
   calculate the distance between two space coordinates.
*/

#include <iostream.h>
#include <math.h>
#include <conio.h>

struct coordinates {
        double X;
        double Y;
        double Z;
};
```

continues

Listing 10.7. continued

```
double distance(coordinates, coordinates);

main()
{
    coordinates coord1, coord2;

    clrscr();

    cout << "Enter X-Y-Z coordinates of first object : ";
    cin >> coord1.X >> coord1.Y >> coord1.Z;

    cout << "Enter X-Y-Z coordinates of second object : ";
    cin >> coord2.X >> coord2.Y >> coord2.Z;

    cout << "\nDistance between objects = "
         << distance(coord1, coord2) << "\n\n\n";

    return 0;

}


double distance(coordinates coord1, coordinates coord2)

{

    double deltaX, deltaY, deltaZ;

    deltaX = coord1.X - coord2.X;
    deltaY = coord1.Y - coord2.Y;
    deltaZ = coord1.Z - coord2.Z;

    return  sqrt(deltaX * deltaX +
                 deltaY * deltaY +
                 deltaZ * deltaZ);
}
```

The two preceding programs code the function distance in a very similar way. This similarity stems from the fact that translating number-crunching code between Pascal and C++ requires less effort than translating other types of code.

Passing Arguments by Reference

C++ enables you to write functions with parameters that pass arguments by reference. These parameters resemble the VAR parameters in Pascal routines. C++ offers two ways to implement such parameters, pointers, and formal reference parameters. (C has no parallel to reference parameters.) The next sections present functions that pass various kinds of data types by reference.

Passing Simple Variables and Arrays

Listing 10.8 is a program that passes both a simple variable and an array by reference using pointers. This program basically sorts the elements of an array and performs the following steps:

- creates an array of integers in a descending order

- sorts the array to arrange its elements in ascending order

- displays the array elements

Listing 10.8 is the source code for the LST10_08.PAS program. This example program uses the following routines:

1. The InitializeArray procedure initializes the array. The routine has one VAR parameter, which passes by reference the arguments for the initialized array.

2. The SwapThem procedure swaps two integers. The routine uses two VAR parameters to pass the arguments for the swapped numbers.

3. The ShellSort procedure sorts an array using the Shell-Metzner method. The routine has one VAR parameter, which passes the argument for the array to be sorted.

4. The DisplayArray procedure displays an array. The routine has one VAR parameter, which passes the argument for the array to be displayed.

293

Listing 10.8. Source code for the LST10_08.PAS program.

```pascal
Program Pass_and_Modify_Array;

Uses CRT;

{ Program will test the speed of sorting an integer array.
 The program will create a sorted array (in descending order)
 and then sort it in the reverse order.
}

CONST ARRAY_SIZE = 1000;

TYPE numbers = ARRAY[1..ARRAY_SIZE] OF WORD;

VAR Ch : CHAR;
    A : numbers;

PROCEDURE InitializeArray(VAR A : numbers);
{ Procedure to initialize array }

VAR i : WORD;

BEGIN
    WRITELN('Initializing integer array');
    WRITELN;
    FOR i := 1 TO ARRAY_SIZE DO
        A[i] := ARRAY_SIZE - i;
END;


PROCEDURE SwapThem(VAR X, Y : WORD);
{ procedure to swap elements X and Y }

VAR temporary : WORD;

BEGIN
    temporary := X;
    X := Y;
    Y := temporary;
END;


PROCEDURE ShellSort(VAR A : numbers) ;
{ Procedure to perform a Shell-Metzner sorting }

VAR offset, i, j : WORD;
    sorted : BOOLEAN;
```

```
BEGIN
    offset := ARRAY_SIZE;
    WHILE offset > 1 DO BEGIN
        offset := offset DIV 2;
        REPEAT
            sorted := TRUE;
            FOR j := 1 TO (ARRAY_SIZE - offset) DO BEGIN
                i := j + offset;
                IF A[i] < A[j] THEN BEGIN
                    SwapThem(A[i],A[j]);
                    sorted := FALSE;
                END;
            END; { FOR j }
        UNTIL sorted;
    END; { End of while-loop }
END;

PROCEDURE DisplayArray(VAR A : numbers);
{ Display array members }

VAR i : WORD;
BEGIN
    FOR i := 1 TO ARRAY_SIZE DO
        WRITE(A[i]:4);
    WRITELN
END;

BEGIN { Main }
    InitializeArray(A);
    WRITELN('Beginning to sort press <cr>');
    Ch := ReadKey; WRITELN;
    ShellSort(A);
    WRITELN('Finished sorting!');
    DisplayArray(A);
END.
```

Listing 10.9 is the source code for LST10_09.CPP, the C++ version of the preceding program example. This version uses functions that parallel the Pascal functions in Listing 10.8. I wrote the names of the Turbo C++ functions in lowercase. Notice that the C++ functions use parameters that are pointers to the word type (a typedef of the unsigned int predefined type). Such pointers effectively pass a single variable and an array by reference. Notice that although the Turbo C++ version declares the numbers array type, the parameters of the initializearray, shellsort, and displayarray functions use the word* pointer type.

Listing 10.9. Source code for the LST10_09.CPP program.

```
/*
    Program will test the speed of sorting an integer array.
    The program will create a sorted array (in descending order)
    and then sort it in the reverse order.
*/

#include <iostream.h>
#include <conio.h>

enum boolean { TRUE, FALSE };
typedef unsigned char byte;
typedef unsigned int word;

const unsigned ARRAY_SIZE = 1000;

// define 'numbers' as an array-type identifier
typedef word numbers[ARRAY_SIZE];

// declare prototype of void functions used
void initializearray(word*);
void swapthem(word*, word*);
void shellsort(word*);
void displayarray(word*);

main()
{
    numbers A;

    initializearray(A);
    cout << "Beginning to sort press <cr>";
    getche(); cout << "\n";
    shellsort(A);
    cout << "Finished sorting!\n";
    displayarray(A);

    return 0;
}

void initializearray(word *A)
// routine to initialize array

{
    int i;

    cout << "Initializing integer array" n;
    for (i = 0 ; i < ARRAY_SIZE; i++)
        *(A++) = ARRAY_SIZE - i + 1;
```

```
}


void swapthem(word *x, word *y)
/* routine that swaps elements x and y */

{

    int temporary = *x;

    *x = *y;
    *y = temporary;
}


void shellsort(word *A)
/* routine to perform a Shell-Metzner sorting */

{
    int offset, i, j;
    boolean sorted;

    offset = ARRAY_SIZE;
    while (offset > 1)  {
        offset /=  2;
        do {
            sorted = TRUE;
            for (j = 0; j < (ARRAY_SIZE - offset); j++)  {
                i = j + offset;
                if (*(A+i) < *(A+j))  {
                    swapthem((A+i),(A+j));
                    sorted = FALSE;
                }
            }
        } while (sorted == FALSE);
    }
}

void displayarray(word *A)
// Display array members

{
    int i;

    for (i = 0; i < ARRAY_SIZE; i++) {
        cout.width(4);
        cout << *(A+i);
    }
    cout << "\n";
}
```

I translated the Numbers-type parameter in the Turbo Pascal version into word* pointer types. Similarly, I translated the VAR parameters of the SwapThem procedure into word* pointers.

Passing Strings by Reference

The following program examples pass strings by formal reference. These examples present a new version of the uppercase function; the uppercase routine does not return a result, and yet it can still alter its arguments. Listing 10.10 is the source code for the LST10_10.PAS program. This Turbo Pascal version uses a VAR parameter to pass STRING80-typed arguments. In fact, the program uses the V- compiler directive to relax the type checking on string parameters. Consequently, the uppercase procedure in the Turbo Pascal version can handle strings of any size and type. The program prompts you to enter a string with lowercase characters. Then, the program converts your input into uppercase and displays it. Listing 10.11 is the source code for the Turbo C++ version of the program, LST10_11.CPP.

Listing 10.10. Source code for the LST10_10.PAS program.

```
Program Pass_and_Modify_String;

{$V-}

{ Turbo Pascal program that passes a string to a procedure to
  return the uppercase version of the string.  The string is
  passed by reference.
}

TYPE STRING80 = STRING[80];
     STRING255 = STRING[255];

VAR strng : STRING80;


PROCEDURE uppercase(VAR strng : STRING80 { in/out });

VAR i : BYTE;

BEGIN
```

```
    { loop to convert each character to uppercase }
    FOR i := 1 TO Length(strng) DO
        strng[i] := UpCase(strng[i]);

END;


BEGIN
    REPEAT
        WRITE('Enter string : ');
        READLN(strng);
        IF strng <> '' THEN BEGIN
            uppercase(strng);
            WRITELN(strng);
            WRITELN;
        END;
    UNTIL strng = '';
    WRITELN; WRITELN;
END.
```

Listing 10.11. Source code for the LST10_11.CPP program.

```
/* C++ program that passes a string to a procedure to
   return the uppercase version of the string.  The string is
   passed by reference.

 */

#include <iostream.h>

void uppercase(char*);

main()
{
    char dummy[81], *strng = dummy;

    do {
        cout << "Enter string : ";
        cin.getline(strng, 80);
        if (*strng != '\0')  {
            uppercase(strng);
            cout << strng << "\n";
        }
    } while (*strng != '\0');
    cout << "\n\n";
}
```

continues

299

Listing 10.11. continued

```
void uppercase(char *strng)

{
    int ascii_shift = 'A' - 'a';

    /* loop to convert each character to uppercase */
    while ( *strng != '\0')
        if (*strng >= 'a' && *strng <= 'z')
            *(strng++) += ascii_shift;
        else
            strng++;

}
```

Examine the Turbo C++ program version. The program uses the following function heading:

```
void uppercase(char *strng)
```

The function passes the base address of the string-typed arguments and returns a void. Notice that the statements in the function increment the address stored in the strng pointer and do not reset that pointer to the initial base address of the string argument. Does this lack of action cause the cout << statement to emit jumbled text? No, because the call to uppercase function passes a copy of the address of strng as defined in function main. When the uppercase function alters the copy of the address, the original address of the argument itself remains intact. This feature enables you to pass a string by reference (informal reference, to be more exact) using a pointer.

Passing Structures by Reference

In this section, I present an example that passes a structure by formal reference. I will make the Turbo C++ version pass the structures as a formal reference parameter instead of using a pointer. The example shows how you can alter the fields (or *data members*, as they are called in C++) of a structure inside a function.

The program fills a 100-element array with random numbers and calculates the mean and standard deviation of the data in that array. Both the Pascal and C++ program versions use a record structure, bastat, that contains three floating-point fields: mean, standard deviation, and degrees of freedom (which is equal to the number of data points minus one). The program performs the statistical calculations inside the basic_stat routine. This routine passes a bastat record structure by reference, enabling the caller to retrieve the statistical results. Listing 10.12 is the source code for the LST10_12.PAS program. Listing 10.13 is the source code for the LST10_13.CPP program.

Listing 10.12. Source code for the LST10_12.PAS program.

```pascal
Program Basic_Statistics;

Uses CRT;

{ Turbo Pascal program that passes a structure by reference to
  alter its value.  This program calculates the mean and standard
  deviation of a randomly generated array.
}

CONST MAX = 100;

TYPE
    bastat = RECORD
        mean,
        sdev,
        degree_freedom : REAL;
    END;

    realArray = ARRAY [1..MAX] OF REAL;


VAR data : realArray;
    i : WORD;
    statistics : bastat;

PROCEDURE basic_stat(VAR x     : realArray;  { input  }
                         count : WORD;        { input  }
                     VAR stat  : bastat       { output });

VAR sum, sumx, sumxx : REAL;
    j : WORD;
```

continues

Listing 10.12. continued

```
BEGIN
    { initialize statistical summations }
    sum := count;
    sumx := 0.0;
    sumxx := 0.0;

    FOR j := 1 TO MAX DO BEGIN
        sumx := sumx + x[j];
        sumxx := sumxx + x[j] * x[j];
    END;

    WITH stat DO BEGIN
        mean := sumx / sum;
        sdev := sqrt((sumxx - sumx * sumx / sum) / (sum - 1));
        degree_freedom := sum - 1.0;
    END;

END;

BEGIN
    ClrScr;

    randomize;

    FOR i := 1 TO MAX DO
        data[i] := random;

    basic_stat(data, MAX, statistics);

    WITH statistics DO BEGIN
        WRITELN;
        WRITELN('Mean = ',mean); WRITELN;
        WRITELN('Sdev = ',sdev); WRITELN;
        WRITELN('Df = ',degree_freedom); WRITELN;
    END;

END.
```

Listing 10.13. Source code for the LST10_13.CPP program.

```
/* C++ program that passes a structure by reference to
   alter its value.  This program calculates the mean and standard
   deviation of a randomly generated array.
*/
```

```
#include <iostream.h>
#include <stdlib.h>
#include <math.h>
#include <conio.h>

const unsigned MAX = 100;

struct bastat {
   double mean;
   double sdev;
   double degree_freedom;
};

typedef unsigned int word;

void basic_stat(double*, word, bastat&);

main()
{

    double data[MAX];
    word i;
    bastat statistics;

    clrscr();

    randomize();

    for (i = 0; i < MAX; i++)
        data[i] = (double) random(100);

    basic_stat(data, MAX, statistics);

    cout << "\n"
        << "Mean = " << statistics.mean << "\n\n"
        << "Sdev = " << statistics.sdev << "\n\n"
        << "Df   = " << statistics.degree_freedom << "\n\n";

}


void basic_stat(double *x, word count, bastat& stat)

{
    double sum = count, sumx = 0.0L, sumxx = 0.0L;
    word j;
```

continues

303

Listing 10.13. continued

```
for (j = 0; j < count; j++)  {
    sumx += *x;
    sumxx += *x * *x;
    x++;
}

stat.mean = sumx / sum;
stat.sdev = sqrt((sumxx - sumx * sumx / sum) / (sum - 1));
stat.degree_freedom = sum - 1.0;

}
```

Compare the two program versions and notice the following:

1. The Turbo Pascal `bastat` record has the following declaration:

```
bastat = RECORD
   mean,
   sdev,
   degree_freedom : REAL;
END;
```

The Turbo C++ `bastat` structure has the following declaration:

```
struct bastat {
   double mean;
   double sdev;
   double degree_freedom;
};
```

2. The Turbo Pascal `basic_stat` procedure has the following heading:

```
PROCEDURE basic_stat(VAR x      : realArray;  { input }
                         count : WORD;       { input }
                     VAR stat  : bastat      { output });
```

The preceding procedure passes the arguments for the x array and record `stat` by reference. The Turbo C++ `basic_stat` function has the following declaration:

```
void basic_stat(double *x, word count, bastat& stat)
```

Notice that the preceding C++ function passes the pointer to the array. In addition, the function declares the `stat` parameter as a reference to the `bastat` structure. This declaration makes the `stat` parameter a temporary alias for its arguments. Because a reference parameter is not exactly the same as a pointer, notice the `stat` parameter accesses the various data members of the `bastat` structure using the dot access operator, not the `->` pointer access operator.

Passing Numerical Matrices by Reference

Number-crunching applications (such as statistical, scientific, and engineering programs) often use numerical matrices. Despite the fact that C++ is not intended to be used primarily for such applications (replacing FORTRAN), matrices are still important data structures. As a programmer, you might find yourself using nonnumerical matrices to store tables of characters or structures. The examples in this section deal with numerical matrices. In the next section, I'll illustrate how to work with character matrices.

Listings 10.14 and 10.15 are based on a benchmark for floating-point operations that I use to test the compilers of various languages. The program creates a matrix with 20 rows and 20 columns. The program assigns 1 to each non-diagonal element and assigns 2 to every diagonal element. The program then inverts the matrix using a separate routine. This approach requires that the matrix-inversion routine pass the matrix by reference, to make the benchmark program more efficient. I coded the program so that it does not display the matrix itself. Instead, I chose to focus on displaying the result, which should be equal to 21. Listing 10.14 is the source code for the LST10_14.PAS program. Listing 10.15 is the source code for the LST10_15.CPP program.

Listing 10.14. Source code for the LST10_14.PAS program.

```
PROGRAM MTINVERT;

{ Program to test speed of floating point matrix inversion.  }
{ The program will form a matrix with ones in every member,  }
{ except the diagonals, which will have values of 2.         }

CONST MAX = 20;

TYPE MATRIX = ARRAY[1..MAX,1..MAX] OF REAL;

VAR A : MATRIX;
    determinant : REAL;
    n : INTEGER;


PROCEDURE CreateMat(VAR X : MATRIX; { output }
                    VAR n : INTEGER { in/out });
```

continues

Listing 10.14. continued

```pascal
VAR j, k : INTEGER;

BEGIN

    IF (n < 0) OR (n > MAX) THEN n := MAX;

    { Creating test matrix }
    FOR j := 1 TO n DO BEGIN
        FOR k := 1 TO n DO
            X[j,k] := 1.0;
        X[j,j] := 2.0;
    END;

END; { CreateMat }


PROCEDURE Invert_Mat(VAR X   : MATRIX;  { in/out }
                         n   : INTEGER; { input  }
                     VAR det : REAL     { output });

    VAR j, k, l : INTEGER;
        pivot, tempo : REAL;

    BEGIN
        det := 1.0;
        IF (n > MAX) OR (n < 2) THEN EXIT;

        FOR j := 1 TO n DO BEGIN
            pivot := X[j,j];
            det := det * pivot;
            X[j,j] := 1.0;
            FOR k := 1 TO n DO
                X[j,k] := X[j,k] / pivot;

            FOR k := 1 TO n DO
                IF k <> j THEN BEGIN
                    tempo := X[k,j];
                    X[k,j] := 0.0;
                    FOR l := 1 TO n DO
                        X[k,l] := X[k,l] - X[j,l] * tempo;

                END;
        END; { End of outer for-loop }

END; { Invert_Mat }
```

```
BEGIN

  WRITELN('Starting matrix inversion');

  n := MAX;
  CreateMat(A, n);
  Invert_Mat(A, n, determinant);
  WRITELN(^G'DONE');
  WRITELN;
  WRITE('Determinant = ',determinant:3, ' ?=? ', MAX+1);
  WRITELN; WRITELN;

END.
```

Listing 10.15. Source code for the LST10_15.CPP program.

```cpp
/* Program to test speed of floating point matrix inversion.
   The program will form a matrix with ones in every member,
   except the diagonals, which will have values of 2.
*/

#include <iostream.h>
#include <stdlib.h>

const unsigned MAX = 20;
typedef double varmat[][MAX];

// define 'matrix' as an array-type identifier
typedef double matrix[MAX][MAX];

void create_mat(double[][MAX], int&);
void invert_mat(double[][MAX], int, double&);

main()
{
  matrix A;
  double determinant;
  int n;

  cout << "\nStarting matrix inversion\n";

  n = MAX;
  create_mat(A, n);
  invert_mat(A, n, determinant);
```

continues

Listing 10.15. continued

```
cout << "\n\007DONE"
     << "\nDeterminant = " << determinant
     << " ?=? " << MAX+1 << "\n\n";

  return 0;

}

void create_mat(varmat x, int &n)

{
  int j, k;

  if (n < 0 || n > MAX)  n = MAX;
  cout << "Matrix size = " << n << "\n";
  /* Creating test matrix */
  for (j = 0; j < n; j++)  {
      for (k = 0; k < n; k++)
          *(*(x+j)+k) = 1.0;
      *(*(x+j)+j) = 2.0;
  }
}

void invert_mat(varmat x, int n, double &det)

{
  int j, k, l;
  double pivot, tempo;

  det = 1.0;
  if (n > MAX || n < 2) exit(0);

  for (j = 0; j < n; j++)  {
      pivot = *(*(x+j)+j);
      det *= pivot;
      *(*(x+j)+j) = 1.0;
      for (k = 0; k < n; k++)
          *(*(x+j)+k) /= pivot;

      for (k = 0; k < n; k++)
          if (k != j)  {
              tempo = *(*(x+k)+j);
              *(*(x+k)+j) = 0.0;
              for (l = 0; l < n; l++)
```

```
            *(*(x+k)+l) = *(*(x+k)+l) -
                          *(*(x+j)+l) * tempo;

        }
    }
}
```

Compare the Turbo Pascal and Turbo C++ listings and observe the following:

1. The Turbo Pascal version defines a type identifier, MATRIX, to model the matrix:

```
TYPE MATRIX = ARRAY[1..MAX,1..MAX] OF REAL;
```

The Turbo C++ version defines two types, varmat and matrix:

```
typedef double varmat[][MAX];
typedef double matrix[MAX][MAX];
```

The varmat type models an open matrix type, whereas the matrix type models a fixed matrix type similar to the Turbo Pascal MATRIX type.

2. The Turbo Pascal version uses the MATRIX type to declare the matrix-related parameters in the following procedures:

```
PROCEDURE CreateMat(VAR X : MATRIX; { output }
                    VAR n : INTEGER { in/out });

PROCEDURE Invert_Mat(VAR X   : MATRIX;  { in/out }
                         n   : INTEGER; { input  }
                     VAR det : REAL     { output });
```

Consequently, the preceding Turbo Pascal procedures handle only matrices that have the MATRIX data type. By contrast, the Turbo C++ version uses the varmat type in declaring the functions that create and invert the matrices:

```
void create_mat(varmat x, int &n)

void invert_mat(varmat x, int n, double &det)
```

The preceding Turbo C++ functions can handle matrices that vary in row numbers. This flexibility is possible because I declared the varmat type in such a way that the first bracket set is empty and the second bracket set has MAX elements. This kind of declaration indicates to the compiler that you wish to keep the size of the first dimension flexible. If you make both brackets empty, you get a compiler error because the compiler cannot handle more than one variable-size dimension in an array type. Using this approach also forces you to use the pointer form to access the elements of the matrix parameter. For example, the following code is the nested loop that initializes the matrix:

309

```
/* Creating test matrix */
for (j = 0; j < n; j++) {
    for (k = 0; k < n; k++)
        *(*(x+j)+k) = 1.0;
    *(*(x+j)+j) = 2.0;
}
```

Keep in mind that the expression `*(x+j)` yields a pointer to a matrix row. Therefore, the expression `*(*(x+j)+k)` accesses the matrix element `x[j][k]`. The C++ functions must have one fixed dimension to determine the offset used in jumping over rows. This information permits pointer arithmetic with arrays of rows. For example, if `*x` points to the first element of row 0, then `*(x+1)` points to the first element of row 1, and so on. Therefore, the size of each row is needed to determine how many bytes to skip to access a specific row.

Passing Pointers to Dynamic Structures

The binary tree is among the popular dynamic data structures. Such structures empower you to build ordered collections of data without prior knowledge of the number of data items. The basic building block for a binary tree is a node. Each node has a field, which is used as a sorting key; optional additional data, called *non-key data*; and two pointers to establish a link with other tree nodes. Dynamic memory allocation enables you to create space for each node and to dynamically set up the links between the various nodes. If you want to learn more about binary tree structure, consult a data structure textbook.

The following programs support simple binary tree operations. To manage a binary tree, you need to maintain a pointer to the root of the tree. In Listings 10.16 and 10.17, I present routines that pass the pointer to the root of the tree by reference to insert, search, and display the data in a binary tree. The programs create an array with random integers and insert these integers in a binary tree. The programs then recursively traverse the nodes of the binary tree to display its data. As a result, the programs display an ordered list of integers. Listing 10.16 is the source code for the Pascal program, LST10_16.PAS. Listing 10.17 is the source code for the C++ program, LST10_17.CPP.

Listing 10.16. Source code for the LST10_16.PAS program.

```pascal
PROGRAM TestBinTree;

{
    Turbo Pascal program that creates an array of integers using
    random numbers.  The array is stored in a binary tree.
    The tree is traversed to obtain an ordered list of the array
    elements.
}

Uses CRT;

CONST SIZE = 20;

TYPE BinTreePtr =  ^Node;

     Node = RECORD
                Value : WORD;
                Left,
                Right : BinTreePtr;
            END;

     NumArray = ARRAY [1..SIZE] OF WORD;

VAR Numbers : NumArray;
    I, Num : WORD;
    TreeRoot : BinTreePtr;
    dummy : CHAR;

PROCEDURE Create(VAR X   : NumArray; { output }
                     Num : WORD      { in/out });
{ Create array using random numbers }
VAR J : WORD;

BEGIN
    IF (Num < 0) OR (Num > SIZE) THEN Num := SIZE;

    Randomize;
    FOR J := 1 TO Num DO
        X[J] := Trunc(Random(1000));

END;

PROCEDURE Insert(VAR Root : BinTreePtr; Item : WORD);
{ Recursive insertion of an element in the binary tree }
```

continues

Listing 10.16. continued

```
BEGIN
    IF Root = NIL THEN BEGIN
        NEW(Root);
        Root^.Value := Item;
        Root^.Left := NIL;
        Root^.Right := NIL
    END
    ELSE
        WITH Root^ DO
            IF Item < Value THEN Insert(Left,Item)
                            ELSE Insert(Right,Item);
END;


PROCEDURE Display_Sort(VAR Root : BinTreePtr);
{ Recursively visit the binary tree nodes }
BEGIN
    IF Root^.Left <> NIL THEN Display_Sort(Root^.Left);
    WRITELN(Root^.Value);
    IF Root^.Right <> NIL THEN Display_Sort(Root^.Right);

END;

BEGIN { MAIN }
    Num := SIZE;
    Create(Numbers, Num);
    WRITE('Created array ....');
    { Building the binary tree }
    TreeRoot := NIL;
    FOR I := 1 TO SIZE DO
        Insert(TreeRoot,Numbers[I]);

    WRITELN('Created Tree');
    WRITELN('Sorted array of number is');
    Display_Sort(TreeRoot);
END.
```

Listing 10.17. Source code for the LST10_17.CPP program.

```
/* C++ program that creates an array of integers using random
   numbers.  The array is stored in a binary tree.  The tree
   is traversed to obtain an ordered list of the array elements
*/
```

```
#include <iostream.h>
#include <stdlib.h>

const unsigned ARRAY_SIZE = 20;

typedef unsigned int word;
typedef struct node* nodeptr;

struct node {
   word value;
   nodeptr left;
   nodeptr right;
};


// define array-type identifier
typedef word num_array[ARRAY_SIZE];

void create(word*, word&);
void insert(nodeptr&, word);
void display_sort(nodeptr);

main()
{

    num_array numbers;
    word i, num = ARRAY_SIZE;
    nodeptr treeroot = NULL;
    create(numbers, num);
    cout << "Created array ....";
    // Building the binary tree
    for (i = 0; i < num; i++)
       insert(treeroot,numbers[i]);

    cout << "Created Tree"
        << "\nSorted array of number is\n";
    display_sort(treeroot);

    return 0;

}

void create(word* x, word &num)
// Create array using random numbers
{
   word j;
```

continues

Listing 10.17. continued

```
    if (num < 1 || num > ARRAY_SIZE)   num = ARRAY_SIZE;

    randomize();
    for (j = 0; j < num; j++)
        *(x + j) = random(1000);

}

void insert(nodeptr& root, word item)
// Recursively insert element in binary tree
{
    if (!root)  {
        root = new node;
        root->value = item;
        root->left = NULL;
        root->right = NULL;
    }
    else {
        if (item < root->value)
            insert(root->left,item);
        else
            insert(root->right,item);
    }
}


void display_sort(nodeptr root)
// Recursively visit the binary tree nodes
{
    if (root->left) display_sort(root->left);
    cout << "\n" << root->value;
    if (root->right) display_sort(root->right);

}
```

Examine the listings for the Turbo Pascal and Turbo C++ versions and notice the following:

1. The Turbo C++ example uses a `typedef` statement to define the `nodeptr` pointer type before the declaration of the node structure.

2. Compare the heading for the data insertion routines:

```
PROCEDURE Insert(VAR Root : BinTreePtr; Item : WORD);
void insert(nodeptr& root, word item)
```

The two headings resemble each other because the Turbo C++ version declares the root parameter as a reference to the node pointer. Such a declaration enables the root to point to a different address (which is the case when you insert the first element in the binary tree). If C++ did not support reference parameters (as is the case with C), then the insert function would need to return a nodeptr type to update the pointer to the root of the binary tree. Therefore, thanks to the reference parameters in C++, you easily translate the code for dynamic data structures from Turbo Pascal to Turbo C++.

Listing 10.18 is the source code for the LST10_18.CPP program, which is similar to LST10_17.CPP except that it handles strings. Each string may contain up to STRING80 characters (including the null terminator). The program prompts you to enter five strings using the following loop:

```
for (j = 0; j < num; j++) {
    cout << "Enter string " << j+1 << " : ";
    cin.getline(*(x + j), STRING80);
}
```

The cin.getline stream function enables the program to obtain strings from the keyboard.

After you enter the data in the array of x strings (actually it is a matrix of characters), the program inserts these strings in the binary tree and then traverses the tree to display the strings you typed in an ascending order.

Notice that the program uses the string comparison function strcmp (which is prototyped in the string.h header file) to compare an inserted string with the strings that are already in the binary tree. The strcmp function returns 1, 0, and −1 if the first argument is greater than, equal to, and less than the second argument, respectively.

Listing 10.18. Source code for the LST10_18.CPP program.

```
/*
   C++ program that sorts an array of strings using a binary
   tree structure.
*/

#include <iostream.h>
#include <stdlib.h>
#include <string.h>
#include <conio.h>
```

continues

315

Listing 10.18. continued

```
const unsigned ARRAY_SIZE = 5;
const unsigned STRING80 = 81;

typedef unsigned int word;

typedef struct node* nodeptr;

struct node {
   char* value;
   nodeptr left;
   nodeptr right;
};

typedef char strarray[ARRAY_SIZE][STRING80];

main()
{
   strarray strings;
   word i, num = ARRAY_SIZE;
   nodeptr treeroot = NULL;

   void getdata(char[][STRING80], word&);
   void insert(nodeptr&, char*);
   void display_sort(nodeptr&);

   clrscr();
   // get array of strings
   getdata(strings, num) ;

   // Building the binary tree
   for (i = 0; i < num; i++)
      insert(treeroot,strings[i]);

   cout << "\nSorted array is\n";
   display_sort(treeroot);
   cout << "\n\n";

   return 0;
}

void getdata(char x[][STRING80], word &num)
// read array of strings
{
   word j;
```

```
    if ((num < 1) || (num > ARRAY_SIZE)) num = ARRAY_SIZE;

    for (j = 0; j < num; j++) {
        cout << "Enter string " << j+1 << " : ";
        cin.getline(*(x + j), STRING80);
    }

}

void insert(nodeptr& root, char* item)
// Insert element in binary tree
{
    if (!root)  {
     root = new node;
        root->value = item;
        root->left = NULL;
        root->right = NULL;
    }
    else {
        if (strcmp(item, root->value) < 0)
            insert(root->left,item);
        else
            insert(root->right,item);
    }
}


void display_sort(nodeptr& root)
// Visit the binary tree nodes recursively
{
    if (root->left)  display_sort(root->left);
    cout << "\n" << root->value;
    if (root->right) display_sort(root->right);

}
```

Accessing Command-Line Arguments

Turbo Pascal enables you to access the number of command-line arguments and strings using the predefined ParamCount and ParamStr functions. C++, like C, enables you to access

317

command-line arguments by supplying and using the following parameters in function main:

```
main(int argc, char* argv[])
```

The argc parameter returns the number of command-line arguments. The argv parameter is a character pointer that accesses the various command-line arguments. The value of argc takes into account the name of the program itself. The expression argv[0] is the pointer to the program's name. The expression argv[1] is a pointer to the first argument, and so on.

The following program examples use command-line arguments, implementing a simple four-function calculator that takes its arguments from the DOS prompt. The general syntax for using the program (assuming you rename the compiled file into CALC.EXE) is:

```
> CALC operand1 operator operand2
```

Listing 10.19 contains the source code for the LST10_19.PAS program. Listing 10.20 shows the source code for the LST10_20.CPP program.

Listing 10.19. Source code for the LST10_19.PAS program.

```
Program Calc;

{ Turbo Pascal program that uses command-line arguments to
  perform one-line calculations.  Only the four basic
  operations are supported.

  For practical use make the filename CALC.EXE, so that when
  you invoke it from DOS you type, for example:

      CALC  355 / 113

}

VAR ok : BOOLEAN;
    opr : CHAR;
    error1, error2, error3 : INTEGER;
    strng : STRING[80];
    result, first, second : REAL;

BEGIN

    IF ParamCount < 3 THEN BEGIN
        WRITELN('Proper usage : <number> <operation> <number>');
        WRITELN; WRITELN;
        HALT;
```

```
END;

Val(ParamStr(1), first, error1);
Val(ParamStr(3), second, error3);
strng := ParamStr(2); { must use a string as a go-between
                        to avoid type mismatch }
opr := strng[1];

IF NOT (opr IN ['+', '-', '*', '/']) THEN
    error2 := 1
ELSE
    error2 := 0;

IF ((error1 + error2 + error2) > 0) THEN BEGIN
    IF error1 > 0 THEN BEGIN
        WRITELN(ParamStr(1));
        WRITELN('^':error1,'bad number');
    END;

    IF error2 > 0 THEN
        WRITELN(opr,' is an invalid operator');

    IF error3 > 0 THEN BEGIN
        WRITELN(ParamStr(3));
        WRITELN('^':error2,'bad number');
    END;

    WRITELN; WRITELN;
    HALT;
END;

ok := TRUE;

CASE opr OF
    '+' : result := first + second;
    '-' : result := first - second;
    '*' : result := first * second;
    '/' : IF second <> 0.0 THEN
              result := first / second
          ELSE BEGIN
              ok := FALSE;
              WRITELN('Cannot divide by zero');
          END;
END; { CASE }

IF ok THEN WRITELN('result = ',result);

END.
```

Listing 10.20. Source code for the LST10_20.CPP program.

```
/* C++ program that uses command-line arguments to
   perform one-line calculations.  Only the four basic
   operations are supported.

   For practical use make the filename CALC.EXE, so that when
   you invoke it from DOS you type, for example:

       CALC  355 / 113

*/

#include <iostream.h>
#include <stdlib.h>
#include <string.h>

main(int argc, char* argv[])
{
    char opr;
    int error1, error2, error3;
    char strng[81];
    double result, first, second;

    /* check for the number of arguments.
       This is a step often performed        */
    if (argc < 4)  {
      // provide simple on-line help
      cout << "Proper arguments : <number> <operation> <number>"
           << "\n\n";
      exit(0);
    }

    // convert operands to double
    first  = atof(argv[1]);
    second = atof(argv[3]);
    strcpy(strng,argv[2]);
    opr = strng[0];

    if (opr != '+' && opr != '-' && opr != '*' && opr != '/')
        error2 = 1;
    else
        error2 = 0;

    if (first == 0.0 || error2 == 1 || second == 0.0) {
        cout << "bad number(s) or operator\n\n";
        exit(0);
    }
```

```
switch (opr) {
    case '+' :
        result = first + second;
        break;
    case '-' :
        result = first - second;
        break;
    case '*' :
        result = first * second;
        break;
    case '/' :
        result = first / second;
        break;
}

cout << "result = " << result << "\n\n";

return 0;

}
```

If you compare the Turbo Pascal and Turbo C++ listings, you will observe that the `if` statements which compare the number of command-line arguments are:

```
IF ParamCount < 3 THEN BEGIN
if (argc < 4)  {
```

The Turbo C++ version compares the `argc` parameter with 4 instead of 3, because the name of the program itself counts as a command-line argument.

If you examine the code carefully, you may notice that a valid second argument can be a multi-character string as long as the first character is a valid operator symbol. Thus, if you enter /%^$#@@ as the second command-line argument, the program picks up the first character (/), ignores the rest, and performs a division operation.

Pointers to Functions

The program compilation process translates the names of variables into memory addresses where data are stored and retrieved. Pointers to addresses can also access these addresses. This translation step holds true for variables and functions alike. The compiler translates the name of a function into the address of executable code. C++ extends the strategy of manipulating variables by using pointers to include functions. The general syntax for declaring a pointer to a function is:

```
returnType (*functionPointer)(<list of parameters>);
```

The preceding form tells the compiler that the functionPointer is a pointer to a function that has the returnType return type and a list of parameters. A few examples of declaring pointers to functions follow:

```
double (*fx)(double x);
void (*sort)(int* intArray, unsigned n);
unsigned (*search)(int searchKey, int* intArray, unsigned n);
```

The first identifier, fx, points to a function that returns a double and has a single double-typed parameter. The second identifier, sort, is a pointer to a function that returns a void type and takes two parameters: a pointer to int and an unsigned. The third identifier, search, is a pointer to a function that returns an unsigned and has three parameters: an int, a pointer to an int, and an unsigned.

C++ enables you to declare an array of function pointers. The general syntax is:

```
returnType (*functionPointer[arraySize])(<list of parameters>);
```

The following code lines are a few examples of declaring arrays of pointers to functions:

```
double (*fx[3])(double x);
void (*sort[MAX_SORT])(int* intArray, unsigned n);
unsigned (*search[MAX_SEARCH])(int searchKey,
                               int* intArray, unsigned n);
```

As with any pointer, you need to initialize a function pointer before using it. This step is simple. You merely assign the bare name of a function to the function pointer. The general syntax is:

```
functionPointer = aFunction;
```

The assigned function must have the same return type and parameter list as the function pointer. Otherwise, the compiler flags an error. The general syntax for assigning a function to an element in an array of function pointers is:

```
functionPointer[index] = aFunction;
```

After you assign a function name to a function pointer, you can use the pointer to invoke its associated function. It will probably be evident why the function pointer must have the same return type and parameter list as the accessed function. The general syntax for the expression that invokes function pointers is:

```
(*functionPointer)(<argument list>);
(*functionPointer[index])(<argument list>);
```

The next Turbo C++ example uses function pointers and performs linearized regression on two observed variables: the independent variable, X, and the dependent variable, Y. The model that relates these two variables is:

```
f(Y) = intercept + slope * g(X)
```

The function f(Y) transforms the data for the Y variable. The function g(X) transforms the data for the X variable. The functions f(Y) and g(X) can be linear, logarithmic, exponential, square root, square, or any other mathematical function. When both f(Y) = Y and g(X) = X, the preceding model becomes the linear regression model, as follows:

```
Y = intercept + slope * X
```

The linearized regression (referring back to the general model) calculates the best values for the slope and intercept for the values of f(Y) and g(X). The regression also provides the correlation coefficient statistic, which represents the fraction of the f(Y) data that is explained by the variation in g(X). A value of 1 represents a perfect fit, and 0 represents a total lack of any correlation between f(Y) and g(X) data.

The next program performs linear regression and carries out the following tasks:

1. Prompts you to enter the number of data. Your input must be in the limit indicated by the program.

2. Prompts you to enter the observed values of X and Y.

3. Prompts you to select the function that transforms the observations for variable X. The program displays a small itemized menu that shows your options. These options indicate the linear, logarithmic, square, square root, and reciprocal functions.

4. Prompts you to select the function that transforms the observations for variable Y. The program displays a small itemized menu that shows your options. These options indicate the linear, logarithmic, square, square root, and reciprocal functions.

5. Performs the regression calculations.

6. Displays the intercept, slope, and correlation coefficient for the linearized regression.

7. Prompts you to supply values for X and calculate the estimated values of Y.

8. Prompts you to select another set of transformation functions.

Listing 10.21 is the source code for the LST10_21.CPP program.

Listing 10.21. Source code for the LST10_21.CPP program.

```
/*
   C++ program that uses pointers to functions to implement
   a linear regression program that supports temporary
   mathematical transformations.  The program also enables
   you to perform projections.
*/

#include <iostream.h>
#include <conio.h>
#include <math.h>

const unsigned MAX_SIZE = 100;

typedef unsigned int word;
typedef unsigned char byte;
enum boolean { FALSE, TRUE };

typedef double vector[MAX_SIZE];

struct regression {
   double Rsqr;
   double slope;
   double intercept;
};

// declare function pointer
double (*fx)(double);
double (*fy)(double);
double (*inv_fy)(double);

// declare function prototypes
void initArray(double*, double*, word);
double linear(double);
double sqr(double);
double reciprocal(double);
void calcRegression(double*, double*, word, regression&,
                    double (*fx)(double), double (*fy)(double));
int select_transf(const char*);

main()
{
    char ok, ans;
    word count;
    double xdata, ydata;
    vector x, y;
    regression stat;
```

```
int trnsfx, trnsfy;

clrscr();

do {
    cout << "Enter array size [2.." << MAX_SIZE << "] : ";
    cin >> count; cout << "\n";
} while ( !(count > 1 && count <= MAX_SIZE) );

initArray(x, y, count);

do {

  trnsfx = select_transf("X");
  trnsfy = select_transf("Y");

  switch (trnsfx) {
   case 0 :
      fx = linear;
      break;
   case 1 :
      fx = log;
      break;
   case 2 :
      fx = sqrt;
      break;
   case 3 :
      fx = sqr;
      break;
   case 4 :
      fx = reciprocal;
      break;
   default :
      fx = linear;
      break;
  }

  switch (trnsfy) {
   case 0 :
      fy = linear;
      inv_fy = linear;
      break;
   case 1 :
      fy = log;
      inv_fy = exp;
      break;
```

continues

325

Listing 10.21. continued

```
        case 2 :
           fy = sqrt;
           inv_fy = sqr;
           break;
        case 3 :
           fy = sqr;
           inv_fy = sqrt;
           break;
        case 4 :
           fy = reciprocal;
           inv_fy = reciprocal;
           break;
        default :
           fy = linear;
           break;
    }

    /*  call function with functional arguments
                                    |       |
                                    V       V */
    calcRegression(x, y, count, stat, fx, fy);

    cout << "\n\n\n\n"
         << "R-square = " << stat.Rsqr << "\n\n"
         << "Slope = " << stat.slope << "\n\n"
         << "Intercept = " << stat.intercept << "\n\n\n"
         << "\nWant to project more data? (Y/N) : ";
    ans = getche();
    while (ans == 'Y' ¦¦ ans == 'y') {
      cout << "\nEnter a value for X : ";
      cin >> xdata;
      ydata = (*inv_fy)(stat.intercept +
                        stat.slope * (*fx)(xdata));
      cout << "Y = " << ydata << "\n\n";
      cout << "\nWant to project more data? (Y/N) : ";
      ans = getche();
    }
    cout << "\nWant to test another transformation? (Y/N) : ";
    ok = getche();
  } while (ok == 'Y' ¦¦ ok == 'y');
  cout << "\n\n";

  return 0;

}
void initArray(double* x, double* y, word count)
```

```
// read data for array from the keyboard
{
    word i;

    for (i = 0; i < count; i++, x++, y++) {
        cout << "X[" << i << "] : ";
        cin >> *x;
        cout << "Y[" << i << "] : ";
        cin >> *y;
    }
}

int select_transf(const char* var_name)
// select choice of transformation
{

    int choice = -1;

    clrscr();
    cout << "select transformation for variable " << var_name
         << "\n\n\n"
         << "0) No transformation\n\n"
         << "1) Logarithmic transformation\n\n"
         << "2) Square root transformation\n\n"
         << "3) Square  transformation\n\n"
         << "4) Reciprocal transformation\n\n";
    while (choice < 0 || choice > 4) {
        cout << "\nSelect choice by number : ";
        cin >> choice;
    }

    return choice;
}

double linear(double x)
{
    return x;
}


double sqr(double x)
{
    return x * x;
}


double reciprocal(double x)
```

continues

Listing 10.21. continued

```
{
    return 1.0L / x;
}


void calcRegression(double* x,
                    double* y,
                    word count,
                    regression &stat,
                    double (*fx)(double),
                    double (*fy)(double))

{
    double meanx, meany, sdevx, sdevy;
    double sum, sumx, sumy;
    double sumxx, sumyy, sumxy;
    double xdata, ydata;
    word i;

    // initialize statistical summations
    sum = (double) count;
    sumx = 0L; sumxx = 0L;
    sumy = 0L; sumyy = 0L;
    sumxy = 0L;

    for (i = 0; i < count; i++) {
        xdata = (*fx)(*(x+i));
        ydata = (*fy)(*(y+i));
        sumx += xdata;
        sumy += ydata;
        sumxx += sqr(xdata);
        sumyy += sqr(ydata);
        sumxy += xdata * ydata;
    }

    meanx = sumx / sum;
    meany = sumy / sum;
    sdevx = sqrt((sumxx - sqr(sumx) / sum)/(sum-1.0));
    sdevy = sqrt((sumyy - sqr(sumy) / sum)/(sum-1.0));
    stat.slope = (sumxy - meanx * meany * sum) /
                    sqr(sdevx)/(sum-1);
    stat.intercept = meany - stat.slope * meanx;
    stat.Rsqr = sqr(sdevx / sdevy * stat.slope);


}
```

The preceding program declares the structure regression as follows:

```
struct regression {
   double Rsqr;
   double slope;
   double intercept;
};
```

The program also declares the following global function pointers:

```
double (*fx)(double);
double (*fy)(double);
double (*inv_fy)(double);
```

The identifiers fx and fy are pointers to the functions that transform the observations for the variables X and Y, respectively. The identifier inv_fy is a pointer to the function that performs the inverse transformation for estimating the values of Y.

The program also declares the function prototypes for the various functions, including the ones that transform data:

```
double linear(double);
double sqr(double);
double reciprocal(double);
```

The initArray function reads the observations for variables X and Y from the keyboard. The program stores the information you enter in the x and y arrays.

The select_transf function displays the itemized menu that displays the various transformations available. The function returns the integer value that you enter in selecting a particular transformation.

The calcRegression function performs the linearized regression. Notice that the function definition, shown in the code that follows, includes the fx and fy parameters that are function pointers. This code shows you that C++ allows the use of function pointers as parameters. This feature resembles the procedural parameters available in Turbo Pascal:

```
void calcRegression(double* x,
                    double* y,
                    word count,
                    regression &stat,
                    double (*fx)(double),
                    double (*fy)(double))
```

The function main uses two switch statements to assign the proper data transformation function to the function pointers fx, fy, and inv_fx. Notice that the function assignment uses the bare name of the function and is void of any parameter list.

The program uses the function pointers in two locations. First, the function main uses the inv_fy pointer in the following statement that estimates the value of Y for a given value of X:

```
ydata = (*inv_fy)(stat.intercept +
                  stat.slope * (*fx)(xdata));
```

In addition, the calcRegression function uses the function pointers fx and fy in the following loop that updates the statistical summations:

```
for (i = 0; i < count; i++) {
    xdata = (*fx)(*(x+i));
    ydata = (*fy)(*(y+i));
    sumx += xdata;
    sumy += ydata;
    sumxx += sqr(xdata);
    sumyy += sqr(ydata);
    sumxy += xdata * ydata;
}
```

Compile and run the program in Listing 10.21. Here is a sample session:

```
Enter array size [2..100] : 4

X[0] : 10
Y[0] : 51
X[1] : 25
Y[1] : 76
X[2] : 30
Y[2] : 88
X[3] : 100
Y[3] : 214


select transformation for variable X


0) No transformation

1) Logarithmic transformation

2) Square root transformation
```

```
3) Square  transformation

4) Reciprocal transformation

Select choice by number : 0


select transformation for variable Y

0) No transformation

1) Logarithmic transformation

2) Square root transformation

3) Square transformation

4) Reciprocal transformation

Select choice by number : 0



R-square = 0.999706

Slope = 1.816602

Intercept = 32.315175



Want to project more data? (Y/N) : y
Enter a value for X : 35
Y = 95.896239


Want to project more data? (Y/N) : n
Want to test another transformation? (Y/N) : n
```

The next program shows you how to use arrays of function pointers and how to declare them as parameters in other functions. I modified the preceding program to produce the next one by replacing the pointers fx and fy with a two-member array of pointers f[2]. The program performs the same tasks as the previous one. The difference is in the coding. Listing 10.22 is the source code for the LST10_22.CPP program.

Listing 10.22. Source code for the LST10_22.CPP program.

```
/*
   C++ program that uses pointers to functions to implement
   a linear regression program that supports temporary
   mathematical transformations.  The program also enables
   you to perform projections.
*/

#include <iostream.h>
#include <conio.h>
#include <math.h>

const unsigned MAX_SIZE = 100;

typedef unsigned int word;
typedef unsigned char byte;
enum boolean { FALSE, TRUE };

typedef double vector[MAX_SIZE];

struct regression {
   double Rsqr;
   double slope;
   double intercept;
};

// declare function pointer
double (*f[2])(double);
double (*inv_fy)(double);

// declare function prototypes
void initArray(double*, double*, word);
double linear(double);
double sqr(double);
double reciprocal(double);
void calcRegression(double*, double*, word, regression&,
                    double (*f[2])(double));
int select_transf(const char*);

main()
{
    char ok, ans;
    word count;
    double xdata, ydata;
    vector x, y;
    regression stat;
    int trnsfx, trnsfy;
```

```
clrscr();

do {
    cout << "Enter array size [2.." << MAX_SIZE << "] : ";
    cin >> count; cout << "\n";
} while ( !(count > 1 && count <= MAX_SIZE) );

initArray(x, y, count);

do {

  trnsfx = select_transf("X");
  trnsfy = select_transf("Y");

  switch (trnsfx) {
   case 0 :
      f[0] = linear;
      break;
   case 1 :
      f[0] = log;
      break;
   case 2 :
      f[0] = sqrt;
      break;
   case 3 :
      f[0] = sqr;
      break;
   case 4 :
      f[0] = reciprocal;
      break;
   default :
      f[0] = linear;
      break;
  }

  switch (trnsfy) {
   case 0 :
      f[1] = linear;
      inv_fy = linear;
      break;
   case 1 :
      f[1] = log;
      inv_fy = exp;
      break;
   case 2 :
      f[1] = sqrt;
```

continues

Listing 10.22. continued

```
            inv_fy = sqr;
            break;
        case 3 :
            f[1] = sqr;
            inv_fy = sqrt;
            break;
        case 4 :
            f[1] = reciprocal;
            inv_fy = reciprocal;
            break;
        default :
            f[1] = linear;
            break;
    }

    calcRegression(x, y, count, stat, f);

    cout << "\n\n\n\n"
         << "R-square = " << stat.Rsqr << "\n\n"
         << "Slope = " << stat.slope << "\n\n"
         << "Intercept = " << stat.intercept << "\n\n\n"
         << "\nWant to project more data? (Y/N) : ";
    ans = getche();
    while (ans == 'Y' || ans == 'y') {
        cout << "\nEnter a value for X : ";
        cin >> xdata;
        ydata = (*inv_fy)(stat.intercept +
                          stat.slope * (*f[0])(xdata));
        cout << "Y = " << ydata << "\n\n";
        cout << "\nWant to project more data? (Y/N) : ";
        ans = getche();
    }
    cout << "\nWant to test another transformation? (Y/N) : ";
    ok = getche();
  } while (ok == 'Y' || ok == 'y');
  cout << "\n\n";

  return 0;

}

void initArray(double* x, double* y, word count)
// read data for array from the keyboard
{
    word i;
```

```
    for (i = 0; i < count; i++, x++, y++) {
        cout << "X[" << i << "] : ";
        cin >> *x;
        cout << "Y[" << i << "] : ";
        cin >> *y;
    }
}

int select_transf(const char* var_name)
// select choice of transformation
{

    int choice = -1;

    clrscr();
    cout << "select transformation for variable " << var_name
        << "\n\n\n"
        << "0) No transformation\n\n"
        << "1) Logarithmic transformation\n\n"
        << "2) Square root transformation\n\n"
        << "3) Square  transformation\n\n"
        << "4) Reciprocal transformation\n\n";
    while (choice < 0 ¦¦ choice > 4) {
        cout << "\nSelect choice by number : ";
        cin >> choice;
    }

    return choice;
}

double linear(double x)
{
    return x;
}


double sqr(double x)
{
    return x * x;
}


double reciprocal(double x)
{
    return 1.0L / x;
}
```

continues

Listing 10.22. continued

```
void calcRegression(double* x,
                    double* y,
                    word count,
                    regression &stat,
                    double (*f[2])(double))

{
    double meanx, meany, sdevx, sdevy;
    double sum, sumx, sumy;
    double sumxx, sumyy, sumxy;
    double xdata, ydata;
    word i;

    // initialize statistical summations
    sum = (double) count;
    sumx = 0L; sumxx = 0L;
    sumy = 0L; sumyy = 0L;
    sumxy = 0L;

    for (i = 0; i < count; i++) {
        xdata = (*f[0])(*(x+i));
        ydata = (*f[1])(*(y+i));
        sumx += xdata;
        sumy += ydata;
        sumxx += sqr(xdata);
        sumyy += sqr(ydata);
        sumxy += xdata * ydata;
    }

    meanx = sumx / sum;
    meany = sumy / sum;
    sdevx = sqrt((sumxx - sqr(sumx) / sum)/(sum-1.0));
    sdevy = sqrt((sumyy - sqr(sumy) / sum)/(sum-1.0));
    stat.slope = (sumxy - meanx * meany * sum) /
                     sqr(sdevx)/(sum-1);
    stat.intercept = meany - stat.slope * meanx;
    stat.Rsqr = sqr(sdevx / sdevy * stat.slope);

}
```

Notice the following aspects of the preceding Turbo C++ program:

1. The declaration of the global array of function pointers f:

   ```
   double (*f[2])(double);
   ```

2. Assigning functions to the members of array f involves using an index, just like with normal arrays.

3. The declaration of calcRegression now has a parameter that represents an array of function pointers:

```
void calcRegression(double* x,
                    double* y,
                    word count,
                    regression &stat,
                    double (*f[2])(double))
```

4. The loop that updates the statistical summations in function calcRegression now looks like:

```
for (i = 0; i < count; i++) {
    xdata = (*f[0])(*(x+i));
    ydata = (*f[1])(*(y+i));
    sumx += xdata;
    sumy += ydata;
    sumxx += sqr(xdata);
    sumyy += sqr(ydata);
    sumxy += xdata * ydata;
}
```

The transforming functions are invoked using (*f[0]) and (*f[1]) along with an argument.

Functions with Varying Arguments

C++ and C enable you to write functions that take on a varying number of arguments. This feature has no parallel in many structured and object-oriented languages, such as Pascal, Modula-2, and BASIC. These languages require that the number of arguments match the number of parameters. In Chapter 7, "Simple Functions," I introduced a C++ language feature that enables you to assign and use default arguments for parameters in your functions. With this feature, you can only reduce the number of arguments in a function call.

The implementation of functions with a varying number of arguments is not terribly complicated. You need to observe the following rules:

1. Include the header file, stdarg.h, in your application.

2. Prototype the varying-argument function as follows:

```
returnType function(<type list of fixed arguments>, ...);
```

3. Declare the varying-argument function as follows:

```
returnType function(<list of fixed arguments>, ...);
```

4. Use the va_list pointer type, exported by the stdarg.h file, to declare a pointer to the list of varying arguments:

```
va_list varArgList;
```

5. Initialize the list of varying argument by calling the va_start function, prototyped in file stdarg.h, as follows:

```
va_start(varArgList, nameOfLastFixedParameter);
```

This step enables the list pointer to access the first argument in the varying argument list.

6. Access each argument in the varying argument list using the va_arg function, which is prototyped in the stdarg.h file. The first argument of the va_arg function is the name of the varying argument list pointer. The second argument is the name of a data type used to typecast the retrieved argument. The va_arg function returns a result that matches its second argument:

```
variable = va_arg(varArgList, type);
```

TIP

Include a special value in the varying argument list that acts as an end-of-list value. Use this value in a conditional loop to determine when you have obtained all the meaningful arguments in the varying argument list.

7. End the process by using the va_end function (also prototyped in stdarg.h). The general syntax for using the va_end function is:

```
va_end(varArgList);
```

The next program is a simple one that returns the largest value in a list of integer arguments. The program declares the vmax function as one with two fixed arguments and a varying argument list. The first parameter is a reference to the result, the largest integer. The second argument is a character pointer that passes a message string. The program uses the constant EOL to identify the end-of-list. The vmax function applies Steps 2 through 7 in declaring the varying list pointer, num_ptr, and using the different va_*xxxx* functions.

The vmax function declares num_ptr to be of type va_list. The function then calls function va_start and supplies it with the two required arguments: the va_list-typed pointer, num_ptr; and the name of the last argument in the fixed argument list, message. The function uses a while loop to invoke the va_arg and supply it the num_ptr and int arguments. The function assigns the result of va_arg to the local variable num. The loop condition also compares the function result with EOL to determine whether to iterate. Once the loop stops iterating, the vmax function calls the va_end function and passes the num_ptr argument. Listing 10.23 contains the source code for the LST10_23.CPP program.

Listing 10.23. Source code for the LST10_23.CPP program.

```
/* C++ program that illustrates functions with a variable
   number of arguments
*/

#include <iostream.h>
#include <stdarg.h>

const int EOL = -1;

void vmax(int&, char*, ...);

main()
{
   int big;

   vmax(big, "The largest of numbers 55, 67, 41 and 28 is ",
                        55, 67, 41, 28, EOL);
   cout << big << "\n";

   return 0;
}


void vmax(int &large, char* message, ...)
{
   int num;
   va_list num_ptr;

   va_start(num_ptr, message);
   cout << message;
   large = -1;
   while ((num = va_arg(num_ptr, int)) != EOL) {
        if (num > large)
```

continues

Listing 10.23. continued

```
            large = num;
    }

  va_end(num_ptr);

}
```

Summary

This chapter touched on various topics related to advanced functions. These topics included

- Passing arrays as function arguments using pointers to the basic types. C++ enables you to declare array parameters using explicit pointer types or using empty brackets. With such parameters, you can write general-purpose functions that work with arrays of different sizes. In addition, these pointers access the array by using its address, instead of making a copy of the entire array.

- Passing strings as function arguments also uses pointers, like the ones used to handle non-character arrays.

- Passing structures as function arguments enables you to shorten the parameter list by encapsulating various related information in C++ structures.

- Passing reference parameters may use pointers or formal references. The formal references become aliases of their arguments. In the case of passing reference to pointers, such reference can update the address of the argument.

- Accessing the command-line arguments using special parameters in function main. These parameters obtain the number of command-line arguments, as well as a pointer to each command-line argument.

- Pointers to functions are valuable tools that enable you to indirectly invoke a function. In fact, using parameters that include pointers to functions enable you to create libraries that can be used with functions not yet written.

- Functions with varying argument lists. C++ offers a special mechanism that enables you to define and use functions that have a varying number of arguments. The star of such a feature is the stdarg.h file, which exports a pointer type, and various functions that make this feature possible.

TP1
TC++

OBJECT-ORIENTED PROGRAMMING BASICS

This chapter is a brief introduction to object-oriented programming (OOP) concepts. If you are familiar with these concepts, you may move on to the next chapter. This chapter discusses the following topics:

- basic concepts of classes and objects

- manipulating objects with methods

- inheritance among classes

- polymorphic behavior of a class hierarchy

The Legacy of Structured Programming

Before I begin the journey into the world of object-oriented programming, it might be wise to glance at the roots of OOP—structured programming. Structured programming promotes order in the code and data structures of a program. This order includes the notion of reusable code and highly independent routines. Interestingly, the Pascal language itself (including Turbo Pascal) has played a major role in promoting structured programming in academic circles.

The approach fostered by structured programming in developing software is primarily procedural. Data structures take second place. The popular top-down software development method requires that you break down your application into major tasks and then repeatedly divide these tasks into smaller subtasks. In general, data manipulation takes shape at the lower-level subtasks.

The OOP Approach

The appeal of procedurally minded structured programming is contrasted by the world of objects that we live in. Look around you—the book you are reading is an object and so is the chair you are sitting on. Your computer system is another object, made up of smaller objects—the screen, the keyboard, the disk drives, the motherboard, and so on. Some objects are highly animated and others are not. Even inactive objects (like the stuff in your garage or attic) occupy space and must be taken into account. Object-oriented programming was conceived by computer scientists who viewed the world as one populated by objects acting and interacting with each other according to their nature. The procedures applied to the objects have taken second place because they depend on the objects themselves. For example, you cannot print a car, drive a light bulb, or wash clothes in your computer! These actions are inappropriate because they are not part of the object's functionality.

Object-oriented programming offers a profoundly new approach to software development. This approach goes beyond simply making data structures primary and procedures secondary. The next section begins to clarify how the basics of object-oriented programming make it very different from structured programming. Many programmers remark that OOP has picked up where structured programming ended.

Classes and Objects

To illustrate the basic notion of classes and objects, I'll use the digital clock that sits near my computer's screen, a CASINO-65 (see Figure 11.1), as an example. This clock is the simplest type of common mass-produced digital clocks. It displays the time and has a few buttons that I use to change or adjust the time. My clock is by no means unique! It is only one particular clock of many that came off the assembly line. It belongs to a class of clocks that represents a specific clock model, the CASINO-65. All the CASINO-65 clocks have the same physical features and functionality. Thus, the clock model represents a class of objects that have the same characteristics and functionality. My clock is merely an instance of the CASINO-65 model. Although it has a lot in common with other CASINO-65 clocks, it has its own state—the particular time setting and rate of deviation from the actual time.

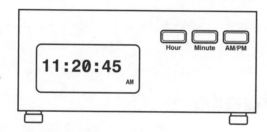

Figure 11.1. A digital clock object.

Methods that Alter the Object's State

The state of my CASINO-65 clock is indicated by the displayed time. When I want to adjust the time, I press the buttons on the front panel. Each button changes the display in a particular way—the hour button advances the hours, the minute button advances the minutes, and the AM/PM button toggles between the AM and PM indicator. When I use these buttons, I send electrical signals to the clock's circuits to alter its state and consequently change the displayed time.

In OOP terms, the clock buttons correspond to the methods that alter the clock's state. Classes encapsulate the data fields and the methods that alter these fields. These methods (the buttons) give functionality to my clock. The electrical signals generated by pressing the clock buttons represent, in OOP terms, the messages that I send to the clock (as an object). In return, the clock responds to these messages. In OOP, the clock-object is the "owner" of the messages. This notion of ownership becomes more relevant when I deal with a class hierarchy in the next chapter.

Definitions

The class is a template for its instances, the objects.

The object is an instance of a class.

The *message* represents what is done to an object. The *method* is how the message is carried out.

Inheritance is a feature that enables a derived class to possess the fields and methods of its ancestor classes.

Inheritance

Suppose the makers of my CASINO-65 clock decide to introduce a new model, the CASINO-66, that has the same features of the 65 plus an alarm. In this case it is likely that the clock manufacturer will build on the 65 model rather than start from scratch. As a result, the new CASINO-66 model is a refinement of the CASINO-65, with a new set of buttons to set the alarm and a switch to turn it on or off. In OOP terms, the CASINO-66 has inherited the features of the 65 model and introduced new operations. The CASINO-66 is a subclass (also called descendant) of the CASINO-65 clocks.

Suppose once more that the CASINO clock makers plan to offer a CASINO-100 model with a clock, alarm, and radio. The clock makers design the CASINO-100 starting with the CASINO-66 model. The radio feature represents the new functionality of the class of CASINO-100 clocks. In OOP terms, the CASINO-100 is a subclass (or descendant) of CASINO-66.

Inheritance is an important concept in object-oriented programming. It enables the spin-off of a new class from an existing one. The new class is the subclass and its parent class is the *superclass*. The first ancestor class is called the *base* class. The CASINO-65 is the base class of the CASINO clocks and the parent of the CASINO-66 clocks. The most significant advantage of inheritance comes from the fact that the new subclass need not reinvent the wheel by redeclaring all the data fields and procedures. Instead, only the new data fields need to be declared. As for the inherited methods, the subclass declares the new methods and the inherited ones that must be overridden. Overriding inherited methods is often necessary to provide an adjusted functionality suitable to the subclass.

Polymorphism

Polymorphism is an important term in object-oriented programming. It is derived from Greek and roughly translates as "multiple forms." A good translation of polymorphism in relation to OOP is perhaps *message abstraction*. To illustrate polymorphism, I'll again use the CASINO clock as the basis for an example.

The CASINO-66 inherited the time features of the CASINO-65. The manufacturer will most likely use the same exterior buttons for both clock models. Suppose the designer of the CASINO-66 had to modify the internal electrical circuits to accommodate both the time and alarm systems. The owner of the CASINO-65 and CASINO-66 clocks would operate the time setting buttons in exactly the same way, without realizing (or even caring) that the time regulating circuits are different. In object-oriented terms, the time buttons of the CASINO-66 model exhibit polymorphic behavior—they perform the same overall task as those of the CASINO-65 using different circuits.

The example can be extended to include the CASINO-100 model, where the physical time and alarm buttons of the CASINO-66 are reused, but a new internal circuit is utilized to manage the interaction between the radio and the alarm system. The time and alarm buttons are polymorphic because they perform the same overall job as the CASINO-66 model, but use different internal circuits. This gives the time button of the three CASINO models a certain level of abstraction.

Polymorphism allows each class to own custom versions of methods that maintain a unified response in a class hierarchy.

Summary

This chapter introduced you to the basics of object-oriented programming:

- Classes are templates or models for objects.

- Objects are instances of classes. Although the various instances of the same class share common capabilities and characteristics, each instance has its own state.

345

- Inheritance is the ability to create classes as descendants of parent classes. The descendant classes inherit the characteristics and operations of the parent class. The derived class also defines new characteristics and operations and can override inherited operations.

- Polymorphism is a valuable object-oriented programming that enables objects to respond to similar messages in their own way.

TURBO PASCAL OOP FEATURES

This chapter is for readers who are not familiar with the object-oriented features of Turbo Pascal. If you are familiar with this topic, you may want to move on to the next chapter, "C++ Classes." This chapter discusses

- declaring base object types
- declaring derived object types
- static versus virtual methods
- dynamic objects

Declaring Base Object Types

The first object-oriented extensions to the Pascal language were implemented by Apple Computer, Inc. with the help of Nicklaus Wirth, the developer of Pascal. The Turbo Pascal OOP features have their roots in Apple Computer implementation. Classes are declared as follows:

```
className = OBJECT ¦ OBJECT(parentClass)
        <list of data fields>
        <headers for the methods>
END;
```

The keyword OBJECT was first used by Apple Computer's Object Pascal and is inherited by Turbo Pascal. This led the Turbo Pascal manual writers to call classes as objects, because the OBJECT keyword is used. Other object-oriented Pascal implementations also use the OBJECT keyword but recognize the defined data types as classes. All other object-oriented languages define classes as the template data types for objects. The best way to deal with this dual system of nomenclature in relation to this book is as follows:

1. The term *object type* refers to the Turbo Pascal OBJECT data type.

2. The term *object variable* refers to the Turbo Pascal variable of type OBJECT.

3. The term *class* is used when discussing C++ classes or classes in general.

4. The term *object* refers to the instance of a C++ class or the instance of a class in general.

With these set guidelines, I'll explain the components of a Turbo Pascal object type:

1. Data fields: these fields are the record-like data fields that belong to an object type. They define the state of the object variables.

2. The headers for the methods are equivalent to the forward declarations for the various functions and procedures encapsulated in the object type to provide the desired functionality. You cannot include the code body in the declaration of an object type.

Object-oriented programming discourages direct access of data fields. Instead, object types should offer access methods to set and query the values of various data fields. This scheme allows controlled access to the data fields and a more robust object type. Some data fields can be set and queried, others can only be queried, and still others are denied access because they are strictly for internal use. Turbo Pascal Version 6.0 first offered the PRIVATE keyword that allows data fields and methods to be declared as private. Borland Pascal 7.0 added the PUBLIC keyword to explicitly declare data fields as public. The general syntax is as follows:

```
className = OBJECT ¦ OBJECT(parentClass)
    PUBLIC
        <list of public data fields>
        <headers for the public methods>
    PRIVATE
        <list of private data fields>
        <headers for the private methods>
    END;
```

The private data fields and methods cannot be accessed by the instances of the object types. I will discuss this topic in greater detail in the next chapter.

An example of an object type hierarchy is shown in Listing 12.1. These object types model the following simple geometric shapes:

1. The TCircle object type models a simple circle and is declared as follows:

```
TCircle = OBJECT
    PROCEDURE SetRadius(R : REAL { input  });
    FUNCTION GetRadius : REAL;
    FUNCTION Area : REAL;
    FUNCTION Circumference : REAL;
  PRIVATE
    Radius : REAL;
END;
```

The object type has one data field, namely, Radius, to store the radius of the circle. Two methods, SetRadius and GetRadius, set and query the value of the private Radius data field, respectively. The Area and Circumference methods return the area and circumference of the circle, respectively. The TCircle is the base object type for the geometric shape hierarchy.

2. The TSphere that models a sphere is declared as follows:

```
TSphere = OBJECT(TCircle)
    FUNCTION Area : REAL;
    FUNCTION Volume : REAL;
END;
```

I declared the TSphere object type as a descendent of TCircle by placing the name of the parent object type in parentheses after the OBJECT keyword. The method Area overrides the inherited one to calculate the surface area of the sphere. The method Volume returns the volume of the sphere. The Radius data field and the methods GetRadius, SetRadius, and Circumference are inherited from TCircle. The GetRadius and SetRadius methods serve the TSphere object type adequately.

3. The TCylinder object type that models a solid cylinder is declared as follows:

```
TCylinder = OBJECT(TCircle)
    PROCEDURE SetHeight(H : REAL { input  });
    FUNCTION GetHeight : REAL;
    FUNCTION Area : REAL;
    FUNCTION BaseArea : REAL;
    FUNCTION Volume : REAL;
  PRIVATE
    Height : REAL;
END;
```

349

The `TCylinder` object type is another descendent of `TCircle`. Because a cylinder has a circular base and a height, it requires radius and height data fields for object type modeling. The radius data field is inherited from `TCircle`. Therefore, the `TCylinder` object type declares the required `Height` data field along with `SetHeight` and `GetHeight` methods to set and query the values of `Height`. The `TSphere` object type overrides the inherited `Area` method to declare its own version. This new version calculates the total surface area as being equal to the lateral area plus twice the base area. The base area is returned by method `BaseArea`. The volume of the solid cylinder is obtained by method `Volume`.

4. The `THollowCylinder` object type that models a hollow cylinder is declared as follows:

```
THollowCylinder = OBJECT(TCylinder)
    InnerRadius : REAL;
    PROCEDURE SetInnerRadius(R : REAL { input  });
    FUNCTION GetInnerRadius : REAL;
    FUNCTION Area : REAL;
    FUNCTION BaseArea : REAL;
  PRIVATE
    InnerRadius : REAL;
END;
```

The `THollowCylinder` object type is a descendent of `TCylinder` because it is a refinement of the solid cylinder. The hollow cylinder has two radii and a height. The data fields for the outer radius and the height are inherited from `TCylinder`. Therefore, the `THollowCylinder` declares the required `InnerRadius` data field along with methods `SetInnerRadius` and `GetInnerRadius` to set and query `InnerRadius`, respectively. The `THollowCylinder` object type defines its own versions of methods `Area` and `BaseArea`. The method `Volume` is inherited from its parent object type because the volume of a hollow cylinder is also equal to the product of the base area and the cylinder height.

As you look at Listing 12.1, notice the following items regarding the various methods:

1. They are all defined outside the object type declaration. This is mandated by the Turbo Pascal compiler.

2. Each method is qualified by the name of the owner object type. This tells the Turbo Pascal compiler two things. First, that the routine is part of an object type. Second, it associates the methods with their respective object types. This certainly removes the ambiguity of associating methods like `Area`, `BaseArea`, and `Volume` with their proper object types.

3. The methods access the data fields without the need for additional qualifiers. The same is said about accessing other methods that belong to the same object type hierarchy. The traditional implementations of object-oriented Pascal require that

you employ the identifier SELF, a reference to the object type itself, to access the various data fields and methods. Thus, for example, Self.Radius is used to access the Radius data field. Borland chose to simplify matters greatly in Turbo Pascal by placing an invisible WITH Self DO inside each method. This absolves you from explicitly qualifying the data fields and methods with Self.

Listing 12.1. Source code for the LST12_01.PAS program.

```pascal
Program Shapes;

Uses Crt;

TYPE
    TCircle = OBJECT
        PROCEDURE SetRadius(R : REAL { input  });
        FUNCTION GetRadius : REAL;
        FUNCTION Area : REAL;
        FUNCTION Circumference : REAL;
      PRIVATE
        Radius : REAL;
    END;

    TSphere = OBJECT(TCircle)
        FUNCTION Area : REAL;
        FUNCTION Volume : REAL;
    END;

    TCylinder = OBJECT(TCircle)
        PROCEDURE SetHeight(H : REAL { input  });
        FUNCTION GetHeight : REAL;
        FUNCTION Area : REAL;
        FUNCTION BaseArea : REAL;
        FUNCTION Volume : REAL;
      PRIVATE
        Height : REAL;
    END;

    THollowCylinder = OBJECT(TCylinder)
        PROCEDURE SetInnerRadius(R : REAL { input  });
        FUNCTION GetInnerRadius : REAL;
        FUNCTION Area : REAL;
        FUNCTION BaseArea : REAL;
      PRIVATE
        InnerRadius : REAL;
    END;
```

continues

351

Listing 12.1. continued

```pascal
PROCEDURE TCircle.SetRadius(R : REAL { input  });
BEGIN
    Radius := R
END;

FUNCTION TCircle.GetRadius : REAL;
BEGIN
    GetRadius := Radius
END;

FUNCTION TCircle.Area : REAL;
BEGIN
    Area := Pi * SQR(Radius);
END;

FUNCTION TCircle.Circumference : REAL;
BEGIN
    Circumference := 2 * Pi * Radius
END;

FUNCTION TSphere.Area : REAL;
BEGIN
    Area := 4 * TCircle.Area
END;

FUNCTION TSphere.Volume : REAL;
BEGIN
    Volume := 4 / 3 * Pi * SQR(Radius) * Radius
END;

PROCEDURE TCylinder.SetHeight(H : REAL { input  });
BEGIN
    Height := H
END;

FUNCTION TCylinder.GetHeight : REAL;
BEGIN
    GetHeight := Height
END;

FUNCTION TCylinder.Area : REAL;
BEGIN
    Area := 2 * BaseArea + TCircle.Circumference * Height;
END;
```

```
FUNCTION TCylinder.BaseArea : REAL;
BEGIN
    BaseArea := TCircle.Area
END;

FUNCTION TCylinder.Volume : REAL;
BEGIN
    Volume := BaseArea * Height
END;

PROCEDURE THollowCylinder.SetInnerRadius(R : REAL { input  });
BEGIN
    InnerRadius := R
END;

FUNCTION THollowCylinder.GetInnerRadius : REAL;
BEGIN
    GetInnerRadius := InnerRadius
END;

FUNCTION THollowCylinder.Area : REAL;
BEGIN
    Area := 2 * BaseArea + TCircle.Circumference * Height
END;

FUNCTION THollowCylinder.BaseArea : REAL;
BEGIN
    BaseArea := Pi * (SQR(Radius) - SQR(InnerRadius))
END;

VAR Circle : TCircle;
    Sphere : TSphere;
    Cylinder : TCylinder;
    Hollow : THollowCylinder;
    AKey : CHAR;

BEGIN
    ClrScr;
    Circle.SetRadius(1);
    WRITELN('Circle Radius        = ', Circle.GetRadius);
    WRITELN('Circle Circumference = ', Circle.Circumference);
    WRITELN('Circle Area          = ', Circle.Area);
    WRITELN;
    Sphere.SetRadius(1);
    WRITELN('Sphere Radius        = ', Sphere.GetRadius);
    WRITELN('Sphere Area          = ', Sphere.Area);
    WRITELN('Sphere Volume        = ', Sphere.Volume);
```

continues

353

Listing 12.1. continued

```
    WRITELN;
    Cylinder.SetRadius(1);
    Cylinder.SetHeight(10);
    WRITELN('Cylinder Radius    = ', Cylinder.GetRadius);
    WRITELN('Cylinder Height    = ', Cylinder.GetHeight);
    WRITELN('Cylinder Base Area = ', Cylinder.BaseArea);
    WRITELN('Cylinder Area      = ', Cylinder.Area);
    WRITELN('Cylinder Volume    = ', Cylinder.Volume);
    WRITELN;
    Hollow.SetRadius(1);
    Hollow.SetInnerRadius(0.5);
    Hollow.SetHeight(10);
    WRITELN('Hollow Radius       = ', Hollow.GetRadius);
    WRITELN('Hollow Inner Radius = ', Hollow.GetInnerRadius);
    WRITELN('Hollow Height       = ', Hollow.GetHeight);
    WRITELN('Hollow Base Area    = ', Hollow.BaseArea);
    WRITELN('Hollow Area         = ', Hollow.Area);
    WRITELN('Hollow Volume       = ', Hollow.Volume);
    WRITELN;
    AKey := ReadKey;
END.
```

The program in Listing 12.1. declares four object variables: one for each object type. The various messages are sent to these objects using the record-like reference style. For example, `Circle.SetRadius(1)` sends a `SetRadius` message to object variable `Circle` with an argument of 1.

The following code is the screen output for program LST12_01.PAS.

```
Circle Radius        = 1.0000000000E+00
Circle Circumference = 6.2831853072E+00
Circle Area          = 3.1415926536E+00

Sphere Radius        = 1.0000000000E+00
Sphere Area          = 1.2566370614E+01
Sphere Volume        = 4.1887902048E+00

Cylinder Radius      = 1.0000000000E+00
Cylinder Height      = 1.0000000000E+01
Cylinder Base Area   = 3.1415926536E+00
Cylinder Area        = 6.9115038379E+01
Cylinder Volume      = 3.1415926536E+01

Hollow Radius        = 1.0000000000E+00
Hollow Inner Radius  = 5.0000000000E-01
```

```
Hollow Height      =  1.0000000000E+01
Hollow Base Area   =  2.3561944902E+00
Hollow Area        =  6.7544242052E+01
Hollow Volume      =  3.1415926536E+01
```

Static Versus Virtual Methods

If you examine the preceding output, you'll see that the volumes of the similarly dimen-sioned solid and hollow cylinders are the same! This is an error because the value for the hollow cylinder must be less than that of the solid cylinder. Where did the program go wrong? The answer lies in the Volume method that the THollowCylinder object type in-herits from TCylinder. The latter object type declares the Volume method as follows:

```
FUNCTION TCylinder.Volume : REAL;
BEGIN
    Volume := BaseArea * Height
END;
```

When the Hollow object variable receives the Volume message it invokes the inherited TCylinder.Volume method. If you single-step through the statement that has Hollow.Volume, you'll find that the method TCylinder.Volume calls the TCylinder.BaseArea method, not THollowCylinder.BaseArea! This is the source of the error. You might wonder why the compiler ignored THollowCylinder.BaseArea. The answer is in the type of methods supported by Turbo Pascal.

Turbo Pascal supports two types of methods: *static* and *virtual*. Each type uses a differ-ent way to resolve nested method calls. The compiler resolves nested static methods at compile time. This is basically the traditional way in which Pascal nested routine calls are resolved. When the program starts executing, the runtime system has all the nested calls figured out and set. Executing the program is a matter of systematically following the se-quence of routine calls. In Listing 12.1, the inherited TCylinder.Volume calls BaseArea. The Turbo Pascal compiler resolves this call by invoking TCylinder.BaseArea. This se-quence is applied for both Cylinder.Volume and Hollow.Volume messages.

Virtual methods offer a more sophisticated and correct way for resolving nested method calls. In fact, polymorphism cannot be achieved without virtual methods. Virtual meth-ods guarantee that the messages sent to object variables are properly interpreted. This correct message dispatch occurs because the nested methods are resolved at runtime instead of compile time. Thus, if methods TCylinder.BaseArea and THollowCylinder.BaseArea are made virtual, the program in Listing 12.1 calculates the correct volume for the hollow cylinder. How and why does this happen? The following steps explain the sequence of events.

1. The message Volume is sent to object variable Hollow.

2. The runtime system attempts to find a TCylinder.Volume method. Because none is declared, it looks at the methods of the parent object type TCylinder.

3. A TCylinder.Volume method is found. It contains a call to the virtual method BaseArea.

4. The runtime system looks at the virtual methods of the original message handler: variable Hollow. A matching virtual BaseArea method is found and is used with TCylinder.Volume.

5. The result of method TCylinder.Volume produces the correct response to the Volume message.

Therefore, making the methods virtual causes the runtime system to carry out additional work in resolving nested method calls in a smarter way. Now that I've explained the advantages of using virtual methods, I'll focus on how you set them up. The basic idea is that the compiler needs to keep track of the virtual methods of the various object types. A special table, called the virtual method table (VMT), is established for this purpose. Turbo Pascal requires that you observe the following guidelines when dealing with virtual methods:

1. The object type that uses virtual methods must declare at least one constructor. A constructor is a special procedure that performs two major tasks. First, it tells the compiler that it needs to set up a VMT table. Second, the constructor performs object variable initialization. Attempting to send a message before invoking the constructor causes your system to hang! An object type is allowed multiple constructors to allow various ways for initializing the instances of object types. The typical constructor name is Init.

2. The VIRTUAL keyword is used to declare methods as virtual. It is placed in a separate statement after the routine heading inside the object type declaration. The VIRTUAL keyword must not appear in the method definition.

3. Once a method is declared virtual it remains virtual. If a method is first declared virtual in a descendent object type, it can override static methods declared by the parent object types.

4. The parameter list of virtual methods cannot be changed by descendent object types (as is the case with static methods).

5. A destructor is needed to remove the instance of the object type and eliminate the associated VMT table. Destructors have no parameter lists. There can be only one destructor for an object type. The typical destructor name is Done.

6. The instances of object types with virtual methods are placed in the heap area instead of the program's data segment.

Listing 12.2 provides the version of the geometric object types that use virtual methods. Notice that the TCylinder and THollowCylinder object types declare the BaseArea methods as virtual. In addition, these object types use a constructor and a destructor. In the case of TCylinder, the SetHeight constructor replaces the SetHeight procedure. Similarly, the SetInnerRadius constructor replaces procedure SetInnerRadius in the THollowCylinder object type. The destructors for these two classes perform nothing. Their main purpose is to indicate to the runtime system that the corresponding VMT tables are no longer needed. Other changes made to the code are:

1. The object types are placed in a library unit. This enables various applications to create instances of these object types.

2. The data fields of the object types are placed in PRIVATE clauses to make them inaccessible to the object variables of client programs. I'll cover more about PRIVATE data members and methods in the next chapter.

Listing 12.2. Source code for the SHAPES.PAS library unit.

```pascal
Unit Shapes;

INTERFACE

TYPE
    TCircle = OBJECT
        PROCEDURE SetRadius(R : REAL { input  });
        FUNCTION GetRadius : REAL;
        FUNCTION Area : REAL;
        FUNCTION Circumference : REAL;
      PRIVATE
        Radius : REAL;
    END;

    TSphere = OBJECT(TCircle)
        FUNCTION Area : REAL;
        FUNCTION Volume : REAL;
    END;

    TCylinder = OBJECT(TCircle)
        CONSTRUCTOR SetHeight(H : REAL { input  });
        DESTRUCTOR Done;
        FUNCTION GetHeight : REAL;
```

continues

Listing 12.2. continued

```
      FUNCTION Area : REAL;
      FUNCTION BaseArea : REAL; VIRTUAL;
      FUNCTION Volume : REAL;
   PRIVATE
      Height : REAL;
END;

THollowCylinder = OBJECT(TCylinder)
      CONSTRUCTOR SetInnerRadius(R : REAL { input  });
      DESTRUCTOR Done;
      FUNCTION GetInnerRadius : REAL;
      FUNCTION Area : REAL;
      FUNCTION BaseArea : REAL; VIRTUAL;
   PRIVATE
      InnerRadius : REAL;
END;

IMPLEMENTATION

PROCEDURE TCircle.SetRadius(R : REAL { input  });
BEGIN
   Radius := R
END;

FUNCTION TCircle.GetRadius : REAL;
BEGIN
   GetRadius := Radius
END;

FUNCTION TCircle.Area : REAL;
BEGIN
   Area := Pi * SQR(Radius);
END;

FUNCTION TCircle.Circumference : REAL;
BEGIN
   Circumference := 2 * Pi * Radius
END;

FUNCTION TSphere.Area : REAL;
BEGIN
   Area := 4 * TCircle.Area
END;
```

```
FUNCTION TSphere.Volume : REAL;
BEGIN
    Volume := 4 / 3 * Pi * SQR(Radius) * Radius
END;

CONSTRUCTOR TCylinder.SetHeight(H : REAL { input  });
BEGIN
    Height := H
END;
DESTRUCTOR TCylinder.Done;
BEGIN
END;

FUNCTION TCylinder.GetHeight : REAL;
BEGIN
    GetHeight := Height
END;

FUNCTION TCylinder.Area : REAL;
BEGIN
    Area := TCircle.Area + TCircle.Circumference * Height;
END;

FUNCTION TCylinder.BaseArea : REAL;
BEGIN
    BaseArea := TCircle.Area
END;

FUNCTION TCylinder.Volume : REAL;
BEGIN
    Volume := BaseArea * Height
END;

CONSTRUCTOR THollowCylinder.SetInnerRadius(R : REAL { input  });
BEGIN
    InnerRadius := R
END;

DESTRUCTOR THollowCylinder.Done;
BEGIN
END;

FUNCTION THollowCylinder.GetInnerRadius : REAL;
BEGIN
    GetInnerRadius := InnerRadius
END;
```

continues

359

Listing 12.2. continued

```
FUNCTION THollowCylinder.Area : REAL;
BEGIN
    Area := BaseArea + TCircle.Circumference * Height
END;

FUNCTION THollowCylinder.BaseArea : REAL;
BEGIN
    BaseArea := Pi * (SQR(Radius) - SQR(InnerRadius))
END;

END.
```

Listing 12.3. shows LST12_03.PAS, a test program for the SHAPES.PAS library unit. Although the program resembles the main program body of Listing 12.1, the Done messages are sent to the Cylinder and Hollow object variables.

Listing 12.3. Source code for the test program LST12_03.PAS.

```
Program TestShapes;

Uses Crt, Shapes;

VAR Circle : TCircle;
    Sphere : TSphere;
    Cylinder : TCylinder;
    Hollow : THollowCylinder;
    AKey : CHAR;

BEGIN
    ClrScr;
    Circle.SetRadius(1);
    WRITELN('Circle Radius        = ', Circle.GetRadius);
    WRITELN('Circle Circumference = ', Circle.Circumference);
    WRITELN('Circle Area          = ', Circle.Area);
    WRITELN;
    Sphere.SetRadius(1);
    WRITELN('Sphere Radius        = ', Sphere.GetRadius);
    WRITELN('Sphere Area          = ', Sphere.Area);
    WRITELN('Sphere Volume        = ', Sphere.Volume);
    WRITELN;
    Cylinder.SetRadius(1);
    Cylinder.SetHeight(10);
```

```
     WRITELN('Cylinder Radius      = ', Cylinder.GetRadius);
     WRITELN('Cylinder Height      = ', Cylinder.GetHeight);
     WRITELN('Cylinder Base Area   = ', Cylinder.BaseArea);
     WRITELN('Cylinder Area        = ', Cylinder.Area);
     WRITELN('Cylinder Volume      = ', Cylinder.Volume);
     WRITELN;
     Cylinder.Done;
     Hollow.SetRadius(1);
     Hollow.SetInnerRadius(0.5);
     Hollow.SetHeight(10);
     WRITELN('Hollow Radius        = ', Hollow.GetRadius);
     WRITELN('Hollow Inner Radius  = ', Hollow.GetInnerRadius);
     WRITELN('Hollow Height        = ', Hollow.GetHeight);
     WRITELN('Hollow Base Area     = ', Hollow.BaseArea);
     WRITELN('Hollow Area          = ', Hollow.Area);
     WRITELN('Hollow Volume        = ', Hollow.Volume);
     WRITELN;
     Hollow.Done;
     AKey := ReadKey;
END.
```

Dynamic Objects

You can use pointers to object types to create dynamic instances of objects. Use the New and Dispose intrinsics for this purpose. Turbo Pascal has extended the syntax of the New and Dispose statements to include calls to constructors and destructors. The general form for the extended New syntax is:

```
New(objectPointer, constructorName(<arguments_list>));
```

This has the same effect as:

```
New(objectPointer);
objectPointer^.constructorName(<argument_list>);
```

The general form for the extended Dispose syntax is:

```
Dispose(objectPointer, destructorName);
```

This replaces the following two statements:

```
objectPointer^.destructorName;
Dispose(objectPointer);
```

Listing 12.4 contains a version of Listing 12.3 that uses pointers to object types instead of object variables. The program creates and later removes the dynamic objects for the TCircle and TSphere object types using the standard-syntax New and Dispose statements. The dynamic objects for the TCylinder and THollowCylinder use the extended syntax with the New and Dispose statements.

Listing 12.4. Source code for the LST12_04.PAS test program.

```
Program TestShapes2;

Uses Crt, Shapes;

VAR Circle : ^TCircle;
    Sphere : ^TSphere;
    Cylinder : ^TCylinder;
    Hollow : ^THollowCylinder;
    AKey : CHAR;

BEGIN
    ClrScr;
    New(Circle);
    Circle^.SetRadius(1);
    WRITELN('Circle Radius        = ', Circle^.GetRadius);
    WRITELN('Circle Circumference = ', Circle^.Circumference);
    WRITELN('Circle Area          = ', Circle^.Area);
    WRITELN;
    Dispose(Circle);
    New(Sphere);
    Sphere^.SetRadius(1);
    WRITELN('Sphere Radius        = ', Sphere^.GetRadius);
    WRITELN('Sphere Area          = ', Sphere^.Area);
    WRITELN('Sphere Volume        = ', Sphere^.Volume);
    WRITELN;
    Dispose(Sphere);
    New(Cylinder, SetHeight(10));
    Cylinder^.SetRadius(1);
    WRITELN('Cylinder Radius      = ', Cylinder^.GetRadius);
    WRITELN('Cylinder Height      = ', Cylinder^.GetHeight);
    WRITELN('Cylinder Base Area   = ', Cylinder^.BaseArea);
    WRITELN('Cylinder Area        = ', Cylinder^.Area);
    WRITELN('Cylinder Volume      = ', Cylinder^.Volume);
    WRITELN;
    Dispose(Cylinder, Done);
    New(Hollow, SetInnerRadius(0.5));
    Hollow^.SetRadius(1);
```

```
    Hollow^.SetHeight(10);
    WRITELN('Hollow Radius        = ', Hollow^.GetRadius);
    WRITELN('Hollow Inner Radius  = ', Hollow^.GetInnerRadius);
    WRITELN('Hollow Height        = ', Hollow^.GetHeight);
    WRITELN('Hollow Base Area     = ', Hollow^.BaseArea);
    WRITELN('Hollow Area          = ', Hollow^.Area);
    WRITELN('Hollow Volume        = ', Hollow^.Volume);
    WRITELN;
    Dispose(Hollow, Done);
    AKey := ReadKey;
END.
```

Summary

This chapter covered the following Turbo Pascal object-oriented programming issues:

- Declaring base object types; Turbo Pascal classes are declared as follows:

```
className = OBJECT ¦ OBJECT(parentClass)
        <list of data fields>
        <headers for the methods>
END;
```

- Declaring derived object types; the general syntax is:

```
className = OBJECT ¦ OBJECT(parentClass)
    PUBLIC
        <list of public data fields>
        <headers for the public methods>
    PRIVATE
        <list of private data fields>
        <headers for the private methods>
END;
```

- Static versus virtual methods; virtual methods are vital tools for implementing polymorphic behavior. They allow for runtime binding to ensure the proper response of an object to a message. When a subclass declares its own version of a virtual method, it cannot alter the parameter list of that method. By contrast, a subclass may override an inherited static method by also changing its parameter list.

- Dynamic objects; Borland extended the syntax for the New and Dispose intrinsics. The extension allows you to invoke the constructor or destructor with the call to New and Dispose, respectively. The general form for the extended New syntax is:

```
New(objectPointer, constructorName(<arguments_list>));
```

This has the same effect as:

```
New(objectPointer);
objectPointer^.constructorName(<argument_list>);
```

The general form for the extended Dispose syntax is:

```
Dispose(objectPointer, destructorName);
```

This replaces the following two statements:

```
objectPointer^.destructorName;
Dispose(objectPointer);
```

C++ CLASSES

C ++ extends the C language by adding object-oriented programming language features. OOP purists, however, do not regard C++ as a true object-oriented programming language. This view is shared by the designers of C++. Nevertheless, C++ has enough OOP extensions to make it quite useful for modeling objects. This chapter focuses on C++ classes and covers the following topics:

- declaring base classes

- declaring a class hierarchy

- constructors and destructors

- static members

- nested data types

- friend functions

- operators and friend operators

- friend classes

- multiple inheritance

This chapter was written with the assumption that you're familiar with the basic concepts of object-oriented programming and the OOP features of Turbo Pascal. If you are not, please read the preceding two chapters.

This chapter does not cover every detail of C++ classes. Instead, it is a broad introduction that enables you to quickly learn how to develop C++ classes. After you feel
comfortable with C++ classes, I suggest that you read a textbook dedicated to cov-
ering C++ programming issues extensively.

Declaring Base Classes

C++ enables you to declare a class that encapsulates data members (equivalent to fields in
Turbo Pascal) and member functions (equivalent to methods in Turbo Pascal). The member functions alter the state of the class instances by changing the various values of one or
more data members. The general syntax for declaring a base class (one that is not derived
from any other class) is:

```
class className
{
    private:
        <private data members>
        <private member functions>

    protected:
        <protected data members>
        <protected member functions>

    public:
        <public data members>
        <public member functions>
};
```

The preceding syntax shows that the declaration involves the class keyword. C++ classes
offer three levels of visibility for the various members (that is, both data members and
member functions):

1. The private section; only member functions of the class can access the private
   members. The class instances are denied access to private members.

2. The protected section; only member functions of the class and its descendant
   classes can access protected members. The class instances are denied access to
   protected members.

3. The public section; specifies members that are visible to the member functions of the class, class instances, member functions of descendant classes, and their instances.

The following rules apply to the various sections:

1. Class sections can appear in any order.

2. Class sections may appear more than once.

3. If no class section is specified, the C++ compiler treats the members as protected.

4. You should avoid placing data members in the public section, unless such a declaration significantly simplifies your design. Data members are typically placed in the protected section to allow their access by member functions of descendant classes.

5. Use member functions to set and query the values of data members. The members that set the data members assist in performing validation and updating other data members, if necessary.

After you declare a class, you can use the class name as a type identifier to declare class instances. The syntax resembles declaring variables.

Listing 13.1 is the source code for the LST13_01.CPP program, an example that declares and uses a C++ class. This program declares the class TCircle to model a circle.

Listing 13.1. Source code for the LST13_01.CPP program.

```
/*
   C++ program that demonstrates a simple class that models
   a circle.
*/

#include <iostream.h>
#include <conio.h>
#include <math.h>

const double pi = 4 * atan(1);

inline double sqr(double x)
{
  return x * x;
}
```

continues

367

Listing 13.1. continued

```cpp
class TCircle
{
  protected:
    double radius;

  public:
    TCircle(double R = 0)
      { radius = R; }
    void setRadius(double R)
      { radius = R; }
    double getRadius() const
      { return radius; }
    double area() const
      { return pi * sqr(radius); }
    double circumference() const
      { return 2 * pi * radius; }
    void showData();
};

void TCircle::showData()
{
  cout << "Circle radius        = " << getRadius()
       << "\nCircle circumference = " << circumference()
       << "\nCircle area          = " << area()
       << "\n\n";
}

main()
{
  TCircle Circle(1);

  clrscr();
  Circle.showData();
  Circle.setRadius(2);
  Circle.showData();
  Circle.setRadius(3);
  Circle.showData();
  getch();
  return 0;
}
```

The TCircle class declares the protected data member, radius, and a number of public member functions. Declaring the data member as protected follows the rules I suggested and prevents the instances of TCircle from directly accessing the member radius.

The TCircle class declares the following member functions:

1. The TCircle constructor that allows you to assign a value to the radius data member when declaring an instance of class TCircle. Constructors and destructors play a more strategic role in C++ than they do in Turbo Pascal. I cover constructors and destructors in more detail later on in this chapter.

2. The setRadius member function that assigns a value to the radius data member.

3. The getRadius member function that returns the value of the radius data member. Notice that the empty parameter list of the function is followed by the const keyword. This keyword tells the compiler that the getRadius function cannot alter the radius data member. In general, member functions that have the const keyword after their parameter lists cannot alter any data member that is either declared in the class or inherited from a parent class.

4. The area member function returns the calculated value of the area. Again, the function declaration has the const keyword after the empty parameter list.

5. The circumference member function yields the calculated circumference.

6. The showData member function displays the value of the radius, the circumference, and the area of the circle. Notice that the class only declares showData—it does not define it. The definition of the showData function appears outside (and after) the class declaration. Observe that the heading of showData is:

```
void TCircle::showData()
```

TCircle:: is a qualifier that informs the compiler of the owner of member function showData. This kind of clarification is more evident in the next example, which contains several versions of showData, each associated with a different class. All the other member functions of class TCircle use single statements. With C++, you can place these short statements in the class declaration (something Turbo Pascal does not allow) rather than outside the class declaration. The compiler treats these member functions as inline, if possible. You still can define the member functions outside the class declaration.

For simplicity, I wrote Listing 13.1 to contain all the code related to the example. Typically, you place the class declaration in a h or .hpp header file, the definition of member functions in a .CPP file, and function main (and other auxiliary functions) in a separate .CPP file.

The program also declares the function main that performs the following relevant tasks:

1. Declares the instance of class TCircle (Circle) and assigns 1 to the radius data member.

2. Invokes the showData member function with the instance Circle. This function call displays the radius, the circumference, and the area of the circle.

3. Assigns a new value for the radius by calling the setRadius member function and supplying it with an argument of 2.

4. Invokes the showData member function to display the current data of the instance Circle.

5. Assigns a new value for the radius by calling the setRadius member function and supplying it with an argument of 3.

6. Invokes the showData member function to display the current data of the instance Circle.

> Notice in the preceding task description that I did not use the notion of sending messages to object Circle. The C++ designers have stated that C++ classes do not implement the same concept of handling messages as pure OOP languages, such as SmallTalk, do.

Compile and run Listing 13.1. The following code is the program output:

```
Circle radius        = 1
Circle circumference = 6.283185
Circle area          = 3.141593

Circle radius        = 2
Circle circumference = 12.566371
Circle area          = 12.566371

Circle radius        = 3
Circle circumference = 18.849556
Circle area          = 28.274334
```

Declaring a Class Hierarchy

With C++, you can declare descendant classes from existing ones. The general syntax for declaring a derived class is:

```
class className : [public] parentClass
{
    private:
        <private data members>
        <private member functions>

    protected:
        <protected data members>
        <protected member functions>

    public:
        <public data members>
        <public member functions>
};
```

The descendant class inherits the members of its ancestor classes (that is, parent class, grandparent class, and so on). The class lineage is indicated by a colon followed by the optional public keyword and the name of the parent class. When you include the public keyword, you allow the instances of the descendant class to access the public members of the parent and other ancestor classes. Conversely, when you omit the public keyword, you deprive the instance of the descendant class from accessing the members of the ancestor classes. This data hiding feature is justified in cases in which the descendant class brings a change in context. The following example helps explain this. Consider a class that implements a dynamic list of unsigned integers:

```
class intList
{
    protected:
        unsigned* head;
        unsigned listSize;
        // other members

    public:
        intList();  // constructor
        ~intList(); // destructor
        int insert(unsigned n);
        int search(unsigned n);
        int remove(unsigned n);
        void clearList();
        // other member functions
};
```

371

You can use the preceding class to implement a class that models a list-based stack of unsigned integers:

```
class intStack : intList
{
    public:
          intStack(); // constructor
          ~intStack(); // destructor
          void push(unsigned n);
          int pop(unsigned& n);
          void clearStack();
};
```

The intStack class is a descendant of class intList. However, you do not want the instances of class intStack to access the public member functions insert, search, and remove because they support operations for lists. By omitting the public class derivation, you force the instances of intStack to use the member functions push, pop, and clearStack. This example shows how the descendant class has changed context yet still makes use of the operations supported by the parent class.

The descendant classes inherit the data members of their ancestor classes. C++ has no mechanism to remove unwanted inherited data members—you are basically stuck with them. In contrast, with C++ you can override inherited member functions. I'll discuss this topic later in this chapter. The descendant classes declare new data members, new member functions, and overriding member functions. Again, you can place these members in the private, protected, or public sections as you see fit in your class design.

Listing 13.2 is the source code for the LST13_02.CPP program, an example that declares a small class hierarchy. This program declares classes that contain a hierarchy of simple geometric shapes: a circle, a sphere, a cylinder, and a hollow cylinder.

Listing 13.2. Source code for the LST13_02.CPP program.

```
/*
   C++ program that demonstrates a small hierarchy of classes
   that models simple geometric shapes
*/


#include <iostream.h>
#include <conio.h>
#include <math.h>

const double pi = 4 * atan(1);
```

```
inline double sqr(double x)
{
  return x * x;
}

class TCircle
{
  protected:
    double radius;

  public:
    TCircle(double R = 0)
      { radius = R; }
    void setRadius(double R)
      { radius = R; }
    double getRadius() const
      { return radius; }
    virtual double area() const
      { return pi * sqr(radius); }
    double circumference() const
      { return 2 * pi * radius; }
    virtual void showData();
};

class TSphere : public TCircle
{
  public:
    TSphere(double R = 0)
      { radius = R; }
    virtual double area() const
      { return 4 * TCircle::area(); }
    virtual double volume() const
      { return 4 / 3 * pi * sqr(radius) * radius; }
    virtual void showData();
};

class TCylinder : public TCircle
{
  protected:
    double height;

  public:
    TCylinder(double H = 0, double R = 0);
    void setHeight(double H)
      { height = H; }
    double getHeight() const
      { return height; }
```

continues

Listing 13.2. continued

```
      virtual double area() const
        { return 2 * baseArea() +
                TCircle::circumference() * height; }
      virtual double baseArea() const
        { return TCircle::area(); }
      virtual double volume() const
        { return baseArea() * height; }
      virtual void showData();
};

class THollowCylinder : public TCylinder
{
  protected:
    double innerRadius;

  public:
    THollowCylinder(double H = 0,
                    double Rin = 0,
                    double Rout = 0);
    void setInnerRadius(double R)
      { innerRadius = R; }
    double getInnerRadius() const
      { return innerRadius; }
    virtual double area() const
      { return 2 * baseArea() +
          TCircle::circumference() * height; }
    virtual double baseArea() const
      { return pi * (sqr(radius) - sqr(innerRadius)); }
    virtual void showData();
};

void TCircle::showData()
{
  cout << "Circle radius        = " << getRadius()
       << "\nCircle circumference = " << circumference()
       << "\nCircle area          = " << area()
       << "\n";
}

void TSphere::showData()
{
  cout << "\nSphere radius        = " << getRadius()
       << "\nSphere area          = " << area()
       << "\nSphere volume        = " << volume()
       << "\n";
}
```

```
TCylinder::TCylinder(double H, double R)
{
  height = H;
  radius = R;
}

void TCylinder::showData()
{
   cout << "\nCylinder radius      = " << getRadius()
        << "\nCylinder height      = " << getHeight()
        << "\nCylinder Base area   = " << baseArea()
        << "\nCylinder area        = " << area()
        << "\nCylinder volume      = " << volume()
        << "\n";
}

THollowCylinder::THollowCylinder(double H, double Rin, double Rout)
{
   height = H;
   radius = Rout;
   innerRadius = Rin;
}

void THollowCylinder::showData()
{
   cout << "\nHollow radius        = " << getRadius()
        << "\nHollow inner radius  = " << getInnerRadius()
        << "\nHollow height        = " << getHeight()
        << "\nHollow Base area     = " << baseArea()
        << "\nHollow area          = " << area()
        << "\nHollow volume        = " << volume()
        << "\n";
}

main()
{
   TCircle Circle(1);
   TSphere Sphere(1);
   TCylinder Cylinder(10, 1);
   THollowCylinder Hollow(10, 0.5, 1);

   clrscr();
   Circle.showData();
   Sphere.showData();
   Cylinder.showData();
   Hollow.showData();
   getch();
   return 0;
}
```

The preceding listing declares the following classes:

1. The class TCircle models a circle and is the base class for the hierarchy of geometric shapes.

2. The class TSphere models a sphere and is a descendant of class TCircle.

3. The class TCylinder models a solid cylinder and is a descendant of class TCircle.

4. The class THollowCylinder models a hollow cylinder and is a descendant of class TCylinder.

Now that I've introduced the classes in the hierarchy, I'll discuss their makeup.

1. The TCircle class is almost identical to the one presented in Listing 13.1. The minor differences include the functions area and showData declared as virtual. Virtual member functions in C++ classes are very similar to virtual methods in Turbo Pascal object types. In fact, the latter were inspired by the C++ virtual member functions.

2. Class TSphere is publicly derived from TCircle by using the public keyword. Although the TSphere class declares no data members, it declares the following constructor and member functions:

   - The TSphere constructor, which allows you to assign a value to the data member radius when declaring a class instance.

   - The virtual member function area, which returns the surface of a sphere.

   - The virtual volume member function, which returns the volume of the sphere.

   - The virtual showData member function, which displays the radius, area, and volume of a class instance.

3. The TCylinder class is publicly derived from TCircle. The descendant class declares a new data member, height, to store the height of the cylinder. The class inherits the TCircle::radius member to store the value for the cylinder's radius. In addition, the class declares the following constructor and member functions:

   - The constructor that allows you to assign values for the radius and height data members when you create a class instance. Notice that the class declaration only declares the constructor but does not define it. Listing 13.2 contains the definition of the TCylinder constructor after the class declaration.

   - The setHeight and getHeight member functions set and retrieve the value stored in the data member height.

- The virtual function area returns the surface area of the cylinder. Notice that the function explicitly invokes the circumference function of TCircle by using the expression TCircle::circumference().

- The baseArea virtual function returns the base area of the circular base.

- The virtual member function volume yields the volume of the cylinder.

- The showData virtual function displays the radius, height, base area, area, and volume of a class instance.

4. The THollowCylinder class is publicly derived from TCylinder. The descendant class declares the innerRadius data member. A hollow cylinder has two radii: an outer radius and an inner radius. This class uses the inherited TCircle::radius member to represent the outer radius. Likewise, the class inherits the TCylinder::height member to store the values for the hollow cylinder's height. In addition, the THollowCylinder class declares the following constructor and member functions:

- The constructor that allows you to assign values to the radii and height of a hollow cylinder when you create a class instance.

- The setInnerRadius and getInnerRadius functions set and retrieve the values of the inner radius, respectively.

- The virtual function baseArea returns the base area of the circular base.

- The virtual member function volume yields the volume of the hollow cylinder.

- The virtual function showData displays the radii, height, base area, area, and volume of a class instance.

The function main performs the following tasks:

1. Declares the instance Circle, of class TCircle, and assigns 1 to the circle's radius.

2. Declares the instance Sphere, of class TSphere, and assigns 1 to the sphere's radius.

3. Declares the instance Cylinder, of class TCylinder, and assigns 10 and 1 to the circle's height and radius, respectively.

4. Declares the instance Hollow, of class THollowCylinder, and assigns 10, 0.5, and 1 to the circle's height, inner radius, and outer radius, respectively.

5. Invokes showData for each class instance.

Examine the following output for the preceding program (Listing 13.2):

```
Circle radius        = 1
Circle circumference = 6.283185
Circle area          = 3.141593

Sphere radius        = 1
Sphere area          = 12.566371
Sphere volume        = 3.141593

Cylinder radius      = 1
Cylinder height      = 10
Cylinder Base area   = 3.141593
Cylinder area        = 69.115038
Cylinder volume      = 31.415927

Hollow radius        = 1
Hollow inner radius  = 0.5
Hollow height        = 10
Hollow Base area     = 2.356194
Hollow area          = 67.544242
Hollow volume        = 23.561945
```

Constructors and Destructors

Although C++ constructors and destructors have inspired Borland programmers to use constructors and destructors in Turbo Pascal, how they work in the two languages differs significantly. In C++, constructors and destructors work automatically to guarantee the appropriate creation and removal of class instance. C++ has the following features and rules regarding constructors:

1. The name of the constructor must be identical to the name of its class.

2. You must not include any return type, not even void.

3. A class can have any number of constructors, including none. In the latter case, the compiler automatically creates one for you.

4. The default constructor is the one that either has neither parameters nor a parameter list where all the parameters use default arguments. Note the following two examples:

```
class complex
{
    protected:
        double real;
        double imag;
```

```
    public:
        complex();
        // other members
};

class Complex
{
    protected:
        double real;
        double imag;

    public:
        Complex(double Real = 0, double Imag = 0);
        // other members
};
```

5. The copy constructor enables you to create a class instance using an existing instance. Note the following example:

```
class complex
{
    protected:
        double real;
        double imag;

    public:
        complex(); // default constructor
        complex(complex& c); // copy constructor
        complex(double Real, double Imag);
        // other members
};
```

> If you do not declare a copy constructor, the compiler creates one for you. Many C++ programmers strongly recommend that you declare copy constructors, especially for classes that model dynamic data structures.

6. The declaration of a class instance (which includes function parameters and local instances) involves a constructor. Which constructor is called? The answer depends on how many constructors you have declared for the class and how you declared the class instance. For example, consider the following instances of the last version of class complex:

```
complex c1; // involves the default constructor
complex c2(1.1, 1.3); // uses the third constructor
complex c3(c2); // uses the copy constructor
```

Because instance c1 specifies no arguments, the compiler uses the default constructor. The instance c2 specifies two floating-point arguments. Consequently, the compiler uses the third constructor. The instance c3 has the instance c2 as an argument. Therefore, the compiler uses the copy constructor to create instance c3 from instance c2.

C++ has the following features and rules regarding destructors:

1. The name of the destructor must begin with the tilde character (~). The rest of the destructor name must be identical to the name of its class.

2. You must not include any return type, not even void.

3. A class can have no more than one destructor. In addition, if you omit the destructor, the compiler automatically creates one for you.

4. The destructor cannot have any parameters.

5. The runtime system automatically invokes a class destructor when the instance of that class is out of scope.

Listing 13.3, a program that illustrates the use of constructors and destructors, contains the source code for the LST13_03.CPP program. The program manipulates dynamic arrays that are modeled by the Array class .

Listing 13.3. Source code for the LST13_03.CPP program.

```
/*
  C++ program that demonstrates constructors and destructors
*/


#include <iostream.h>
#include <conio.h>

const unsigned MIN_SIZE = 10;
enum boolean { false, true };

class Array
{
   protected:
     unsigned *dataPtr;
     unsigned size;
```

```
  public:
    Array(unsigned Size = MIN_SIZE);
    Array(Array& ar)
      { copy(ar); }
    ~Array()
      { delete [] dataPtr; }
    unsigned getSize() const
      { return size; }
    boolean store(unsigned x, unsigned index);
    boolean recall(unsigned& x, unsigned index);
    Array& copy(Array& ar);

};

Array::Array(unsigned Size)
{
  size = (Size < MIN_SIZE) ? MIN_SIZE : Size;
  dataPtr = new unsigned[size];
}

Array& Array::copy(Array& ar)
{
  delete [] dataPtr; // delete the current array
  // make size of instance equal to size of argument
  size = ar.size;
  // recreate new array
  dataPtr = new unsigned[size];
  // copy elements
  for (unsigned i = 0; i < size; i++)
    dataPtr[i] = ar.dataPtr[i];
  return *this;
}

boolean Array::store(unsigned x, unsigned index)
{
  if (index < size) {
    dataPtr[index] = x;
    return true;
  }
  else
    return false;
}

boolean Array::recall(unsigned& x, unsigned index)
{
  if (index < size) {
    x = dataPtr[index];
```

continues

Listing 13.3. continued

```
    return true;
  }
  else
    return false;
}

main()
{
  Array Ar1;
  Array Ar2(20);
  unsigned x;

  for (unsigned i = 0; i < Ar1.getSize(); i++)
    Ar1.store(i * i, i);

  for (i = 0; i < Ar2.getSize(); i++)
    Ar2.store(i + 2, i);

  clrscr();
  cout << "Array Ar1 has the following values:\n\n";
  for (i = 0; i < Ar1.getSize(); i++) {
    if (Ar1.recall(x, i))
      cout << "Ar1[" << i << "] = " << x << "\n";
    else
      cout << "Ar1[" << i << "] = nonexistent\n";
  }

  cout << "\n\nPress any key to continue...";
  getch();

  clrscr();
  cout << "Array Ar2 has the following values:\n\n";
  for (i = 0; i < Ar2.getSize(); i++) {
    if (Ar2.recall(x, i))
      cout << "Ar2[" << i << "] = " << x << "\n";
    else
      cout << "Ar2[" << i << "] = nonexistent\n";
  }

  cout << "\n\nPress any key to continue...";
  getch();

  Ar1.copy(Ar2);

  clrscr();
  cout << "Expanded array Ar1 (=Array Ar2)"
       << " has the following values:\n\n";
```

```
    for (i = 0; i < Ar1.getSize(); i++) {
      if (Ar1.recall(x, i))
        cout << "Ar1[" << i << "] = " << x << "\n";
      else
        cout << "Ar1[" << i << "] = nonexistent\n";
    }
    cout << "\n\nPress any key to end the program...";
    getch();

    return 0;
}
```

The class Array declares two data members, two constructors, a destructor, and four member functions. The data member dataPtr is the pointer to the elements of the dynamic array. The data member size stores the size of the array. I coded the class such that the array size never goes below a minimum value defined by the MIN_SIZE global constant.

The class defines two constructors. The first constructor, Array (unsigned), has a single parameter that uses a default argument. This argument allows the compiler to use this constructor as the default constructor. The second constructor is the copy constructor, which merely invokes the copy function to duplicate the elements of one array into the targeted class instance.

The destructor preforms the simple, yet necessary, task of removing the dynamically allocated space.

The Array class declares the following member functions:

1. The getSize function returns the current size of the array.

2. The boolean store function stores the x parameter at the array index specified by the index parameter. The function returns true if the argument of parameter index is within valid range. Otherwise, the function yields false.

3. The boolean recall function retrieves the value of the array element at the index specified by the index parameter. The function returns true if the argument of the index parameter is within valid range. Otherwise, the function yields false. The reference parameter x returns the accessed value.

4. The copy function duplicates the targeted class instance using the array specified by the ar parameter. Notice that the copy function returns a reference to class Array. In addition, the ar parameter is also a reference parameter. Using reference parameters enables you to skip creating a copy of the argument— a step that involves calling the copy constructor of class Array. The copy function performs the following tasks:

383

- deletes the element of the targeted class instance

- assigns the size member of the argument to the size member of the targeted class instance

- creates a new dynamic array whose size matches that of parameter ar

- uses a `for` loop to copy the elements of array ar into the elements of the targeted class instance

- returns the object `*this`

> When you write a member function that returns the reference to the host class, always return `*this`. The identifier `this` (which is equivalent to the identifier SELF in Turbo Pascal) points to the targeted class instance, and the expression `*this` returns the targeted instance itself.

The function `main` manipulates the two instances, `Ar1` and `Ar2`, of class `Array`. The function creates these instances using the following statements:

```
Array Ar1;
Array Ar2(20);
```

The `main` function creates instance `Ar1` using the first constructor, acting as the default constructor. By contrast, the function builds the instance `Ar2` by supplying the first constructor with an explicit size. If you place a breakpoint at any statement in the first constructor and run the program, you'll notice that the program execution stops twice at the breakpoint—once for each instance.

The `main` function assigns values to the instances `Ar1` and `Ar2` and displays them. Then the function uses the `copy` member function, to copy the size and elements of instance `Ar2` into instance `Ar1`. After copying the arrays, the function `main` displays the elements of the update instance `Ar1`.

Static Members

In many applications, you need to use special data members that conceptually belong to the class rather than any class instance. A few cases where such data members are useful include:

1. Tracking the number of class instances.

2. Allocating a special memory block for the various class instances.

3. Using arrays of structures to implement a micro database commonly used by the various class instances.

C++ allows you to use static data members for such purposes. You need to observe the following rules:

1. Declare the static data member by placing the static keyword before the member's data type.

2. You can access the static members inside the member functions just like any other nonstatic data members.

3. Initialize the static members outside the class declaration, even if these members are protected or private.

4. The static data members exist separately from the class instances. Therefore, you can access them before you create any class instance.

With C++, you can also declare static member functions to access the static data members. To declare a static member function, place the static keyword before the function's return type. Static member functions *must never* return the expression *this and should not access nonstatic data members. When you access a public static data member or static member function, you need to use the class name as a qualifier. Listing 13.4, the source code for the LST13_04.CPP program, is a simple application of static data members. This program is based on the last one and uses static members to keep track of the number of instances of class Array.

Listing 13.4. The source code for the LST13_04.CPP program.

```
/*
  C++ program that demonstrates static members
*/


#include <iostream.h>
#include <conio.h>

const unsigned MIN_SIZE = 10;
enum boolean { false, true };
```

continues

Listing 13.4. continued

```
class Array
{
   protected:
     unsigned *dataPtr;
     unsigned size;
     static unsigned countInstances;

   public:
     Array(unsigned Size = MIN_SIZE);
     Array(Array& ar);
     ~Array();
     unsigned getSize() const
       { return size; }
     static unsigned getCountInstances()
       { return countInstances; }
     boolean store(unsigned x, unsigned index);
     boolean recall(unsigned& x, unsigned index);
     Array& copy(Array& ar);

};

Array::Array(unsigned Size)
{
  size = (Size < MIN_SIZE) ? MIN_SIZE : Size;
  dataPtr = new unsigned[size];
  countInstances++;
}

Array::Array(Array& ar)
{
  copy(ar);
  countInstances++;
}

Array::~Array()
{
  delete [] dataPtr;
  countInstances—;
}

Array& Array::copy(Array& ar)
{
  delete [] dataPtr; // delete the current array
  // make size of instance equal to size of argument
  size = ar.size;
  // recreate new array
  dataPtr = new unsigned[size];
```

```
    // copy elements
    for (unsigned i = 0; i < size; i++)
      dataPtr[i] = ar.dataPtr[i];
    return *this;
}

boolean Array::store(unsigned x, unsigned index)
{
  if (index < size) {
    dataPtr[index] = x;
    return true;
  }
  else
    return false;
}

boolean Array::recall(unsigned& x, unsigned index)
{
  if (index < size) {
    x = dataPtr[index];
    return true;
  }
  else
    return false;
}

// initialize the static member
unsigned Array::countInstances = 0;

main()
{
  Array Ar1;

  unsigned x;

  for (unsigned i = 0; i < Ar1.getSize(); i++)
    Ar1.store(i * i, i);


  clrscr();
  cout << "Array Ar1 has the following values:\n\n";
  for (i = 0; i < Ar1.getSize(); i++) {
    if (Ar1.recall(x, i))
      cout << "Ar1[" << i << "] = " << x << "\n";
    else
      cout << "Ar1[" << i << "] = nonexistent\n";
  }
```

continues

387

Listing 13.4. continued

```
cout << "\nThere are " << Array::getCountInstances()
     << " instance(s) of class Array"
     << "\nPress any key to continue...";
getch();

{
  Array Ar2(20);

  clrscr();
  for (i = 0; i < Ar2.getSize(); i++)
    Ar2.store(i + 2, i);

  cout << "Array Ar2 has the following values:\n\n";
  for (i = 0; i < Ar2.getSize(); i++) {
    if (Ar2.recall(x, i))
      cout << "Ar2[" << i << "] = " << x << "\n";
    else
      cout << "Ar2[" << i << "] = nonexistent\n";
  }

  cout << "\nThere are " << Array::getCountInstances()
       << " instance(s) of class Array"
       << "\nPress any key to continue...";
  getch();
  Ar1.copy(Ar2);
}

clrscr();
cout << "Expanded array Ar1 (=Array Ar2)"
     << " has the following values:\n\n";
for (i = 0; i < Ar1.getSize(); i++) {
  if (Ar1.recall(x, i))
    cout << "Ar1[" << i << "] = " << x << "\n";
  else
    cout << "Ar1[" << i << "] = nonexistent\n";
}
cout << "\nThere are " << Array::getCountInstances()
     << " instance(s) of class Array"
     << "\nPress any key to continue...";
getch();

return 0;

}
```

The new version of class `Array` declares the static `countInstances` member to keep track of the number of class instances. Notice that the program initializes the static data member outside the class declaration using the following statement:

```
unsigned Array::countInstances = 0;
```

In addition, notice that the constructors increment the member `countInstances`. By contrast, the destructor decrements the static data member. These actions enable the class to keep track of the current number of instances as client functions create and destroy them.

The class also declares the static member function `getCountInstances` to return the value stored in the `countInstances` member. The various member functions access the member `countInstances` just like the other two nonstatic data members.

I modified function `main` to declare the instance `Ar2` in a nested block. This declaration enables the instance `Ar2` to come into being later in function `main` and to be removed before the end of the function. When function `main` displays the elements of instances `Ar1` or `Ar2`, it also includes the current number of class instances. The function displays this information by calling the static function `getCountInstances`. Notice that this function requires the code to qualify it using the class name, `Array`.

Nested Data Types

One of the problems that plagues C programmers is name space pollution. This problem results from declaring too many identifiers, thus making the declaration of new ones likely to conflict with existing ones. C++ allows classes to reduce this problem by enabling you to declare enumerated types, structures, and even classes, that are nested in classes. Although these nested types are still accessible outside their host class, you need the class name to qualify them. Consequently, this approach reduces the chances of creating new names that conflict with others.

Listing 13.5, the source code for the LST13_05.CPP program, is an example of types nested in classes. The program declares a class that models dynamic stacks of unsigned integers. The stack uses single-linked lists as the underlying structure.

Listing 13.5. Source code for the LST13_05.CPP program.

```
/*
  C++ program that demonstrates types that are nested in classes
*/


#include <iostream.h>
#include <string.h>
#include <conio.h>

class Stack
{

  protected:
    // nested structure
    struct StackNode {
        unsigned nodeData;
        StackNode *nextPtr;
    };

    // nested enumerated type
    enum boolean { false, true };

    unsigned height;   // height of stack
    StackNode *top; // pointer to the top of the stack

  public:
    Stack();
    ~Stack()
      { clear(); }

    void push(unsigned);
    boolean pop(unsigned&);
    void clear();
};


Stack::Stack()
{
    height = 0;
    top = NULL;
}

void Stack::clear()
{
    unsigned x;
```

```
    while (pop(x))
      /* do nothing */;
}

void Stack::push(unsigned x)
{
    StackNode *p;

    if (top) {
        p = new StackNode; // allocate new stack element
        p->nodeData = x;
     p->nextPtr = top;
     top = p;
    }
    else {
        top = new StackNode;
     top->nodeData = x;
     top->nextPtr = NULL;
    }
    height++;
}

Stack::boolean Stack::pop(unsigned& x)
{
    StackNode *p;

    if (height) {
        x = top->nodeData;
     p = top;
     top = top->nextPtr;
     delete p; // deallocate stack node
     height—;
     return true;
    }
    else
     return false;
}

main()
{
  unsigned x;
  Stack::boolean ok;
  Stack intStk;

  clrscr();
  intStk.push(1);
  intStk.push(10);
```

continues

391

Listing 13.5. continued

```
intStk.push(100);
intStk.push(1000);
intStk.push(10000);

cout << "Popping off data from integer stack\n\n";
ok = intStk.pop(x);
while (ok) {
  cout << x << "\n";
  ok = intStk.pop(x);
}
cout << "\n";
getch();
return 0;
}
```

The class `Stack` declares two nested types:

1. The `StackNode` structure, which contains the `nodeData` and `nextPtr` data members. The `nodeData` member stores a list element (emulating a stack element). The `nextPtr` member is the pointer to the next list node.

2. The `boolean` enumerated type. I declared the `boolean` type as a nested type instead of a global one, for the sake of this demonstration. In contrast, the class implementation does not require using the `StackNode` structure outside the class (that is, there are parameters in a member function that use that structure type).

The `Stack` class declares a set of data members, a constructor, a destructor, and a number of member functions. These functions support the basic stack operations such as pushing data, popping data, and clearing the stack. These member functions use the nested types to support the various operations. I want to point out two particularly interesting pieces of code from Listing 13.5:

1. The definition of the `pop` member function uses the fully qualified name of the nested boolean type:

   `Stack::boolean Stack::pop(unsigned& x)`

2. The function `main` declares the boolean variable `ok`, again by using the fully qualified name of the nested boolean type:

   `Stack::boolean ok;`

The test program performs the trivial tasks of pushing and popping data on to and off of the stack, respectively.

Friend Functions

C++ allows member functions to access all the data members of a class. In addition, C++ grants the same privileged access to friend functions. Friend functions are ordinary functions that have access to all data members of one or more classes. The declaration of friend functions appears in the class and begins with the `friend` keyword. Other than using the special keyword, friend functions look very much like member functions (except they cannot return a reference to the befriended class, because such results require returning the `*this` self-reference). However, when you define friend functions outside the declaration of their befriended class, you need not qualify the function names with the name of the class.

Friend classes can accomplish tasks that are awkward, difficult, and even impossible with member functions.

Listing 13.6, the source code for the LST13_06.CPP program, is a simple example for using friend functions. This program performs a very simple manipulation of complex numbers.

Listing 13.6. Source code for the LST13_06.CPP program.

```
/*
  C++ program that demonstrates friend functions
*/

#include <iostream.h>
#include <string.h>
#include <conio.h>

class complex
{
  protected:
    double real;
    double imag;

  public:
    complex(double Real = 0, double Imag = 0)
      { assign(Real, Imag); }
    complex(complex& c);
    void assign(double Real = 0, double Imag = 0);
    void assign(complex& c);
```

continues

393

Listing 13.6. continued

```
      double getReal() const
        { return real; }
      double getImag() const
        { return imag; }
      friend complex add(complex& c1, complex& c2);
};

complex::complex(complex& c)
{
  real = c.real;
  imag = c.imag;
}

void complex::assign(double Real, double Imag)
{
  real = Real;
  imag = Imag;
}

void complex::assign(complex& c)
{
  real = c.real;
  imag = c.imag;
}

complex add(complex& c1, complex& c2)
{
  complex result(c1);

  result.real += c2.real;
  result.imag += c2.imag;
  return result;
}

main()
{
  complex c1(1, 1);
  complex c2(2, 2);
  complex c3;

  clrscr();
  c3.assign(add(c1, c2));
  cout << "(" << c1.getReal() << " + i" << c1.getImag() << ")"
       << " + "
       << "(" << c2.getReal() << " + i" << c2.getImag() << ")"
       << " = "
```

```
        << "(" << c3.getReal() << " + i" << c3.getImag() << ")"
        << "\n\n";

  getch();
  return 0;
}
```

The complex class, which models complex numbers, declares two data members, two constructors, a friend function (the highlight of this example), and a set of member functions. The real and imag data members store the real and imaginary components of a complex number.

The class has two constructors. The first constructor has two parameters (with default arguments) that enable you to build a class instance using the real and imaginary components of a complex. Because the two parameters have default arguments, the constructor doubles up as the default constructor. The second constructor, complex(complex&), is the copy constructor that allows you to create class instances by copying the data from existing instances.

The complex class declares the following member functions:

1. The overloaded assign function assigns values to the real and imag data members. The first version of assign has two double-typed parameters, whereas the second version has a complex-type parameter. The two versions of the assign function parallel the two constructors in their parameter lists.

2. The getReal function returns the value stored in the data member real.

3. The function getImag yields the value stored in the data member imag.

The complex class declares the add friend function to add two complex numbers. To keep the program short, I did not implement complementary friend functions that subtract, multiply, and divide class instances. What is so special about the friend function add? Why not use an ordinary member function to add a class instance? To answer these questions, I'll present the declaration of the alternate add member function:

```
complex& add(complex& c)
```

The preceding declaration states that the function treats the c parameter as a second operand. Here's how the add member function works:

```
complex c1(3, 4), c2(1.2, 4.5);
c1.add(c2); // adds c2 to c1
```

First, the add member function works as an increment and not as an addition function. Second, the targeted class instance is always the first operand. Though this is not a

395

problem for operations like addition and multiplication, it is a problem for subtraction and division. That is why the add friend function works better by giving you the freedom of choosing how to add the class instances.

The add friend function returns a class instance. The function creates a local instance of class complex and returns that instance.

The function main uses the member function assign and the friend function add to perform simple complex operations. In addition, the function main invokes the functions getReal and getImag with the various instances of class complex to display the components of each instance.

Operators and Friend Operators

The last program used a member function and a friend function to implement complex math operations. The approach is typical in C and Pascal because these languages do not support user-defined operators. On the other hand, with C++ you can declare operators and friend operators. These operators include +, -, *, /, %, ==, !=, <=, <, >=, >, +=, -=, *=, /=, %=, [], and (). Consult a C++ language reference book for more details on rules for using these operators. C++ treats operators and friend operators as special member functions and friend functions.

The general syntax for declaring operators and friend operators is:

```
// unary operator
returnType operator operatorSymbol(operand);
// binary operator
returnType operator operatorSymbol(firstOperand, secondOperand);
// unary friend operator
friend returnType operator operatorSymbol(operand);
// binary operator
friend returnType operator operatorSymbol(firstOperand,
                                          secondOperand);
```

The client function uses the operators and friend operators just like predefined operators. Therefore, you can create operators to support the operations of classes that model, for example, complex numbers, strings, arrays, and matrices. These operators enable you to write expressions that are far more readable than expressions that use named functions.

Listing 13.7, the source code for LST13_07.CPP, is a program that demonstrates operators and friend operators. I created this program by modifying and expanding the last one.

Listing 13.7. Source code for the LST13_07.CPP program.

```cpp
/*
  C++ program that demonstrates operators and friend operators
*/

#include <iostream.h>
#include <string.h>
#include <conio.h>

class complex
{
   protected:
     double real;
     double imag;

   public:
     complex(double Real = 0, double Imag = 0)
       { assign(Real, Imag); }
     complex(complex& c);
     void assign(double Real = 0, double Imag = 0);
     double getReal() const
       { return real; }
     double getImag() const
       { return imag; }
     complex& operator =(complex& c);
     complex& operator +=(complex& c);
     friend complex operator +(complex& c1, complex& c2);
     friend ostream& operator <<(ostream& os, complex& c);
};

complex::complex(complex& c)
{
  real = c.real;
  imag = c.imag;
}

void complex::assign(double Real, double Imag)
{
  real = Real;
  imag = Imag;
}
```

continues

397

Listing 13.7. continued

```
complex& complex::operator =(complex& c)
{
  real = c.real;
  imag = c.imag;
  return *this;
}

complex& complex::operator +=(complex& c)
{
  real += c.real;
  imag += c.imag;
  return *this;
}

complex operator +(complex& c1, complex& c2)
{
  complex result(c1);

  result.real += c2.real;
  result.imag += c2.imag;
  return result;
}

ostream& operator <<(ostream& os, complex& c)
{
  os << "(" << c.real
     << " + i" << c.imag << ")";

  return os;
}

main()
{
  complex c1(1, 1);
  complex c2(2, 2);
  complex c3;
  complex c4(4, 4);

  clrscr();
  c3 = c1 + c2;
  cout << c1 << " + " << c2 << " = " << c3 << "\n\n";
  cout << c3 << " + " << c4 << " = ";
  c3 += c4;
  cout << c3 << "\n\n";
  getch();
  return 0;
}
```

The new class complex replaces the assign(complex&) member function with the = operator. The class also replaces the friend function add with the friend operator +:

```
complex& operator =(complex& c);
friend complex operator +(complex& c1, complex& c2);
```

The = operator has one parameter, a reference to an instance of complex class, and also returns a reference to the same class. The + friend operator has two parameters (both are references to instances of class complex) and yields a complex class type. The statements in these two operators are no different than the ones in their counterpart functions in Listing 13.6.

I also took this opportunity to add two new operators:

```
complex& operator +=(complex& c);
friend ostream& operator <<(ostream& os, complex& c);
```

The += operator is a member of class complex and takes one parameter, a reference to an instance of class complex, and yields a reference to the same class. The other new operator is the friend operator <<, which illustrates how to write a stream extractor operator for a class. The friend operator has two parameters: a reference to class ostream (the output stream class) and a reference to class complex. The << operator returns a reference to class ostream. This type of value enables you to chain stream output with other predefined types or other classes (assuming that these classes have a << friend operator). The definition of << friend operator has two statements. The first one outputs strings and the data members of class complex to the output stream parameter os. The friendship status of operator << allows it to access the real and imag data members of its complex-typed c parameter. The second statement in the operator definition returns the first os parameter.

The function main declares four instances of class complex: c1, c2, c3, and c4. The instances c1, c2, and c4 are created with nondefault values assigned to the data members real and imag. The function tests using the operators =, +, <<, and +=. The program illustrates that, by using operators and friend operators, you can write more readable code which supports a higher level of abstraction. Comparing Listings 13.6 and 13.7 proves the correctness of this preceding statement.

Listing 13.8 illustrates an interesting and special use of the [ ] operator. This program uses a dynamic array to calculate, store, and display factorials.

Listing 13.8. Source code for the LST13_08.CPP program.

```
/*
  C++ program that demonstrates using the [] operator
*/

#include <iostream.h>
#include <string.h>
#include <conio.h>

const unsigned MIN_SIZE = 10;
const double BAD_VALUE = -1.0e+30;

class Array
{
   protected:
     double *dataPtr;
     unsigned size;
     double badIndex;

   public:
     Array(unsigned Size = MIN_SIZE);
     ~Array()
       { delete [] dataPtr; }
     unsigned getSize() const
       { return size; }
     double& operator [](unsigned index);
};

Array::Array(unsigned Size)
{
  size = (Size < MIN_SIZE) ? MIN_SIZE : Size;
  badIndex = BAD_VALUE;
  dataPtr = new double[size];
}

double& Array::operator [](unsigned index)
{
  if (index < size)
    return *(dataPtr + index);
  else
    return badIndex;
}

main()
{
  Array factorial(15);
```

```
  clrscr();
  factorial[0] = 1;
  factorial[1] = 1;
  for (unsigned i = 2; i < factorial.getSize(); i++)
    factorial[i] = i * factorial[i-1];

  for (i = 0; i < factorial.getSize(); i++)
    cout << i << "! = " << factorial[i] << "\n";
  getch();
  return 0;
}
```

The class Array models a dynamic array of floating-point numbers with minimal functionality. The class declares three data members: dataPtr, size, and badIndex. The dataPtr member is a pointer used to access the dynamic array of doubles. The size member stores the number of elements in a class instance. The badIndex member provides a value for out-of-range indices.

The highlight of the Array class is the [ ] operator. This operator has one parameter that passes the arguments for the array indices. The operator returns a reference to the type double. If the argument of parameter index is within the valid range, the operator returns a reference to the sought array element. Otherwise, the operator yields the reference to the data member badIndex.

The versatility of the [ ] operator comes from the fact that it returns a reference type. Such a return type enables the operator to be used on both sides of an assignment operator. This is exactly what you see in the first for loop located in the function main. Notice that function main accesses the individual elements of array factorial using the [ ] operator as if it were an array of a predefined data type! Thus, using the operator [ ] enables you to support a level of abstraction for class-based arrays that is similar to the abstraction offered for arrays of predefined types.

Friend Classes

Just as there are friend functions and friend operators, there are friend classes. C++ enables you to specify an across-the-board friendship between two classes. The general syntax for declaring a friend class is:

```
class className : [public] parentClass
{
```

401

```
        friend class befriendedClass;

    private:
        <private data members>
        <private member functions>

    protected:
        <protected data members>
        <protected member functions>

    public:
        <public data members>
        <public member functions>
};
```

Many C++ programmers have mixed feelings about using friend classes. Conceptually, a good class design should determine a safe interface with other classes, so that you don't need to use class friendship. I have had the opportunity to code two versions of the same set of classes: one using friendship and the other without such an access privilege. I've concluded you should use friendship between classes only to achieve significant increase in application speed—using the access member functions of a class may add significant overhead. To bypass that overhead, use friendship between classes.

Listing 13.9 puts class friendship to work. The program performs simple manipulation of numerical arrays and matrices.

Listing 13.9. Source code for the LST13_09.CPP program.

```
/*
  C++ program that demonstrates friend classes
*/

#include <iostream.h>
#include <string.h>
#include <conio.h>

const unsigned MIN_SIZE = 5;
const unsigned MIN_ROWS = 2;
const unsigned MIN_COLS = 2;
const double BAD_VALUE = -1.0e+30;

class Array
{
    // declare that class Matrix is a friend
    friend class Matrix;
```

```
    protected:
      double *dataPtr;
      unsigned size;
      double badIndex;

    public:
      Array(unsigned Size = MIN_SIZE);
      ~Array()
        { delete [] dataPtr; }
      unsigned getSize() const
        { return size; }
      double& operator [](unsigned index);
};

class Matrix
{
    protected:
      double *dataPtr;
      unsigned maxRows;
      unsigned maxCols;
      double badIndex;

    public:
      Matrix(unsigned Rows = MIN_ROWS, unsigned Cols = MIN_COLS);
      ~Matrix()
        { delete [] dataPtr; }
      unsigned getMaxRows() const
        { return maxRows; }
      unsigned getMaxCols() const
        { return maxCols; }
      double& operator ()(unsigned row, unsigned col);
      void copyRow(Array& arr, unsigned row);
      void copyCol(Array& arr, unsigned col);
};

Array::Array(unsigned Size)
{
  size = (Size < MIN_SIZE) ? MIN_SIZE : Size;
  badIndex = BAD_VALUE;
  dataPtr = new double[size];
}

double& Array::operator [](unsigned index)
{
  if (index < size)
    return *(dataPtr + index);
```

continues

Listing 13.9. continued

```
  else
    return badIndex;
}

Matrix::Matrix(unsigned Rows, unsigned Cols)
{
  maxRows = (Rows < MIN_ROWS) ? MIN_ROWS : Rows;
  maxCols = (Cols < MIN_COLS) ? MIN_COLS : Cols;
  badIndex = BAD_VALUE;
  dataPtr = new double[maxRows * maxCols];
}

double& Matrix::operator ()(unsigned row, unsigned col)
{
  if (row < maxRows && col < maxCols)
    return *(dataPtr + row + col * maxRows);
  else
    return badIndex;
}

void Matrix::copyRow(Array& arr, unsigned row)
{
  // delete array and recreate it to fit maxCols elements
  delete [] arr.dataPtr;
  arr.size = maxCols;
  arr.dataPtr = new double[arr.size];
  for (unsigned col = 0; col < maxRows; col++)
    arr[col] = *(dataPtr + row + col * maxRows);
}

void Matrix::copyCol(Array& arr, unsigned col)
{
  // delete array and recreate it to fit maxCols elements
  delete [] arr.dataPtr;
  arr.size = maxRows;
  arr.dataPtr = new double[arr.size];
  for (unsigned row = 0; row < maxCols; row++)
    arr[row] = *(dataPtr + row + col * maxRows);
}

main()
{
  const unsigned ARR_SIZE = 10;
  const unsigned ROWS = 3;
  const unsigned COLS = 3;
```

```
    Array ar(ARR_SIZE);
    Matrix mat(ROWS, COLS);

    clrscr();
    // assign values to array ar
    for (unsigned i = 0; i < ar.getSize(); i++)
      ar[i] = 2.5 + i * i;

    // assign values to matrix at
    for (unsigned row = 0; row < mat.getMaxRows(); row++)
      for (unsigned col = 0; col < mat.getMaxCols(); col++)
        mat(row, col) = 5.5 + row + 10 * col;

    cout << "Array ar contains the following elements:\n\n";
    for (i = 0; i < ar.getSize(); i++)
      cout << "ar[" << i << "] = " << ar[i] << "\n";
    cout << "\nPress any key to continue...";
    getch();

    clrscr();
    cout << "Matrix mat contains the following elements:\n\n";
    for (row = 0; row < mat.getMaxRows(); row++)
      for (col = 0; col < mat.getMaxCols(); col++)
        cout << "mat[" << row << "," << col << "] = "
             << mat(row, col) << "\n";
    cout << "\nPress any key to continue...";
    getch();

    // copy row 0 of matrix mat into array ar
    mat.copyRow(ar, 0);
    clrscr();
    cout << "Array ar contains the following elements:\n\n";
    for (i = 0; i < ar.getSize(); i++)
      cout << "ar[" << i << "] = " << ar[i] << "\n";
    cout << "\nPress any key to continue...";
    getch();

    // copy col 0 of matrix mat into array ar
    mat.copyCol(ar, 0);
    clrscr();
    cout << "Array ar contains the following elements:\n\n";
    for (i = 0; i < ar.getSize(); i++)
      cout << "ar[" << i << "] = " << ar[i] << "\n";
    cout << "\nPress any key to end the program...";
    getch();

    return 0;
}
```

The program declares two classes: Array and Matrix. These classes are somewhat similar. The class Array is the same one I used in Listing 13.8. I designed class Matrix to resemble class Array. I also made class Matrix a friend of class Array by placing the following declaration in class Array:

```
friend class Matrix;
```

Note that I'm using the () operator (the iterator operator in C++) to act as an extended version of the [] operator. Why use the () operator to access the element of a matrix? The answer lies in the fact that the [] operator can only accept one parameter, which must have an integer-compatible type. By contrast, the () operator can take any number and any type of parameter! Therefore, the () operator is suitable for indexing matrices and other multidimensional arrays.

The Matrix class has two special member functions: copyRow and copyCol. These functions, as their names suggest, copy matrix rows and columns into the Array-typed reference parameter arr. These functions resize the ar array to match the size of a row or column. This process is possible only by making class Matrix a friend of class Array. This relation enables the member functions of class Matrix to access the data members of class Array, dataPtr and size, to perform the required operations.

The function main performs the following tasks:

1. Declares the instance ar of class Array. The array stores 10 elements.

2. Declares the instance mat of class Matrix. The matrix contains three rows and three columns.

3. Assigns values to the array ar.

4. Assigns values to matrix mat.

5. Displays the elements of array ar.

6. Displays the elements of matrix mat.

7. Copies row 0 of the matrix mat into the array.

8. Displays the new elements of array ar.

9. Copies column 0 of the matrix mat into the array.

10. Displays the new elements of array ar.

Multiple Inheritance

C++ supports two types of class inheritance: single inheritance and multiple inheritance. Under single inheritance, a class has only one parent class. By contrast, under multiple inheritance, a class may have many parent classes.

Multiple inheritance is perhaps the most controversial feature of C++. Many programming-language scientists and programmers feel that multiple inheritance is a recipe for disaster. They regard containment (that is, declaring classes that contain data members that are themselves instances of other classes) as a much better, safer alternative to multiple inheritance.

Multiple inheritance, like containment, builds on the HasA notion. This notion looks at the class as containing the parent classes instead of refining them. For example, you can model an airplane by creating classes for the different components—the engine, the wings, the wheels, the fuel system, the hydraulic system, and so on. Then you create a class that models the airplane by using multiple inheritance to inherit from all the components. This scheme applies the HasA notion and not the IsA notion— an airplane is not a type of wing or an engine, or any other component. Instead, an airplane has a wing, engines, and other components.

The general syntax for declaring a class using multiple inheritance is:

```
class className : [public][virtual] parent1,
                  [public][virtual] parent2, ...
{

    private:
        <private data members>
        <private member functions>

    protected:
        <protected data members>
        <protected member functions>

    public:
        <public data members>
        <public member functions>
};
```

The public keyword works the same in multiple inheritace as it does in a single inheritance class derivation. The virtual keyword is needed for the parent classes that share a common ancestor class.

407

Listing 13.10, the source code for MINHERIT.CPP, is an example of using multiple inheritance. This program emulates a class that solves simultaneous equations (I say emulates because I actually use much shorter code to perform a simple matrix-array manipulation). The solution of simultaneous equations involves the following equation:

A X = B

in which A is the matrix of coefficients, B is the right-hand vector (array), and X is the solution vector (array).

Listing 13.10. Source code for the LST13_10.CPP program.

```
/*
   C++ program that demonstrates multiple inheritance
*/

#include <iostream.h>
#include <conio.h>

class Array
{
  protected:
    unsigned arrSize;
    double *arrPtr;

  public:
    Array(unsigned ArraySize)
      { arrPtr = new double[arrSize = ArraySize]; }
    ~Array()
      { delete [] arrPtr; }

    void arrStore(double x, unsigned index)
      { arrPtr[index] = x; }
    void arrRecall(double& x, unsigned index)
      { x = arrPtr[index]; }
};

class Matrix
{
  protected:
    unsigned maxRows;
    unsigned maxCols;
    double *matPtr;

  public:
    Matrix(unsigned Rows, unsigned Cols)
```

```
      { maxRows = Rows;
        maxCols = Cols;
        matPtr = new double[Rows * Cols];
      }
    ~Matrix()
      { delete [] matPtr; }

    void matStore(double x, unsigned row, unsigned col)
      { matPtr[row + maxRows * col] = x; }
    void matRecall(double& x, unsigned row, unsigned col)
      { x = matPtr[row + maxRows * col]; }
};

class SimultEqn : public Array, public Matrix
{
   protected:
     double *solnPtr;

   public:
     SimultEqn(unsigned Rows, unsigned Cols) :
       Array(Cols), Matrix(Rows, Cols)
     { solnPtr = new double[Rows]; }

     ~SimultEqn()
       { delete [] solnPtr; }
     void solve();
     void solnRecall(double& x, unsigned index)
       { x = solnPtr[index]; }

};

void SimultEqn::solve()
{
  double x, y;

  for (unsigned row = 0; row < maxRows; row++) {
    solnPtr[row] = 0;
    for (unsigned col = 0; col < maxCols; col++) {
      matRecall(x, row, col);
      arrRecall(y, col);
      solnPtr[row] += x * y;
    }
  }
}

main()
{
```

continues

Listing 13.10. continued

```
SimultEqn se(2,2);
double z;

clrscr();

for (unsigned i = 0; i < 2; i++)
  se.arrStore(1.0 + i, i);

for (i = 0; i < 2; i++)
  for (unsigned j = 0; j < 2; j++)
    se.matStore(2.5 + i + j, i, j);

se.solve();
cout << "Array B:\n";
for (i = 0; i < 2; i++) {
  se.arrRecall(z, i);
  cout << z << "\n";
}

cout << "\nMatrix A:\n";
for (i = 0; i < 2; i++) {
  for (unsigned j = 0; j < 2; j++) {
    se.matRecall(z, i, j);
    cout << z << " ";
  }
  cout << "\n";
}

cout << "\nArray X:\n";
for (i = 0; i < 2; i++) {
  se.solnRecall(z, i);
  cout << z << "\n";
}
cout << "\n\nPress any key to end the program...";
getch();
return 0;
}
```

Listing 13.10 declares the following classes:

1. Class Array, which models a dynamic numerical array.

2. Class Matrix, which models a dynamic numerical matrix.

3. Class `SimultEqn`, a child of `Array` and `Matrix` classes, which models a simultaneous-equations solver.

The `SimultEqn` class inherits the data members to support array `B` and matrix `A` from the classes `Array` and `Matrix`, respectively. To manage the dynamic array of solutions `X`, the class declares the protected pointer `solnPtr`. This pointer is similar to the `arrPtr` in class `Array`. The class `SimultEqn` declares a constructor, a destructor, and a few functions.

The constructor for class `SimultEqn` invokes the constructors of classes `Array` and `Matrix`. In addition, the constructor allocates the dynamic space for the `X` array using the `solnPtr` member. The class destructor deletes the dynamic space accessed by member `solnPtr`. The dynamic space for matrix `A` and array `B` is deallocated by the destructors of classes `Matrix` and `Array`, respectively.

The `SimultEqn::solnRecall` member function enables you to recall dynamic data for the `X` solution array. The `solve` function simulates solving the simultaneous equations. This function uses the array and matrix access functions inherited from classes `Array` and `Matrix`.

The `main` function creates `se`, an instance of class `SimultEqn`, with two rows and two columns. The function uses `for` loop statements to assign values to array `B` and matrix `A`. Then the function calls function `SimultEqn::solve` to manipulate the arrays and matrix. Finally, function `main` uses another set of `for` loops to display array `B`, matrix `A`, and array `X`.

Summary

This chapter introduced C++ classes and discussed the following topics:

- Declaring base classes to specify the various `private`, `protected`, and `public` members. C++ classes contain data members and member functions. The data members store the state of a class instance, and the member functions query and manipulate that state.

- Declaring a class hierarchy enables you to derive classes from existing ones. The descendant classes inherit the members of their ancestor classes. C++ classes are able to override inherited member functions by defining their own versions. If you override a non-virtual function, you may declare the new version using a different parameter list. In contrast, you cannot alter the parameter list of an inherited virtual function.

411

- Constructors and destructors support the automatic creation and removal of class instances. Constructors are special members that must have the same name as the host class. You may declare any number of constructors or none at all. In the latter case, the compiler creates one for you. Each constructor enables you to create a class instance in a different way. There are two special kinds of constructors: the default constructor and the copy constructor. In contrast with constructors, C++ allows you to declare only one destructor that has no parameters. The runtime system automatically invokes the constructor and destructor when a class instance comes into and goes out of its scope.

- Static members are special members that conceptually belong to the class itself rather than any particular instance. C++ supports static data members and member functions. There is only one copy of a static data member, regardless of how many class instances exist. Static data members enable you to store data relevant to the class itself, such as the number of instances or an information table commonly used by all of the class instances.

- Nested data types appear in class declaration. These types include enumerated types, structures, and even classes. Nested types represent a vehicle to limit the problem of name space pollution. You can refer to a nested type outside its class, but you need to qualify it with the name of the host class.

- Friend functions are special non-member functions that may access `protected` and `private` data members. These functions enable you to implement operations that are more flexible than those offered by member functions.

- Operators and friend operators enable you to support various operations, such as addition, assignment, and indexing. These operators empower you to offer a level of abstraction for your classes. In addition, they assist in making the expressions that manipulate class instances more readable and more intuitive.

- Friend classes can access all data members of a befriended class. Such a relation enables the friend class to quickly and flexibly alter instances of the befriended classes. Such instances are typically parameters that appear in the member functions of the befriended class.

- Multiple inheritance is a scheme that enables you to derive a class from multiple parent classes. The descendant class has access to the various members of the parent classes.

BASIC STREAM FILE I/O

This chapter introduces file I/O operations using the C++ stream library. Unlike the stdio.h library, which was standarized by the ANSI C committee, the C++ stream library has not yet been standardized by the C++ ANSI committee. You have a choice of using either file I/O functions in the stdio.h file or those in the C++ stream library. These two I/O libraries offer much power and flexibility. This chapter presents basic and practical operations that enable you to read and write data to files and discusses the following topics:

- common stream I/O functions

- sequential stream I/O for text

- sequential stream I/O for binary data

- random-access stream I/O for binary data

To learn more about the C++ stream library, consult a C++ language reference book, such as Stanley Lipman's *C++ Primer*, second edition (Addison-Wesley).

The C++ Stream Library

The C++ stream I/O library is made up of a hierarchy of classes that are declared in several header files. The iostream.h header file that I've used so far is only one of these header files. Other files include io.h, istream.h, ostream.h, ifstream.h, ofstream.h, and fstream.h. The io.h header file declares low-level classes and identifiers. The istream.h and ostream.h files support the basic input and output stream classes. The iostream.h combines the operations of the classes in the above two header files. Similarly, the ifstream.h and ofstream.h files support the basic file input and output stream classes. The fstream.h file combines the operations of the classes in the ifstream.h and ofstream.h header files. In addition to the header files that I've mentioned, other stream library files offer even more specialized stream I/O. The C++ ANSI committee should define the standard stream I/O library and end any confusion regarding which classes and header files are part of the standard stream library and which ones are not.

Common Stream I/O Functions

In this section, I present stream I/O functions common to both sequential and random-access I/O:

1. The open function, which enables you to open a file stream for input, output, append, and both input and output. The function also permits you to specify whether the related I/O is binary or text. The declaration of the open function is:

    ```
    void open(const char* filename,
              int mode,
              int m = filebuf::openprot);
    ```

    The parameter filename specifies the name of the file to open. The parameter mode indicates the I/O mode. Note the following list of arguments for parameter mode that are exported by the io.h header file:

in	open stream for input
out	open stream for output
ate	set stream pointer to the end of the file
app	open stream for append mode

`trunc`	truncate file size to 0 if it already exists
`nocreate`	raises an error if the file does not already exist
`noreplace`	raises an error if the file already exists
`binary`	open in binary mode

> The file stream classes offer constructors that include the action (and have the same parameters) of the function `open`.

2. The `close` function closes the stream. The function takes no arguments and is declared as follows:

```
void close();
```

3. The set of basic functions that checks the error status of a stream operation. These functions include:

- The `good()` function, which returns a nonzero value if no error occurs in a stream operation. The declaration of function `good` is:

```
int good();
```

- The `fail()` function, which returns a nonzero value if an error occurs in a stream operation. The declaration of function `fail` is:

```
int fail();
```

- The overloaded operator `!` is applied to a stream instance to determine the error status.

The C++ stream libraries offer additional functions to set and query other aspects and types of stream errors.

Sequential Text Stream I/O

The functions and operators involved in sequential text I/O are simple. Moreover, you've already read about most of these functions in earlier chapters. The functions and operators include the following:

1. The stream extractor operator `<<`, which writes strings and characters to a stream.

2. The stream inserter operator `>>`, which reads characters from a stream.

3. The `getline` function, which reads strings from a stream. The declaration of the overloaded `getline` function is:

```
istream& getline(signed char* buffer,
                 int size,
                 char delimiter = '\n');

istream& getline(unsigned char* buffer,
                 int size,
                 char delimiter = '\n');
```

The parameter buffer is a pointer to the string receiving the characters from the stream. The parameter size specifies the maximum number of characters to read. The parameter delimiter specifies the delimiting character that causes the string input to stop before reaching the number of characters specified by parameter size. The parameter delimiter has the default argument of `'\n'`.

Listing 14.1, the source code for LST14_01.CPP, is a simple program that reads a text file, replaces the occurrences of a specific character in that file, and writes the output to a new file.

Listing 14.1. Source code for the LST14_01.CPP program.

```
/*
   C++ program that demonstrates sequential file I/O
*/

#include <iostream.h>
#include <fstream.h>
#include <conio.h>

enum boolean { false, true };

main()
{
  const unsigned NAME_SIZE = 64;
  const unsigned LINE_SIZE = 128;

  fstream fin, fout;
  char inFile[NAME_SIZE + 1], outFile[NAME_SIZE + 1];
  char line[LINE_SIZE + 1];
```

```
char findChar, replChar;
unsigned i;
boolean ok;

clrscr();

do {
  ok = true;
  cout << "Enter input file : ";
  cin.getline(inFile, NAME_SIZE);
  cout << '\n';
  fin.open(inFile, ios::in);
  if (!fin) {
    cout << "Cannot open file " << inFile << "\n\n";
    ok = false;
  }
} while (!ok);

do {
  ok = true;
  cout << "Enter output file : ";
  cin.getline(outFile, NAME_SIZE);
  cout << '\n';
  fout.open(outFile, ios::out);
  if (!fout) {
    cout << "File " << inFile << " is invalid\n\n";
    ok = false;
  }
} while (!ok);

cout << "\nEnter character to find : ";
cin >> findChar;
cout << "\nEnter character to replace : ";
cin >> replChar;
cout << "\n";

// loop to replace the characters
while (fin.getline(line, LINE_SIZE)) {
  for (i = 0; line[i] != '\0'; i++)
    if (line[i] == findChar)
      line[i] = replChar;
  // write line to the output file
  fout << line << "\n";
  // echo updated line to the screen
  cout << line << "\n";
}
```

continues

417

Listing 14.1. continued

```
// close streams
fin.close();
fout.close();

cout << "\nPress any key to end the program...";
getch();
return 0;
}
```

The preceding program example declares no classes and instead focuses on using file streams to input and output text. Function `main` performs the following relevant tasks:

1. Declares the input and output file streams, `fin` and `fout`, respectively.

2. Clears the screen and prompts you to enter the input filename. The function uses a `do-while` loop to validate your input and to carry out the following subtasks:

   - Setting the `ok` flag to true.

   - Displaying the prompting message.

   - Obtaining your input using the `getline` function. Here the loop uses the `getline` function with the standard input stream `cin`.

   - Opening the input file stream `fin` using function `open`. The arguments for function `open` are the name of the input file and the expression `ios::in`, which specifies input-mode only.

   - Using the overloaded operator `!` to test if the stream was successfully opened. If not, the loop displays an error message and assigns false to the `ok` variable.

3. Clears the screen and prompts you to enter the output filename. The function uses a `do-while` loop to validate your input in a manner similar to Step 2. Notice that in this case, stream function `open` has arguments `outFile` (the name of the output file) and `ios::out` (the expression that specifies output-mode only).

4. Prompts you to enter the character to find.

5. Prompts you to enter the replacement character.

6. Uses a `while` loop to process the input lines by performing the following subtasks:

- Reading a line from the input file stream. This subtask applies the `getline` function to the `fin` stream.

- Scanning the characters of the line read to locate and replace the characters that match the character in variable `findChar`.

- Writing the updated line to the output file stream `fout`.

- Echoing the updated line to the standard output stream `cout`.

7. Closes the input and output file streams.

Sequential Binary File Stream I/O

The C++ stream library offers the following stream functions for sequential binary file stream I/O:

1. The `write` function sends multiple bytes to an output stream. The overloaded function has the following declarations:

```
ostream& write(const signed char* buff, int num);
ostream& write(const unsigned char* buff, int num);
```

The `buff` parameter is the pointer to the buffer that contains the data to be sent to the output stream. The `num` parameter indicates the number of bytes in the buffer that are sent to the stream. The `write` stream function resembles the Pascal intrinsic `BlockWrite`.

2. The `read` function receives multiple bytes from an input stream. The overloaded function has the following declarations:

```
istream& read(signed char* buff, int num);
istream& read(unsigned char* buff, int num);
```

The `buff` parameter is the pointer to the buffer that receives the data from the input stream. The `num` parameter indicates the number of bytes to read from the stream. The `read` stream function resembles the Pascal intrinsic `BlockRead`.

Listing 14.2, the source code for LST14_02.CPP, is an example that performs sequential binary stream I/O. The program declares a class that models dynamic numerical arrays. The stream I/O operations enable the program to read and write both the individual array elements and an entire array in binary files.

Listing 14.2. Source code for the LST14_02.CPP program.

```cpp
/*
   C++ program that demonstrates sequential binary file I/O
*/

#include <iostream.h>
#include <fstream.h>
#include <conio.h>

const unsigned MIN_SIZE = 10;
const double BAD_VALUE = -1.0e+30;
enum boolean { false, true };

class Array
{
   protected:
     double *dataPtr;
     unsigned size;
     double badIndex;

   public:
     Array(unsigned Size = MIN_SIZE);
     ~Array()
       { delete [] dataPtr; }
     unsigned getSize() const
       { return size; }
     double& operator [](unsigned index);
     boolean writeElem(fstream& os, unsigned index);
     boolean readElem(fstream& is, unsigned index);
     boolean writeArray(const char* filename);
     boolean readArray(const char* filename);
};

Array::Array(unsigned Size)
{
   size = (Size < MIN_SIZE) ? MIN_SIZE : Size;
   badIndex = BAD_VALUE;
   dataPtr = new double[size];
}

double& Array::operator [](unsigned index)
{
   if (index < size)
     return *(dataPtr + index);
   else
     return badIndex;
}
```

```
boolean Array::writeElem(fstream& os, unsigned index)
{
   if (index < size) {
     os.write((unsigned char*)(dataPtr + index), sizeof(double));
     return (os.good()) ? true : false;
   }
   else
     return false;
}

boolean Array::readElem(fstream& is, unsigned index)
{
   if (index < size) {
     is.read((unsigned char*)(dataPtr + index), sizeof(double));
     return (is.good()) ? true : false;
   }
   else
     return false;
}

boolean Array::writeArray(const char* filename)
{
   fstream f(filename, ios::out | ios::binary);

   if (f.fail())
     return false;
   f.write((unsigned char*) &size, sizeof(size));
   f.write((unsigned char*)dataPtr, size * sizeof(double));
   f.close();
   return (f.good()) ? true : false;
}

boolean Array::readArray(const char* filename)
{
   fstream f(filename, ios::in | ios::binary);
   unsigned sz;

   if (f.fail())
     return false;
   f.read((unsigned char*) &sz, sizeof(sz));
   // need to expand the array
   if (sz != size) {
     delete [] dataPtr;
     dataPtr = new double[sz];
     size = sz;
   }
```

continues

421

Listing 14.2. continued

```
    f.read((unsigned char*)dataPtr, size * sizeof(double));
    f.close();
    return (f.good()) ? true : false;
}

main()
{
  const unsigned SIZE1 = 10;
  const unsigned SIZE2 = 20;
  Array ar1(SIZE1), ar2(SIZE1), ar3(SIZE2);
  fstream f("ar1.dat", ios::out | ios::binary);

  clrscr();
  // assign values to array ar1
  for (unsigned i = 0; i < ar1.getSize(); i++)
    ar1[i] = 10 * i;

  // assign values to array ar3
  for (i = 0; i < SIZE2; i++)
    ar3[i] = i;

  cout << "Array ar1 has the following values:\n";
  for (i = 0; i < ar1.getSize(); i++)
    cout << ar1[i] << "   ";
  cout << "\n\n";

  // write elements of array ar1 to the stream
  for (i = 0; i < ar1.getSize(); i++)
    ar1.writeElem(f, i);
  f.close();

  // reopen the stream for input
  f.open("ar1.dat", ios::in | ios::binary);

  for (i = 0; i < ar1.getSize(); i++)
    ar2.readElem(f, i);
  f.close();
  // display the elements of array ar2
  cout << "Array ar2 has the following values:\n";
  for (i = 0; i < ar2.getSize(); i++)
    cout << ar2[i] << "   ";
  cout << "\n\n";

  // display the elements of array ar3
  cout << "Array ar3 has the following values:\n";
  for (i = 0; i < ar3.getSize(); i++)
```

```
  cout << ar3[i] << "  ";
cout << "\n\n";

// write the array ar3 to file AR3.DAT
ar3.writeArray("ar3.dat");
// read the array ar1 from file AR3.DAT
ar1.readArray("ar3.dat");

  // display the elements of array ar1
cout << "Array ar1 now has the following values:\n";
for (i = 0; i < ar1.getSize(); i++)
  cout << ar1[i] << "  ";
cout << "\n\n";


cout << "\nPress any key to end the program...";
getch();
return 0;
}
```

The preceding program declares a version of class Array that resembles versions presented in the preceding chapter. The main difference is that I added the following four member functions to perform sequential binary file stream I/O:

1. The writeElem function writes a single array element to an output stream:

```
boolean writeElem(fstream& os, unsigned index);
```

The os parameter represents the output stream. The index parameter specifies the array element to write. The writeElem function returns true if the argument for the index is valid and the stream output proceeds without any error. After the writeElem writes an array element, the internal stream pointer advances to the next location.

2. The readElem function reads a single array element from an input stream:

```
boolean readElem(fstream& is, unsigned index);
```

The is parameter represents the input stream. The index parameter specifies the array element to read. The readElem function returns true if the argument for the index is valid and the stream input proceeds without any error. After the readElem reads an array element, the internal stream pointer advances to the next location.

The writeElem and readElem functions permit the same class instance to write and read data elements from multiple streams.

3. The writeArray function writes all elements of the array to a binary file:

```
boolean writeArray(const char* filename);
```

423

The parameter filename specifies the name of the output file. The function opens an output stream and writes the value of the data member size and then writes the elements of the dynamic array. The writeArray function returns true if it successfully writes the array to the stream. Otherwise, the function yields false. The function opens a local output stream using the open stream function and supplying it with the filename and I/O mode arguments. The I/O mode argument is the ios::out | ios::binary expression, which specifies that the stream is opened for binary output only. The function makes two calls to the stream function write: the first call writes the data member size, and the second call writes the elements of the dynamic array.

4. The readArray function reads all elements of the array from a binary file:

```
boolean readArray(const char* filename);
```

The parameter filename specifies the name of the input file. The function opens an input stream and reads the value of the data member size and then reads the elements of the dynamic array. The readArray function returns true if it successfully reads the array to the stream. Otherwise, the function yields false. The function opens a local input stream using the open stream function and supplying it with the filename and I/O mode arguments. The I/O mode argument is the expression ios::in | ios::binary, which specifies that the stream is opened for binary input only. The function makes two calls to the stream function read: the first call reads the data member size, and the second call reads the elements of the dynamic array. Another feature of function readArray is that it resizes the instance of class Array to accommodate the data from the binary file. This means that the dynamic array accessed by the class instance may either shrink or expand, depending on the size of the array stored on file.

These member functions indicate that the program performs two types of sequential binary stream I/O. The first type of I/O, implemented in functions readElem and writeElem, involves items that have the same data type. The second type of I/O, implemented in functions readArray and writeArray, involves items that have the different data types.

Function main performs the following relevant tasks:

1. Declares three instances of class Array: ar1, ar2, and ar3. The first two instances have the same dynamic array size, whereas instance ar3 has a larger dynamic array than the other two.

2. Declares the file stream f and opens it (using a stream constructor) to access file AR1.DAT in binary output mode.

3. Assigns values to instances ar1 and ar3.

4. Displays the elements of instance ar1.

5. Writes the elements of array ar1 to the output file stream f. This task uses a loop that calls the writeElem function and supplies it with the arguments f (the file stream) and i (the loop control variable).

6. Closes the output file stream.

7. Opens the file stream f to access the data file AR1.DAT. This time, the function specifies a binary input mode.

8. Reads the elements of instance ar2 (which has not yet been assigned any values) from the input file stream f. This task uses a loop that calls the readElem function and supplies it with the arguments f (the file stream) and i (the loop control variable).

9. Closes the input file stream.

10. Displays the elements of instance ar2. These elements match those of instance ar1.

11. Displays the elements of instance ar3.

12. Writes the entire instance ar3 using function writeArray. The argument for the writeArray function call is the filename AR3.DAT.

13. Reads the array in file AR3.DAT into instance ar1. This task uses the readArray function and supplies it the argument for the filename AR3.DAT.

14. Displays the new elements of instance ar1.

Random-Access File Stream I/O

Random-access file stream operations also use the read and write stream functions presented in the last section. The stream library offers a number of stream seeking functions to enable you to move the stream pointer to any valid location. Function seekg is one such function. This overloaded function has the following declaration:

```
istream& seekg(long pos);
istream& seekg(long pos, seek_dir dir);
```

425

The pos parameter in the first version specifies the absolute byte position in the stream. In the second version, the pos parameter specifies a relative offset based on the argument for parameter dir. The argument for the latter parameter is:

ios::beg	from the beginning of the file
ios::cur	from the current position of the file
ios::end	from the end of the file

Listing 14.3, the source code for LST14_03.CPP, is an example that uses random-access file stream I/O. This program implements a virtual (disk-based) array. Accessing the different array elements requires random-access I/O.

Listing 14.3. Source code for the LST14_03.CPP program.

```
/*
    C++ program that demonstrates random-access binary file I/O
*/

#include <iostream.h>
#include <fstream.h>
#include <conio.h>
#include <stdlib.h>

const unsigned MIN_SIZE = 10;
const double BAD_VALUE = -1.0e+30;
enum boolean { false, true };

class VmArray
{
   protected:
     fstream f;
     unsigned size;
     double badIndex;

   public:
     VmArray(unsigned Size, const char* filename);
     ~VmArray()
       { f.close(); }
     unsigned getSize() const
       { return size; }
     boolean writeElem(double x, unsigned index);
     boolean readElem(double& x, unsigned index);
     void Combsort();
};
```

```
VmArray::VmArray(unsigned Size, const char* filename)
{
  size = (Size < MIN_SIZE) ? MIN_SIZE : Size;
  badIndex = BAD_VALUE;
  f.open(filename, ios::in ¦ ios::out ¦ ios::binary);
  if (f.good()) {
    // fill the file stream with zeros
    double x = 0.0;
    f.seekg(0);
    for (unsigned i = 0; i < size; i++)
      f.write((unsigned char*) &x, sizeof(double));
  }
}

boolean VmArray::writeElem(double x, unsigned index)
{
   if (index < size) {
     f.seekg(index * sizeof(double));
     f.write((unsigned char*)&x, sizeof(double));
     return (f.good()) ? true : false;
   }
   else
     return false;
}

boolean VmArray::readElem(double &x, unsigned index)
{
   if (index < size) {
     f.seekg(index * sizeof(double));
     f.read((unsigned char*)&x, sizeof(double));
     return (f.good()) ? true : false;
   }
   else
     return false;
}

void VmArray::Combsort()
{
   unsigned i, j, gap = size;
   boolean inOrder;
   double xi, xj;

   do {
     gap = gap * 8 / 11;
     if (gap < 1)
       gap = 1;
```

continues

427

Listing 14.3. continued

```
      inOrder = true;
      for (i = 0, j = gap; i < (size - gap); i++, j++) {
        readElem(xi, i);
        readElem(xj, j);
        if (xi > xj) {
          inOrder = false;
          writeElem(xi, j);
          writeElem(xj, i);
        }
      }
    } while (!(inOrder && gap == 1));
}

main()
{
  VmArray ar(20, "ar.dat");
  double x;

  clrscr();
  // assign random values to array ar
  for (unsigned i = 0; i < ar.getSize(); i++) {
    x = (double) (1 + random(1000));
    ar.writeElem(x, i);
  }

  cout << "Unsorted arrays is:\n";
  for (i = 0; i < ar.getSize(); i++) {
    ar.readElem(x, i);
    cout << x << "\n";
  }

  cout << "\nPress any key to sort the array...";
  getch();

  ar.Combsort();

  clrscr();
  cout << "Sorted arrays is:\n";
  for (i = 0; i < ar.getSize(); i++) {
    ar.readElem(x, i);
    cout << x << "\n";
  }

  cout << "\nPress any key to end the program...";
  getch();
  return 0;
}
```

The VmArray class models a disk-based dynamic array that stores all its elements in a random-access binary file. Notice that the class declares an instance of class fstream, and that there is no pointer to a dynamic array. The class declares a constructor, a destructor, and a number of member functions.

The class constructor has two parameters: Size and filename. The Size parameter specifies the size of the virtual array. The filename parameter names the binary file that stores the elements of a class instance. The constructor opens the stream f using the open stream function and supplies the argument of the filename parameter and the I/O mode expression ios::in ¦ ios::out ¦ ios::binary. This expression specifies that the stream is opened for binary input and output mode (that is, random-access mode). If the constructor successfully opens the file stream, it proceeds with filling the file with zeros. The class destructor performs the simple task of closing file stream f.

The writeElem and readElem functions support the random access of array elements. These functions use the seekg stream function to position the stream pointer at the appropriate array element. writeElem then calls the write stream function to store an array element (supplied by the x parameter). In contrast, the readElem function calls the read stream function to retrieve an array element (returned by the x parameter). Both functions return Boolean results that indicate the success of the I/O operation.

The VmArray class also declares the Combsort function to sort the elements of the virtual array. This function uses the readElem and writeElem member functions to access and swap the array elements.

Function main performs the following relevant tasks:

1. Declares the ar instance of class VmArray. This instance stores 20 elements in the AR.DAT binary file.

2. Assigns random values to the elements of instance ar. This task uses a loop that creates random numbers and assigns them to the local variable x. Then the loop writes the value in x to the instance ar by calling the function writeElem. The arguments for the call to writeElem are x and i (the loop control variable).

3. Displays the unsorted elements of instance ar.

4. Sorts the array by invoking the Combsort member function.

5. Displays the sorted elements of instance ar.

429

Summary

This chapter briefly introduced the C++ stream I/O library and discussed the following topics:

- Common stream I/O functions—these stream functions include open, close, good, fail, and the operator !. Function open, as the name suggests, opens a file for stream I/O and supports alternate and multiple I/O modes. Function close shuts down a file stream. Functions good and fail indicate the success or failure of a stream I/O operation.

- Sequential stream I/O for text. C++ enables you to perform this kind of stream I/O using the << and >> operators, as well as the getline stream function. The << operator can write characters and strings (as well as the other predefined data types). The >> operator is suitable for obtaining characters. The getline function enables your applications to read strings from the keyboard or from a text file.

- Sequential stream I/O for binary data uses the write and read stream functions to write and read data from any kind of variable. These functions resemble the Pascal block I/O intrinsics BlockWrite and BlockRead.

- Random-access stream I/O for binary data uses the seekg function in conjunction with the read and write functions. The seekg function enables you to move the stream pointer to either absolute or relative byte locations in the stream.

INDEX

Symbols

437

M

macro-based constants, 36
macros
  _ _CDECL_ _, 101
  _ _cplusplus_ _, 101
  _ _DATE_ _, 101
  empty, 112
  _ _FILE_ _, 101
  _ _LINE_ _, 101
  _ _MSDOS_ _, 101
  _ _OVERLAY_ _, 101
  _ _PASCAL_ _, 101
  _ _STDC_ _, 101
  _ _TCPLUSPLUS_ _, 102
  _ _TEMPLATES_ _, 102
  _ _TIME_ _, 102
  _ _TURBOC_ _, 102
  VIDEO_ADDR, 277-278
main function, 2, 318
managing strings, 244
matrices, 230
  accessing with pointers, 241
  numerical, passing, 305-310
Matrix class, 406
matrix data type, 309
median function, 282-286
member functions, 369
message abstraction, *see* polymorphism
messages, 344

methods, 344
  Area
    TCircle class, 349
    THollowCylinder class, 350
  BaseArea
    TCylinder class, 350
    THollowCylinder class, 350
  Circumference, 349
  GetHeight, 350
  GetInnerRadius, 350
  GetRadius, 349
  SetHeight, 350
  SetInnerRadius, 350
  SetRadius, 349
  static, 355-361
  virtual, 355-361
  Volume, 349-350
modifiers, data type, 29-30
modulus (%) operator, 54
_ _MSDOS_ _ macro, 101
multidimensional arrays, 224, 230
  accessing, 14-15
  declaring, 230
  elements, storing, 230-231
  initializing, 235
  matrices, 230
  translating to C++, 230
multiple inheritance, 407-411
multiply (*) operator, 54

N

names, array, 258
nested
  data types, 389-392
  if-else statement, 117-118
  loops, 146, 150-151
New statement, 361-363
nextPtr data member, 392
nodeData data member, 392

R

S

DISK OFFER

All the programs (as well as a special string library file that contains a `string` class with extensive string manipulation functions) discussed in this book are available on a disk produced by the author. Enclose a check for $12.00 (if you reside outside the United States, Canada, or Mexico, enclose a check for $16.50 drawn on a United States bank) and this form to:

> Namir C. Shammas
> 3928 Margate Drive
> Richmond, VA 23235

Name _____

Company _____

Street or P.O. Box _____

City _____

State (or province and country) _____

Zip or postal code _____

Disk size: 5.25" _____ or 3.5" _____